Embracing Change

Embracing Change

Postmodern Interpretations
of the *I Ching*
from a Christian Perspective

Jung Young Lee

Scranton: University of Scranton Press
London and Toronto: Associated University Presses

Associated University Presses
440 Forsgate Drive
Cranbury, NJ 08512

Associated University Presses
25 Sicilian Avenue
London WC1A 2QH, England

Associated University Presses
P.O. Box 338, Port Credit
Mississauga, Ontario
Canada L5G 4L8

The paper used in this publication meets the requirements
of the American National Standard for Permanence of Paper
for Printed Library Materials Z39.48-1984

Library of Congress Cataloging in Publication Data:

Lee, Jung Young.
    Embracing change : postmodern interpretations of the I ching from
a Christian perspective / Jung Young Lee
        p. cm.
    Includes bibliographical references and index.
    ISBN 0-940866-23-4 (alk. paper)
    1. I ching. 2. Christianity. I. I ching. English. 1994
II. Title.
PL2464.Z9C485   1994
299'.51282--dc20   92-85296
                                                           CIP

PRINTED IN THE UNITED STATES OF AMERICA

This book is affectionately dedicated
to
my wife, Gy, and my children,
Sue and Jonathan,
who have shared with me
their living wisdom of change

Contents

Acknowledgments

I regard this book as a compendium that, together with my previous works, provides a new, comprehensive introduction to the *I Ching* for those who have been primarily influenced by the Western, Christian tradition. This volume adds the "head" to my former three works: *The Principle of Change* (the "torso"), *The I Ching and Modern Man* (the "feet"), and *The Theology of Change* (the "arms").

While it is impossible to mention everyone who has contributed to this book, I must recognize James Legge, Richard and Hellmut Wilhelm, Carl Jung, and Arthur Waley in the West, as well as Professor Chung-ho Lee, a renowned Korean *I Ching* scholar, who read the entire manuscript and carefully compared my translations of the main text of the *I Ching* with the original Chinese version, corrected my translations, and added new insights to my interpretation. In particular, my translation of line five of hexagram 31 (Influence) owes a great deal to his interpretation. The constructive comments of Dr. Young-chan Ro of George Mason University and Dr. Paul Nagano at Berkeley assisted me to improve the manuscript, and Judith Kurth carefully proofread, typed, and added new insights in preparing the manuscript for publication. Thanks are also due to Yoon Dong-cheol, who prepared the index. Most especially, I must acknowledge my indebtedness to my wife, Gy, and my children, Sue and Jonathan, to whom this book is dedicated.

Introduction

What is the *I Ching?* Is it really worthy of study? How can we study it? These are some questions that I am often asked. In response, I started to teach the *I Ching* or the Book of Change in 1969. Although I have taught the book for twenty years, I still feel inadequate to answer all of the questions that people ask about it. What I have attempted here is to present some essential facts about it in a systematic fashion. Since most of those who have asked me about the *I Ching* have done so from a Judeo-Christian background, I have decided to address this book primarily to Christians or to people who have been deeply influenced by the Christian tradition in the West.

Although countless commentaries on the *I Ching* have been written through the centuries, no one has claimed to be an expert on this book. I do not myself claim to know everything about the *I Ching.* Since I am writing this book chiefly with Christians and general readers in mind, I have no intention of making any special contributions to sinology. However, I have not suspended my scholarly interest in Oriental philosophy. Although this book deals with the *I Ching* itself, its implications for the study of Oriental thought are profound. In this respect, insights into the meaning of the *I Ching* are helpful in furthering our understanding of the Eastern mentality.

This book is written also to correct one of the most common misunderstandings about the *I Ching,* and that is that it is a book of the occult and of magical spells. Because of this misunderstanding, many Christians seem to question the idea of using the *I Ching* in theological thinking. When I was teaching at the Graduate Theological Union in San Francisco some time ago, I required my students to read the *I Ching* along with books on Christian theology. One of my students told me that her roommate at the seminary was so uncomfortable at seeing the *I Ching* lying in the room that she decided to move out.

Some time ago, I had occasion to speak about the Book of Change in one of the most progressive churches in Chicago. In spite of their liberal orientation, more than half of that congregation thought that the *I Ching* and the Christian faith were incompatible. Although the *I Ching* has become one of the most important books for understanding Eastern civilization, many Christians retain the mentality of the seventeenth-century Jesuit missionaries, who denounced it as an insane and heretical book. I spent hours helping people in that congregation to understand the profound meaning and wisdom of the *I Ching*.

The present book is, then, written in part to eliminate serious Christian misunderstandings about the *I Ching*. In order to do this, I have tried to present it as objectively as possible, although I am not totally free from having some personal biases. Because I have written this text with Christians in mind, I have tried to relate it to the Christian faith. Nevertheless, the only way to truly eliminate our bias is to present the *I Ching* just as it is.

I am also writing this book for those who read the *I Ching* for the purpose of divination only. Most people want to know more about the *I Ching* because of their interest in divination. The *I Ching*, however, is much more than a divination book; and to use it for the purpose of divination only is to misuse it. Hsun Tzu once said that anyone who knows the book well does not use it merely for divination. I hope to show that the *I Ching* is a profound book of Eastern wisdom, and that divination is a very small part of it. I have also attempted to convince the reader that there is a proper religious method that might be called divination, which requires a general knowledge of the *I Ching*.

I am writing this work not simply to help Christians understand what the *I Ching* is all about, but to aid them in understanding their own faith as well. The study of the *I Ching* should not be simply an exercise in intellectual curiosity; it should be a process of rediscovering and enriching one's own faith as well. There are sure to be readers, however, who are not interested in the Christian response to the *I Ching;* and for their sake I have used italics when reflecting upon the Christian faith, and those individuals may skip the italicized sections.

Let me remind Christian readers that the method used to interpret Scripture in this book is symbolic interpretation, which is somewhat similar to the so-called "allegorical interpretation" practiced extensively by Augustine, Origen, Jerome, Clement, and others. Although symbolic interpretation may not be acceptable to many contemporary Western scholars, it has been practiced extensively in the East. Moreover, the cultural, historical, and literary backgrounds of the East are so different from those of the West that the historical, literary, and critical methods of interpretation have very limited value in a creative dialogue between East and West. As an Asian, it is natural for me to be more allegorical than analytical in my interpretation of Scripture, because I believe that everything has its inner or spiritual meaning. In this age of renewed interest in spirituality and in dialogue between East and West, the symbolic and spiritual interpretation of the Christian faith may provide a new challenge to a global community of faith.

In addition, as the reader will note from reading the chapter concerning symbolism, symbolic interpretation permits us to address the broader issue of language raised by feminists and other disenfranchised individuals. In this connection, the *I Ching* is a powerful vehicle for redefining and refocusing human judgment systems and reaffirming the totality of human value and worth.

Because the *I Ching* is one of the most revered books, and the earliest cosmological book, in East Asian civilization, it is impossible to know fully the mind of Eastern people without understanding this book. As Carl Jung said, "This work [the *I Ching*] embodies, as perhaps no other, the spirit of Chinese culture, for the best minds of China have collaborated upon it and contributed to it for thousands of years."[1] This book has served as a basis for the development of East Asian civilization, and thus the study of the *I Ching* by those of the Christian faith can contribute toward the mutual understanding of East and West.

Nevertheless, the *I Ching* has been regarded as one of the most difficult books to study. Even students of the East have trouble understanding it without a good background knowledge of Chinese classical works. What is needed is a comprehensive introduction of the *I Ching* for Christians in this global and ecumenical age.

In order to provide the necessary background of the *I Ching,* I have decided to deal initially with a few facts about the book itself. In the first chapter, I will try to answer questions that people usually ask about the book. The second chapter of my book deals with the philosophy of the *I Ching.* In that chapter, I will deal extensively with the nature and process of change, which is the essential focus of the *I Ching.* In the third chapter, symbols are discussed in detail, since the *I Ching* is none other than a book of symbols. Next, I offer useful guidelines for the interpretation of these symbols. The fifth chapter deals with the rationale for and the techniques of divination. Divination is treated toward the end because, in the Eastern view, it is impossible to divine without proper background knowledge of the *I Ching.* A hasty approach to divination cannot produce any reliable result. Finally, I will present the significance of the *I Ching* for various fields of study in our own time. A fresh translation of the main text is added for the sake of reference. In it, I have attempted to clarify many ambiguous passages found in other translations.

Embracing Change

1

About the
I Ching

In this chapter, I hope to provide an overview of the *I Ching* in its totality. Beginners always want to know something about the book itself before deciding whether they would like to study it seriously. The best way for me to provide the beginner with some idea as to the nature of the *I Ching* is to answer some of the questions that beginners usually ask. The most common question, of course, is deceptively simple, since the answer is so complex. That question is: "What is the *I Ching?*"

Basic Facts about the *I Ching*

What is the *I Ching?* It is the Chinese book of change. *I* (*Yi*) in Chinese means "change" and *Ching* (*Jing*) in Chinese means "classic" or "book." Therefore, *I Ching* is usually translated as "The Book of Change." The *I Ching* is also known as the *Chou I* or the Chou Book of Change, so called after the Chou dynasty. Since the present Book of Change is thought to have been written by the founder of the Chou dynasty, the *I Ching* of our day—as distinguished from earlier editions—is called the *Chou I*. I will discuss the earlier editions later in dealing with the origin of this book.

I or "change" comprises, then, the essence of the book. Change can be understood as the power that transforms and governs the world. Since the *I Ching* is none other than a book about change, I will deal with the idea of change in my next chapter. Everything I say in this book, then, presupposes change. Change is the key to understanding cosmic phenomena. It reflects the natural law that governs everything. Signifying the ultimate reality, change is analogous to the Christian idea of God.[1] The claim that change is the essence of all things in the world means that dynamism is an intrinsic part of the cosmos. The world as depicted in the *I Ching* is a dynamic whole, a worldview closely related to the biblical conception. It is quite different from the static worldview of most Hellenic thinking, of course, but quite similar to the dynamic and changing worldview of Hebrew thought. I think, therefore, that the worldview of the *I Ching* is much more compatible with the Judeo-Christian worldview than with that of Greek philosophy (with the exception, of course, of Heraclitus). As I expound upon the idea of change later in this book, the similarity between the *I Ching's* worldview and the Judeo-Christian worldview will become evident.

Change in the *I Ching* is represented as the interaction between yin and yang, or negative and positive forces. Change is here expressed in the symbols of broken and unbroken lines. The broken line symbolizes yin, or the negative force in the world, and the unbroken line symbolizes yang, or the positive force in the world. The broken and unbroken lines are combined to form hexagrams, or diagrams each having six lines. All of the possible combinations of yin and yang lines yield sixty-four hexagrams. In other words, when the two variables (yin and yang) are arranged in six columns with a horizontal row for every possible permutation of the variables, the number of rows required is 2^6 or 64. The process is identical to that of formatting a truth table in logic with the two values, *T* and *F,* and six variables.[2]

Thus, the *I Ching* contains sixty-four hexagrams, signifying all possible patterns of changing process. These sixty-four patterns of changing process can best be understood as sixty-four archetypes or germinal situations of cosmic activity.

Ching means "a classic," which differentiates it from an ordinary book. It also means "a canonical book" or "a sacred book." The *I Ching* has been regarded as one of the most important of the Confucian classics. Its prestige was clearly demonstrated in Chinese history. When the tyrant Ch'in Shi-hung-ti, the emperor who built the Great Wall, burned all of the Confucian books in 215 B.C., the *I Ching* alone was spared.

As one of the Confucian classics, therefore, the *I Ching* is regarded as a sacred book. In this respect, it is similar to the Old and New Testaments of the Judeo-Christian tradition. However, it is important to know that the canonical books of the Confucian tradition are quite different from those of the Judeo-Christian heritage. The former stress wisdom, while the latter emphasize divine revelation. In other words, the Confucian tradition lays more stress upon the human aspect. The *I Ching,* therefore, is more precisely a book of unusual wisdom rather than the witness of divine revelation. It is best understood as a book that reveals the wisdom of the sages rather than the everyday wisdom of the common people. The *I Ching* can best be compared with the wisdom literature of the Old Testament, such as Ecclesiastes or Proverbs. It focuses upon practical life and natural phenomena. As a book of extraordinary wisdom, it is incompatible with superstition or magic.

The *I Ching* is also a source of scientific knowledge. The Swiss psychiatrist Carl Jung correctly characterized the *I Ching* as the standard work of Chinese science. When asked by the president of the British Anthropological Society to explain why so highly intellectual a people as the Chinese had produced no science, Jung answered, "This must really be an optical illusion, because the Chinese did have a 'science' whose 'standard work' was the *I Ching.*"[3] In fact, the *I Ching* became the basis for the development of astronomy, music, medicine, and other arts and sciences in China.

The *I Ching* served as more than a basis for scientific development in China; it was and is also a book of philosophy. The development of highly refined schools of Neo-Confucian philosophy during the Sung dynasty in the eleventh and twelfth centuries A.D. can be, as we shall see later, attributed to the study of the *I Ching*. In many respects, the *I Ching* became the focal point of intellectual and scientific development in early China, and is still relevant to our understanding of our world and human nature. That is why I believe the *I Ching* is an essential handmaiden of theology, just as science and philosophy have been for the Christian faith.

The *I Ching* can also be understood as a book attempting to describe the natural phenomena of the universe. It contains the archetypes of cosmic phenomena, which are expressed in terms of binary symbols, yin and yang, or negative and positive forces. We can transpose these archetypes into every possible situation of our life on all levels of existence and in all their aspects: individual or collective, personal or social, conscious or unconscious. The *I Ching,* as a book of archetypes, transcends time and space. It is therefore relevant to all of humanity, in all walks of life. It has its origin in China, but with its cosmic dimensions, it belongs to the whole human race.

Because it contains the archetypes or germinal patterns of all possible conditions in the universe, the *I Ching* has also been used as a book of divination. Knowing the germinal condition, we can discern the possible outcomes of that condition. "Divination," then, as the word is used here, means merely the tapping of archetypal conditions that eventually blossom in the future. In other words, divination, as a part of human wisdom, is the art of intuitive thinking by which we search for a potential outcome to a particular situation that can be applied to our personal and social life. As will be discussed later, the divination of the *I Ching* is different from other forms of divination. In the *I Ching,* divination is the exploration of the wellspring of our decision to act in relation to changing conditions. Because our freedom to decide for or against action is an intrinsic part of the divination process of the *I Ching,* it has very little to do with fatalism or supernaturalism. It employs a self-help technique based on certain ancient oracles, which in turn can best be understood as the primordial wisdom of the East Asian people.

The Contents of the *I Ching*

With these germinal ideas about the *I Ching* now in hand, let me discuss the
content of the book. When we open the *I Ching,* at first glance we see the
separation of the main text from the appendixes (the supplementary text which is
known as the Ten Wings). Most English editions of the *I Ching* do not contain
the appendixes, but a few—for instance, James Legge's translation (published by
Oxford University Press) or the Richard Wilhelm translation (Princeton University Press)—contain both the main text and the appendixes. The citations used
throughout this book come from my own translations.

THE MAIN TEXT

The main text, consisting of the sixty-four hexagrams, is also divided into two
sections: the first (or former) and second (or latter) texts. The first section
consists of the first thirty hexagrams, and the second section contains the
remaining thirty-four hexagrams. This division is consistent with the bipolar
principles of yin and yang. In most English translations, the division is not
marked. The significance of the division lies in the basic principle that change
always occurs through yin and yang interaction. Just as yin complements yang,
the former section complements the latter. Perhaps it can be compared with the
division of the Christian Bible into Old and New Testaments. The Old
Testament complements the New Testament, just as the former section of the
main text of the *I Ching* complements the latter section. The former deals
primarily with cosmic phenomena, and the latter with human affairs. They
belong together and complement one another. Each would be incomplete without
the other.

Each hexagram consists of six rows of divided and/or undivided lines. The
divided line (— —) represents the yin force; the undivided line (———) represents
the yang force. In their totality, these sixty-four hexagrams comprise the *I Ching*
itself. All other writings on the *I Ching* are merely interpretations of the
hexagrams. The hexagrams are autonomous and complete units of germinal
situations, but are also interdependent with the whole process of change. Each
hexagram, therefore, must be studied in relation to other hexagrams. Thus, no
hexagram remains constant. Each changes and is transformed into a new
hexagram. The sixty-four hexagrams are mutually transforming, without
themselves ceasing to exist. They are not static and eternal forms, such as Plato,
for example, describes. They are moving and flowing patterns, like waves of
water or the motion of the dancer, which cannot be transfixed in a static
category. The hexagrams, therefore, must be understood as the interdependent
patterns of process.

Because the hexagram consists merely of lines, it transcends cultural and linguistic differences. Just as numbers are universal, the lines that form the hexagram are also universal. Thus, the hexagram is directly accessible to all peoples. It is the simplest and most direct symbol of events. If we compare its archetype with the Christ-event itself, it can communicate to us directly without cultural and linguistic intermediation. Zen Buddhism uses this kind of intuitive communication as a means of transmitting the Law or Dharma. Likewise, the archetypal hexagram is accessible to us directly, without cultural or religious mediation. It is comparable with the direct Christian experience of the Christ-event through the subjective presence of the Holy Spirit. Since direct and intuitive perception of archetypes proliferate into all kinds of interpretation, human languages are needed to provide a normative understanding of archetypes. In the *I Ching,* the written text of the appendixes is precisely the resymbolization for human comprehension of the simple and direct linear symbols.

The most concise expression of the hexagrams in words is through their names. The name of each hexagram reveals simply and concisely its symbolic function. As opposed to Western thought, which asks "What's in a name?" and, with Shakespeare, replies that "a rose by any other name would smell as sweet," East Asian civilization lays great importance on names. Careful selection of a name is required, because a name is representative of content. Far from regarding the theory of natural names as illogical, a name is felt to be more than an arbitrary sign designating the entity; a name is viewed as the actual interpretation of that which it represents. When a baby is born, his or her name is carefully chosen according to various factors that affect the baby. The so-called rectification of names has been one of the most important aspects of Confucian teaching. A name must be right, for its meaning must correspond with the entity that is named. In the case of a hexagram, its name summarizes its meaning and character.

The importance of names in the Judeo-Christian tradition cannot be ignored. For example, the name "Christ" or "Son of God" has profound implications for our understanding of Christianity. "Christ" is not just a symbol, which can be used to designate just anyone for the sake of convenience. Christ is the name that represents his uniqueness. It would not be proper to call everyone Christ. Paul makes quite clear the importance of the name when he says, "God has highly exalted him and bestowed on him the name which is above every name, that at the name of Jesus every knee should bow, in heaven and on earth and under the earth" (Phil. 2:9, 10). Jesus also asked us to pray in his name. Thus, most of our prayers end in his name. However, in the West, the significance of names seems to be lost, and less attention is paid to the meaning of names. The I Ching *reminds us that we should take the name of Jesus seriously, as we have been taught in Scripture. A name is more than a mere symbol; it is a unique and irreplaceable symbol.*

A brief text accompanies each hexagram. This text is called the "Judgment" (*T'uan*). The name represents the hexagram, but the Judgment is the decision made with regard to it. The Judgment on the hexagram can, therefore, be compared with a decision of a trial judge, whose decision proclaims a definitive value judgment on the case. Like a legal case, the hexagram is evaluated in terms of both present and future predicaments. The Judgment, thus, is a form of advice which provides a diagnosis of the present condition, a prediction of possible evolution into future conditions, and a prescription for action. Some of the terminology used in the Judgments (i.e., "correct," "success," "good fortune," or "misfortune," among others) is helpful in illustrating the nature of the Judgment. By looking at these words, we see that they represent diagnostic values.

Let us consider the Judgment of hexagram 6, for example. Hexagram 6 is named Conflict (*Sung*). The Judgment of this hexagram reads as follows:

> Conflict. Sincerity is obstructed. The middle way brings good fortune. The end bring misfortune. It is advantageous to see the great person, but it is not advantageous to cross the big river.

In this Judgment, the present condition is described in the first sentence: "Sincerity is obstructed." The second and third sentences indicate future predicaments (good fortune or misfortune). The final sentence prescribes the action to take. In this Judgment, the option for action is included. The Judgment is, then, the most important text of the hexagram.

The Judgment may be compared with the kerygma, the preaching of the Gospel, which has been regarded as the most important message in the Christian church. The concept of the Judgment in the I Ching *illuminates the Christian understanding of the Gospel. Just as the Judgment consists of the present predicament, the possible outcome eventuating, and a prescription for action, the essential message of Jesus also contains these three basic ingredients: the present condition of every human being as a sinner; the possibility of a future condition of salvation or the new humanity; and a prescription for action: to love God and to love one's neighbors. These three aspects of the message symbolize the Gospel.*

Just as the Judgment is based on the hexagram, the kerygma is based on the Jesus-event. The Jesus-event is primary, and the kerygma is derivative. The problem is that most theological works written in the past were developed on the basis of the kerygma, rather than on the Jesus-event. This is a mistake. Just as most people simply read the Judgment before examining the hexagram itself, many Christians read the Gospel without first having direct experience of the Jesus-event, or without being confronted by the Jesus-event through the Holy Spirit. The I Ching *can help to open Christians to the new insight that their dogmatic rigidity of the past was caused by an undue emphasis on kerygma.*

What is needed is to see that kerygma is nothing more than the expression of the living event of Christ. The relationship between the hexagram and the Judgment highlights the Christian's need to reexamine the relationship between the Christ-event and the kerygma. Just as the Judgment is dependent upon having a hexagram to "judge," the kerygma is dependent on the living presence of Christ. Moreover, the Judgment cannot be understood in isolation. It is always read with the hexagram. Likewise, the kerygma alone produces nothing but intellectual speculation and a dead faith. When it is read and understood along with the living event of Christ, it becomes a living and practical faith.

In most English translations of the *I Ching,* a brief text on the Symbol (or Image) of the hexagram is found. For example, in Wilhelm's translation the Symbol appears in the main texts, but in Legge's translation, it does not appear. The Symbol does not in fact belong to the main text, but belongs to the third and fourth wings of the appendixes. The reason that it is included in the main text is that it is a most helpful commentary for our understanding of the structural aspects of the hexagram, and thus seems to complement the Judgment. The former states the nature of the hexagram, while the latter indicates the decision issuing from it. The Symbol, therefore, displays interest in the nature of human, social, and cosmic conditions. Let me illustrate it from the image of hexagram 23: "The mountain adheres to the earth: it is the symbol of breaking apart. Thus superior persons increase their strength, and their people can secure peace." From this example, it is clear that the Symbol began with the structure of symbols—the symbols of mountain and earth—and then passed to the condition of superior persons and their relation to the peace of society.

In the New Testament the counterparts of the Image are parables and metaphors that Jesus used in his teaching. The parables and metaphors belong to the essential teachings of Christ, but they are somewhat different from the kerygma. Just as the Judgment is different from the Symbol, so also the parables and metaphors of the New Testament should be differentiated from the kerygma.

Finally, each line of the hexagram has its own text, which is known as the judgment on the line. In this text, I have decided to use a small letter *j* in the word "judgment" to indicate the judgment on the line, and a capital *J* in the word "Judgment" for the Judgment on the hexagram.

The judgment is understood as a microcosmic reflection of the Judgment on the hexagram as a whole. Because of its microcosmic character, it has a function similar to that of the Judgment. What distinguishes the judgment on the line from the Judgment on the hexagram is its dependence on the latter. In other words, the judgment on the line is always relative to the Judgment on the hexagram. The former represents the part, and the latter represents the whole.

The judgment on the line begins with the lowest line of the hexagram and ends with the uppermost line, representing the process of evolvement from the beginning to the end of the hexagram as a whole. It is confined within the hexagram and describes the stages of development. The judgment on the line is, then, a description of its individual predicament in relation to the other lines in the hexagram. Although its expression is patterned after the Judgment on the hexagram, it is similar to the Symbol as well. It is concerned with the decision that applies the line to individual, social, and cosmic contexts.

If the Judgment on the hexagram reminds us of the kerygma, the apostolic preaching on the Christ-event, the judgment on the lines helps us to see the specific parts of the original preaching that constitute the whole Gospel. The original preaching of Peter in Acts, for example, can be divided into several parts: 1) the age of fulfillment as foretold by the prophets; 2) Christ's ministry, his death and his resurrection; 3) the exaltation of Christ as the Lord of mankind; 4) the coming of the Holy Spirit; 5) the fulfillment; and 6) the appeal for repentance and the newness of life. These parts seem to comprise some order of movement for the fulfillment of God's promise. If the original preaching of Peter is compared with the Judgment on the hexagram as a whole, the six components can be compared with the judgments on the six lines of the hexagram. They describe the processes and mutual interdependence. It is important to observe that the kerygma consists of several components, although these components are not as clearly delineated as the judgment on the lines of the hexagram.

To summarize the main texts of the *I Ching,* there is revealed a hierarchy of symbolism. The names and Judgment are expressions of the hexagram in words. The hexagrams themselves are simple, even primordial, symbols transcending words and cultural and temporal expressions. The hexagrams are the products of the divided and undivided lines, the symbols of the negative and positive forces in the world. That is to say, the negative and positive, or yin and yang, forces are symbolized through the divided and undivided lines; the divided and undivided lines constitute sixty-four hexagrams, and these hexagrams are interpreted in words that formulate the names, judgments, and symbols.

This hierarchical structure of symbolism in the I Ching *is reminiscent of the hierarchy of authority in the New Testament. The creative power of God seems to manifest itself in bipolar relationships: heaven and earth; light and darkness; water and land; male and female; good and evil; and so on. Such bipolar relationships are expressed in the story of the Creation in the Book of Genesis. The bipolar relationship is cumulatively manifested in the death and resurrection of Christ. These dialectical poles of death and resurrection summarize the Christ-event, being the primordial expressions of Christian experience. Like the hexagram, the Christ-event is the essence of the Christian faith. From this event, the kerygma evolved out of the apostolic ministry of the early church. The original preaching of the Gospel became the basis of doctrines and church teachings. The hierarchy of authority in the New Testament witness is then comparable with the hierarchical symbolism in the main text of the* I Ching. *Just as doctrinal statements became necessary to interpret the complex nature of divine revelation, the supplementary texts of the* I Ching *have been helpful for the interpretation of the hexagrams.*

THE SUPPLEMENTARY TEXTS

The supplementary texts are certain Confucian commentaries known as the Ten Wings (*Shih I*). They are called the Ten Wings because they consist of ten commentaries that assist the interpreter to understand the symbolism. Wings symbolize the power of flight and, in Western terms, it might be said that the Ten Wings help the interpreter ascend to meaningful comprehension of the hexagrams.

The Ten Wings are to the main text very much as the commentaries are to the New Testament, or as the Talmud is to the Torah. These commentaries include both exegetical and philosophical interpretations of the main text. Therefore, they can be compared with the church's interpretations of the Gospel in Christianity, which likewise include both exegetical and theological commentaries upon the divine revelation. For example, the theological works of St. Thomas or of John Calvin are comparable to the Ten Wings in the I Ching.

The first two wings are called the Commentary on the Judgment (*T'uan Chuan*). This commentary clarifies the meaning and significance of the Judgment on the hexagram. See, for example, hexagram 37, the Family (*Chia Jên*). The Judgment on this hexagram reads: "The family. The correctness of a woman is advantageous."

The Commentary on the Judgment explains the Judgment on this hexagram as follows:

> The family. The correct place of a woman is inside, while the correct place of a man is outside. The correct place of both man and woman signifies the great righteousness revealed in heaven and earth. In the family, the parents are strict rulers. Let the father be a father and the son a son. Let the elder brother be an elder brother and the younger brother be a younger brother. Let the husband be a husband and the wife a wife. Then the house is correct. When the house is in order, everything under heaven will be firmly established.

In this commentary, the correctness of a woman is explained in detail. In early East Asia, the woman was confined to the family and therefore she was understood as the family person. She stayed inside, but her husband worked outside. Therefore, the woman and the family are closely related. In the commentary, the Confucian value is stressed. The rectification of names and the proper order in the family both signify correctness. As we see in this illustration, the Commentary on the Judgment is primarily an exegetical work on the Judgment.

This commentary can be compared to the exegetical works on the kerygma in the Christian faith. Many biblical scholars have attempted to expound the apostolic preaching of the Christ-event. Thus, most biblical commentaries on the Gospel are comparable to the Commentary on the Judgment. Because it is an exegetical commentary, it should be read along with the Judgment in the main text.

The third and fourth wings are the Commentary on the Symbols (*Hsiang Chuan*). I have previously discussed this commentary in discussing the main text. The symbols in the main text are abbreviations of the Commentary on the Symbols. You will recall that the Commentary on the Symbols belongs to the supplementary texts, although many recent editions of the *I Ching* place it in the main text because of its usefulness for our understanding of the attributes of the hexagram. Here, the symbol is simply the image of the hexagram. The symbol is interpreted in terms of the two constituent trigrams (diagrams of three divided and/or undivided lines). The following is hexagram 7, the Army (*Shih*), which consists of the trigram Earth above and the trigram Water below.

The Commentary on the Symbols says: "Water is in the center of the Earth. It is the symbol of the Army. The superior person, therefore, draws strength from the people through his generosity." Here, the relationship between the two symbols of Earth and Water plays an important role in our interpretation of the symbol of the Army.

Just as the metaphors and parables in the New Testament convey the symbolic meanings of the Christ-event, this commentary on the symbols provides a symbolic interpretation of the germinal situation.

The fifth and sixth wings comprise the most comprehensive and scholarly treatise of all on the main text. They are called the Great Commentary (*Ta Chuan*), or sometimes the Commentary on the Appended Judgments (*Hsi Tz'u Chuan*). The Great Commentary expounds the basic philosophy of the *I Ching*. In this respect, this is the most important commentary for the understanding of the principle of change. The bipolar relationship of yin and yang, the formation of trigrams and hexagrams, the implications of oracles and the instruction on divination techniques are discussed in great detail. This commentary, therefore, attempts to answer many questions and respond to many issues about the *I Ching*. Why does change operate in terms of yin and yang? Why does the hexagram consist of two trigrams? Is this combination an arbitrary creation or is it based on a definite law? Why are the fifty yarrow stalks used for the consultation of the *I Ching?* The Great Commentary attempts to answer these and other questions. This is, perhaps, the philosophical masterpiece within the *I Ching*.

The Great Commentary is much like the great theological treatises of Christianity. Some of the great theological works, such as Thomas Aquinas's Summa theologiae *for the Roman Catholic church, John Calvin's definitive work entitled* Christianae religionis institutio *for the Reformed church, or, in our own time, Karl Barth's* Kirchliche Dogmatik *readily come to mind. These great theological works reflect the Christian attempt to understand the depth of the Christ-event as expressed in Scripture. They are indispensable guides for understanding the message of Christ and the Christian faith. Who is God? Why did Jesus come to the world? Who was Jesus? What is the church? These theological works, like the Great Commentary of the* I Ching, *attempt to answer many of the questions and address issues that concern the Christian faith.*

The seventh wing is the Commentary on the Text (*Wen Yen*). This commentary contains important essays interpreting the main text of the *I Ching*. However, it deals with the first and second hexagrams only, and is thus believed to be merely a remnant of a commentary on the entire text. It deals not only with the first two hexagrams as a whole, but also with each individual line. It would have been a most valuable commentary had its entire text been preserved, but that, unfortunately, is not the case.

The eighth wing is the Discussion of the Trigrams (*Shuo Kua*), which is almost essential for understanding the *I Ching*. It deals with the symbolic correlation of yin and yang and the philosophical background of the trigrams. The commentary is very brief, however, consisting of only eleven paragraphs. This commentary provides very important information concerning the two distinctive arrangements of the trigrams: the Earlier Heaven arrangement and the Later Heaven arrangement. The significance of these arrangements will be discussed later. In the last part of the eighth wing, the symbolic implications of the eight trigrams are discussed in detail. Let me illustrate the symbolic meanings of the first hexagram, Heaven, as described in this commentary.

> Heaven is round, the king, the father, jade, metal, cold, and ice. It is deep red, a good horse, an old horse, a lean horse, a wild horse, and fruit tree.

The Discussion of the Trigrams is similar to a serious type of biblical scholarship that attempts to understand and analyze important terms or ideas in the New Testament. Understanding the deeper meaning of such terms as the Christ, Sin, Death, Resurrection, Reconciliation, and the Kingdom of God is, in fact, fundamental to our understanding of the kerygma. Through the analysis of these terms and their symbolic significance, Christians learn to relate the Gospel to today's world.

The ninth wing is the Sequence of the Hexagrams (*Hsu Kua*), which attempts to trace the order of the hexagrams. The first and second hexagrams,

Heaven and Earth, are the great yang and the great yin. Since they are the bases for the generation of all other hexagrams, the Sequence of the Hexagrams begins with the third hexagram, called Difficulty. The Sequence of the Hexagrams explains why this hexagram arises out of the combination of the first and second hexagrams. It says, "After the first and second hexagrams a being develops. This being fills the gap between Heaven and Earth. This means that Difficulty follows Heaven and Earth. Difficulty means to fill up the gap." Thus the Sequence of the Hexagrams attempts to explain the order in which the hexagrams develop. Although some explanations are not totally convincing, this commentary is nonetheless helpful in understanding any one hexagram in its relationship with others.

This wing is comparable to the chronological study of the life of Jesus and the historical development of the Christian faith. Chronology is helpful in putting the various events in perspective. It is easy to categorize things chronologically, and a chronological overview of the sequence of events as they occurred over time is a useful tool for studying the Gospel. This wing is a rational thought-style that attempts to explain the order of events in a systematic fashion. Any such attempt to explain an existing order or sequence can help us understand any one event in relation to other events.

The last wing is the Miscellaneous Notes on the Hexagrams (*Tsa Kua*), which offers a brief note on each hexagram. For example, the commentary on the first hexagram says, "Heaven is firm." On the second hexagram it says, "Earth is weak." While these brief notes do not add anything new to the existing texts, they provide concise summaries on each hexagram.

This last wing is much like the use of key words in important passages of the Bible. When looking for a specific verse, it is helpful to look for a key word in the concordance that represents the verse. Using appropriate key words aids in utilizing the concordance to locate the needed passage. Thus the key word or concept is an important means of identification.

The Ten Wings as a whole are an indispensable tool for the study of the *I Ching*. Among them, the Commentary on the Symbols is the most important. Many English editions of the *I Ching,* therefore, include this commentary in the main text. Perhaps the Great Commentary and the Discussions of the Trigrams are the most helpful tools dealing with the philosophical and theoretical foundations of the process of change. They can be compared with the great theological and dogmatic treatises in Christianity. Without them, the *I Ching* might easily be misunderstood as a mere divination book. The rest of the Ten Wings is primarily exegetical works. They are helpful for the interpretation of the *I Ching,* and without them the *I Ching* would be incomplete. Because they complement the main text, they ultimately became a part of it.

In some respects, the Ten Wings are more than mere supplementary texts. They have become indispensable aids to the main text. Because of their integral value to the text, they may be regarded as definitive works, basic to all other commentaries. Although hundreds of commentaries and essays have been written on the *I Ching,* none can claim the same authority as the Ten Wings. The Ten Wings, then, are like the Talmud in Judaism, or the works of Aquinas in Roman Catholicism. Therefore, since all other commentaries are little more than varying reflections on the Ten Wings, I will adhere closely to the texts of the Ten Wings when I expound upon the principles of the process of change.

The Origin and Development of the *I Ching*

The origin of the *I Ching* is uncertain. The question of identity of the author, the era of its production, and the sources for the main text are matters that have been debated for many centuries. In particular, sinologists have long attempted to reconstruct the authorship of the *I Ching.* The present book is not intended to satisfy the specialist's interest in such academic debates. Such an endeavor would be like the form criticism developed and debated in the West. Just as textual criticism in New Testament studies in Christianity has aroused the interest of scholars, so also textual criticism of the *I Ching* has been the focus of studies by sinologists. For those not versed in classical Chinese, however, such criticism means very little. For such nonspecialists, the traditional approach is more helpful than that of the sinologists. I do not, however, accept uncritically the traditional authorship of the *I Ching.* As will become readily apparent, I hope to creatively use tradition to reconstruct the origin and development of the *I Ching.*[4]

In the study of the Old and New Testaments, Christians have similar problems. The authorship of the Pentateuch was traditionally attributed to Moses, that of the Psalms to King David, and that of the Gospels to the four Apostles. Scholars, using critical and analytical methods, may question and even disprove their received authorship. However, most Christians are less interested in these scholarly speculations than in knowing how the Old and New Testaments originated and developed. For them, proving or disproving the authorship of the texts is not important. Likewise, I am not interested in form criticism when I deal with the origin and development of the I Ching.

In the Discussion of the Trigrams, the authors of the *I Ching* are described as holy sages: "The holy sages formed the *I Ching* in ancient times" (chapter 1). The same idea is also expressed in the Great Commentary: "The holy sages formed the hexagrams in order to clearly define good fortune and misfortune" (1:2). These statements in the Ten Wings suggest that the *I Ching* is a book of unusual wisdom. Sages are by definition wise persons, and thus their writings are books of wisdom. However, the authorship of the *I Ching* is attributed to the *holy* sages, not just any sages. This makes the *I Ching* more than a wisdom book; it renders it a book of transcendental wisdom. This illuminates the comparison of the *I Ching* with the wisdom literature of the Old Testament.

Who, then, were the holy sages? Since they were regarded as the authors of the *I Ching,* I must refer to tradition to identify their names. According to tradition and legend, the king Fu Hsi (2953–2838 B.C.) was known as the author of the eight trigrams and hexagrams in the *I Ching.* Later, King Wen, founder of the Chou dynasty (1150–249 B.C.) is said to have rearranged the hexagrams and given them the Judgments. His son, Tan, who was the duke of the Chou dynasty, allegedly composed the texts on the lines of the hexagrams. The Ten Wings were then composed as supplements by Confucius or the Confucian School. Although tradition attributes the authorship of the *I Ching* to these holy sages, it is impossible to accept this idea unconditionally.

Like the conditional acceptance of the authorship of the I Ching, *those whose knowledge of the history of Judaism is great often challenge the Judeo-Christian tradition that cites Moses as the author of the Pentateuch, King David as the author of the Psalms, and King Solomon as the author of the wisdom books in the Old Testament.*

What I hope to do in this text is to provide a reliable and informed treatment of the authorship of the *I Ching* without denying tradition. Since the authorship of the Ten Wings or the Supplementary Commentaries has been the subject of intense academic speculation, I will not comment on them in this text. It is probably best understood that the Ten Wings was written by Confucian followers and attributed to Confucius. I will, therefore, focus my discussion upon the origin and formation of the main text of the *I Ching.*

Although tradition attributes the authorship of the book to the holy sages, or at least to certain individuals, I prefer to regard the writing as a process, holding that the main text of the *I Ching* was developed in several stages. This does not deny the tradition, but reinterprets it in process terms. Tradition attributes the book to such great sages as King Fu Hsi, King Wen, the duke of Chou, and Confucius, just as many books of the Old Testament were attributed to great leaders like Moses, King David, and King Solomon. However, behind these great individuals was a long history that impacted upon the creation of each book.

I regard the making of the main text of the *I Ching* to have occurred in four stages of development in Chinese history. The first stage was that dealing with the oracles of divination, without any special reference to cosmological implications. The second stage was the creation of the eight trigrams that became the basis for the primitive cosmology. The third stage was the systematic formulation of the sixty-four hexagrams and the Judgments, and the fourth and final stage culminated in the elaboration and explanation of the lines of the hexagram.

These stages of development are similar to the probable formation of the

Gospel. Although individual authors such as Matthew, Mark, Luke, and John had much to do with the writing of the Gospels, there must have been stages of development. In the first stage, the sayings of Jesus had not yet been connected with the witness of his followers. The second stage must have been, then, the correlation of the sayings of Jesus with the testimony of witnesses and the local traditions of that day. The third stage would likely have been the borrowing of sources from other traditions to complete the narratives. Perhaps the final stage might be the editing and elaborating of the story as a whole. I believe that seeing the formation of the Scriptures in terms of process is the most logical way to understanding them and, at the same time, does not deny traditional authorship. In the same way, most Confucian classics, including the *I Ching,* went through many stages of development.

The first stage, which initiated the formation of the *I Ching,* grew out of the use of the oracle bones associated with the practice of divination. According to the Book of Rites (*Li Chi*), regarded as one of the oldest Confucian classics, the divination oracles were consulted through the use of certain plants and tortoise shells. The Book of Rites says, "The ancient kings made use of the stalks of the divining plant and the tortoise shell; arranged their sacrifices; burned their offerings of silk" (7:2). The "ancient kings" in this context might be synonymous with the holy sages who were believed to be the authors of the *I Ching.* They will be discussed extensively in later sections of this text.

The use of the divining plant seems to have coexisted with the use of the tortoise shell in the early days. However, the tortoise shell was more commonly used than the divining plant. The importance of the tortoise shell for oracles is clearly illustrated in the number of offerings dedicated to it. As is described in the Book of Rites, "In the various articles of tribute the tortoises were placed in front of all other offerings, because the shell gave knowledge of the future" (9:7). The divination oracles invoked by means of the tortoise shell were not only more important but also much older than those called upon by the use of divination stalks. In the Book of Songs (*Shih Ching*), a document that purports to stem from the twenty-third century B.C. (II, 2:18), divination by means of the tortoise shell is already mentioned. Somewhat later, divination through divining plants is found (Book of Songs, V, 4:20, 31). It is uncertain why the tortoise shell was the first object to be used for divination. It seems possible that the tortoise was thought to have the most mysterious and oracular powers of all living creatures because it survived longer than any other then-known living being. In the minds of these primitive people, the life of the tortoise was so long that it became the symbol of immortality; and because of its immortality, it was aware of the future. In divination, the ventral surface of the tortoise was incised with a red-hot stylus so that the shell cracked and crack-lines formed. The diviner then read the oracles from the pattern of the cracks. This kind of divination seems to be still used every year by the Shinto priest in Ise, Japan, to choose the plot on which to grow the sacred crops.

A simpler process of divination seems to have developed later: divination by means of the stalks of a divining plant. Divining both by the tortoise shell and the divining plant continued apace for some time in Chinese history. In the Book of Songs, the use of both methods is well illustrated in the following account of a faithful wife who waits for her husband to return from the battle-ground: "The transport wagons did not come. Great was the distress of my sorrowing heart. For he did not arrive when the time was due, so that I am full of grief. Yet I have divined by the tortoise shell and by the stalks; and they agree in saying that he is near. My soldier [husband] is at hand."[5] For some time, both methods thus coexisted. However, because of the complexity of reading oracles from the cracks of the tortoise shell, divination by stalks was likely more popular, and finally replaced the more cumbersome method of divination by tortoise shells, although it is difficult to pinpoint when the actual transition occurred in history.

The *I Ching* that has come down to us today has its origin in the use of a fixed number of milfoil stalks. Because the use of stalks for divination was easier than the use of tortoise shells and because the Chinese character *I* can also mean "easy," Book of Easy is a possible translation of the title *I Ching*. This could also explain why the *I Ching* has the alternate name of *Chou I*. It was named Chou because it was composed by people of the Chou dynasty, and *I* possibly because its technique for divination was simple.[6]

Now that I have reconstructed the initial stage of the development of the *I Ching,* I must pause to acknowledge the fact that the divination process is often perceived by the Western mind as offensively primitive. Although divination has been misunderstood as an occult and superstitious practice, its real meaning lies in the search for the unknown, for one's destiny. This is a most primitive form of human yearning for transcendent wisdom. Divination as a human search for transcendence has profound implications for the development of civilization. It is best understood as a germ from which developed both science and religion. Therefore, although divination is not a religion, it can nonetheless be considered a vehicle for spiritual expression.

Divination oracles are reminiscent of the sayings of Jesus, and also of the prophecies that were the bases for the entire Judeo-Christian movement. There is a clear distinction, however, between the prophecies in the Old Testament and the divination oracles of the I Ching. *The prophecies were not intended to predict the future but to proclaim the divine will, while the divination oracles in the* I Ching *do not reveal divine will, but do predict the future. The prophecies, then, begin with the divine, while the divination oracles begin with the human search. In this respect, the two practices complement one another. Just as the prophecies marked the beginning of Western religion, the divination oracles comprised the initial stage of the development of the* I Ching.

Before discussing the second stage of development and formation of the *I Ching,* let me make it clear that the stages are not stages of historical process. The distinction between the first and second stages of development is one of logic rather than one based upon historical evidence. For the first stage, I discussed divination oracles; for the second stage, I will discuss the works of the ancient kings or holy sages who have been traditionally regarded as the originators of these oracles.

The second stage deals with the correlation of cosmic process with the oracles in terms of the trinitarian principles of the world. In the Christian faith, the Trinity has to do with divine nature. However, in Eastern Asian tradition, trinitarian principles of the world include the object (that which has form, the Earth), the subject (human beings), and the content (that which is formless, Heaven). This enumeration finds a striking parallel in the subtitle of a synoptic work by the British empirical philosopher of religion F. R. Tennant: "The world, the soul, and God."[7] According to this trinity, the human being is the center, Heaven is above, and the Earth below. It pertains to a worldview and, therefore, is called a trinitarian principle of the world. It forms the basis, in fact, of Asian cosmology. In other words, the trinitarian principle is expressed in the eight trigrams, the diagrams of three divided or undivided lines, which represent all things in the world.

According to Chinese tradition, trigrams were first used in a mysterious map. This map is known as the River Map (*Ho T'u*), for it was discovered coming from the Yellow River in China. The Great Commentary describes the importance of the map as well as the writing:

> Therefore: Heaven produced spiritual things, which were perceived by the holy sages. The transformation of Heaven and Earth was imitated by them. They put images in Heaven to indicate good fortune and misfortune. They reproduced these images. The Yellow River brought forth the map, and the Lo River brought forth the writing. The holy sages patterned the *I Ching* after them. (1:11)

The River Map was, therefore, believed to be the basis for the formation of the *I Ching.* Traditional students of the *I Ching,* therefore, took the map as a blueprint of the *I Ching.* As the Great Commentary remarked, the holy sages patterned the *I Ching* after both the map and the writing. Because the writing from the Lo River became the basis for a technique of divination, I will discuss this writing in the chapter on divination.

According to popular belief, the map was drawn on the back of a dragon-horse coming out of the Yellow River. This belief is recorded in the Book of Rites: "The map was borne by a horse" (8:4). Confucius himself seemed to believe in this map, and he mentioned it in his *Analects* (9:8). What, then, is the significance of this map printed on a dragon-horse? It is the dragon-horse itself that seems to underscore the importance of the map.

The dragon-horse is found in many important places in East Asia. It may be found on the roof of a temple or at the gate of a palace. According to tradition, the dragon-horse can literally see spiritual beings, and it is believed to guard against evil spirits. Moreover, the dragon-horse represents creative power and is, therefore, the symbolic animal of the first hexagram in the *I Ching*. Since there has never actually existed such a creature, it is generally believed to have been a vision.

This vision of a map on a dragon-horse is similar to the Book of Revelation, where John sees various visions of the spiritual world. However, in Revelation the dragon represents the satanic force, whereas in the I Ching *it represents creative force. The contrast is apparently one conditioned by cultural difference.*

This mystical vision is the basis for the formation of the *I Ching*. Those who received the vision were the holy sages. Who in fact were these individuals? According to Chu Chun-sheng (A.D. 1755–1858), there were three persons or sages who received this vision.[8] According to the people of Hsia dynasty (2205–1766 B.C.) Lien Shan received the map, so it was called *Lien Shan*. According to the people of the Shang dynasty (1766–1150 B.C.), Kuei Ts'ang received this map, so it was called *Kuei Ts'ang*. According to the people of the Chou dynasty (1122–256 B.C.), Fu Hsi, the legendary king, secured the map and called it *Fu Hsi*. Fu Hsi's arrangement became the basis for King Wen's arrangement of hexagrams in the present *I Ching*. Both the *Lien Shan* and *Kuei Ts'ang* arrangements were lost, and there is no trustworthy knowledge of them other than their titles. The only book that survived is the *I Ching* which contains the Fu Hsi arrangement of eight trigrams based upon the map.

The original map which Fu Hsi received from the Yellow River was thought to be lost in the eleventh century B.C. However, the map was believed to have been reconstructed at the time of the restoration of the ancient classics during the Han dynasty. Is the reconstructed map, then, identical with the original map? We can only accept it on faith. There is no way to prove that the map reconstructed by the so-called school of Five Movements (*Wu Hsing*) is identical with the River Map.

Uncritical students of the *I Ching,* therefore, accept the reconstructed map as the authentic one. Figure 1 shows what is commonly accepted as a map identical with the original one.

Although it is impossible to verify the authenticity of this map, its intrinsic merit commends it for careful study. Let us see, then, how Fu Hsi may have been able to construct the eight trigrams from it. The map is made of black and white circles. If we count the circles, we find that all of the dark circles come to even numbers such as 2, 4, 6, 8, and 10. All of the light circles, on the other hand, come to odd numbers: 1, 3, 5, 7 and 9. The Great Commentary explains the numbers: "The number 1 belongs to Heaven, 2 to Earth, 3 to Heaven, 4 to

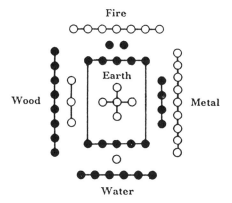

Earth, 5 to Heaven, 6 to Earth, 7 to Heaven, 8 to Earth, 9 to Heaven, and 10 to the Earth" (1:11). Thus, the odd numbers represent Heaven, and the even numbers represent Earth. Yang is the primordial symbol of Heaven, and yin is that of Earth. Thus, the odd numbers are yang numbers and the even numbers are yin numbers. What is significant here is the division of the numbers into two groups—yin and yang. This marks the beginning of the bipolar relationship in the process of change. Everything can be classified into these two groups.

The Great Commentary explains the numerical classification further:

> The heavenly numbers are five, and the earthly numbers are also five. The numbers of these two series correspond with each other, and each one has another that may be considered its complement. The heavenly numbers amount to 25 and the earthly to 30. The numbers of both Heaven and Earth amount in sum to 55. Because of these numbers, changes and transformations are possible. Thus the spiritual powers are achieved. (1:9)

What the commentary tries to say is self-evident. There are five heavenly numbers: 1, 3, 5, 7, and 9; also, there are five earthly numbers: 2, 4, 6, 8, and 10. When the five heavenly numbers are added together, it amounts to 25. Likewise, when the five earthly numbers are added together, it comes to 30. Therefore, the total of the numbers for both heaven and earth amounts to 55, which represents everything in the world.

What is the significance of adding these numbers? Is it not a meaningless game of arithmetic? On the contrary, there is a profound meaning behind it. First of all, the numbers are different, but are united together for the whole. Thus, the commentary attempts to convey the complementary relationship between yin and yang, or the heavenly and earthly numbers. Although they are opposite in character, their mutual complementarity makes the whole possible. There is also another important idea that most Western people fail to notice in this map: that is, the importance of numbers themselves. If the River Map was the basis for the formation of the *I Ching,* it follows that the *I Ching* is based upon numbers. In other words, numerology is correctly regarded as they key to understanding the *I Ching.* Whenever I go to East Asia and discuss the *I Ching,* the question of numbers always arises.

The importance of numerology is also apparent in the Book of Revelation. Those who read and try to understand Revelation cannot escape the significance placed upon numbers. Numbers seem to carry special meanings or even powers. They are more than mere signs—as in our own culture scholars from Pythagoras to Sir James Jeans have also held. The significance of numbers will become more evident as I discuss the formation of the eight trigrams.

The question is, then, how Fu Hsi formed the eight trigrams from the map. First of all, there is a hypothesis that Fu Hsi, if he was really the author of the eight trigrams, failed to construct the trigrams using the circles of the map. He then decided to replace the circles with lines for convenience. The whole or undivided line (———) was used for light circles, and the divided line (— —) represented the dark circles. In this way, the group of odd numbers became undivided lines, and the even numbers became divided lines. The undivided line symbolizes the yang force, and the divided line the yin force. By observing the map carefully, one can notice that the inner formation—five light circles and ten dark circles—comprises the nucleus, which is also known as the Great Ultimate. What one needs, therefore, is to pay attention to the circles on the outer sides of the map.

These circles are divided into four groups: two groups of dark circles and two groups of light circles. The first group of dark circles, which represents water, is the number 6 because it consists of six circles; another group of dark circles, which represents wood, is number 8 because of its eight circles. Both 6 and 8 are even numbers, and therefore they represent yin forces. The number 6 is assigned to the "old yin," which is symbolized with two broken lines (☷), while the number 8 is assigned to the "young yin," which is symbolized with a broken line below and an unbroken line above (☳). In the same manner, one can see the two groups of light circles, which represent fire and metal. The group that represents fire has seven circles, and therefore it is the number 7. The group that represents metal has nine light circles, and therefore it is the number 9. Both 7 and 9 are odd numbers, and represent yang forces. The number 9 is assigned to the "old yang," which is symbolized by two undivided lines (☰). The number 7 is assigned to the "young yang," which is symbolized with an undivided line below and a divided line above (☱). Now, let us look at the four lineal symbols which have been constructed from the outer circle of the map. These four symbols or four duograms represent the four seasons and the four directions. They are comparable, in Western logic, to the formatting of a truth table from two variables where the number of rows is 2^2 or 4. They are frameworks of cosmology because they signify the dimensions of time and the three directions of space. Thus, they become the bases for the formation of the eight trigrams.

By adding one more line to the four duograms, the eight trigrams are formed. The reason for adding an additional line is explained in the Great Commentary: "Therefore, the *I* is in the Great Ultimate beginning. The two primary powers produce the four symbols, the four symbols produce the eight trigrams" (1:11). The ultimate beginning, which is change itself, evolves into two primary powers, the yin and yang forces. The two powers produce four symbols or four duograms, and the four symbols produce eight trigrams. They are Heaven ☰, Earth ☷, Thunder ☳, Wind ☴, Water ☵, Fire ☲, Mountain ☶, and Lake ☱. I will elaborate upon these trigrams later.

Why was it necessary to add another line to form the trigrams? As noted before, the trinitarian principle of the wold is expressed in the trigrams. To achieve it, one must add, as in logic, a third variable—by which one generates four more rows of T's and F's ($2^3 = 8$). Heaven and Earth represent the two primary forces of yang and yin. However, Heaven and Earth cannot complete the world. What is needed between them is a human being. Therefore, by adding one more line to the duograms, the trigrams are completed. This means that human beings are added to Heaven and Earth to complete the trinitarian principle of the cosmos. In this way, Fu Hsi may have been able to construct the eight trigrams from the River Map.

The second stage of development of the *I Ching,* then, was the symbolic construction of the trinitarian principle of the cosmos based upon the vision coming from the Yellow River. *This is reminiscent of the apocalyptic literatures of the Old and New Testaments. The various visions have concrete messages to convey to the world. Certainly, visions are not mere illusions. They often convey powerful impressions—impressions that can transform the world. One such powerful vision occurred in the life of the apostle Paul. The vision of Christ that he saw on his way to Damascus actually transformed Paul's life. The vision that Fu Hsi received was that of a simple map; but it served as the basis for the development of the most profound wisdom for the world. The map of the Yellow River also reminds me of the seven seals in Revelation. Just as with the opening of the seals, the map was opened and the cosmic principles of change were revealed.*

The third stage deals with the creation of the hexagrams and the composition of the Judgments. Was Fu Hsi, who formulated the eight trigrams from the River Map, responsible also for the creation of the sixty-four hexagrams? It is probable that Fu Hsi, even if he was not a legendary king, was capable of constructing the hexagrams through combinations of trigrams. In fact, any logic student, having been shown how to ring all the changes on two values (T and F), taken two or three at a time, can go on to construct a sixty-four-row truth table from T's and F's taken six at a time. According to tradition, the natural arrangement of sixty-four hexagrams was regarded as the creation of King Fu Hsi. We should not, however, take this too literally. King Fu Hsi represents the beginning of Chinese civilization. In this respect, the origin of the hexagrams is coincident with the origin of Chinese civilization. However, the present form of arrangement of the hexagrams in the *I Ching* is commonly attributed to King Wen, the founder of the Chou dynasty. It is possible, therefore, that King Wen used the already existing forms of the hexagrams and merely rearranged them to suit his own purposes. After rearranging them, he added a Judgment to each. The Great Commentary seems to support this idea: "At the end of the Yin dynasty and the rise of the Chou dynasty, the *I* was given. This was the time when King Wen and the tyrant Chou Hsin were fighting against each other. Thus the Judgments of this book often warn against danger" (2:11).

According to tradition, the Judgments on the hexagrams were composed by King Wen when he was held captive for seven years by the last ruler of the Yin dynasty. During this time, he was able to rearrange the sixty-four hexagrams and prescribe the Judgments for them.

There is an interesting story that illustrates the tragedy of the great diviner, King Wen. According to the story, his wisdom in divination was tested by the tyrant Chou Hsin while Wen was in prison. In order to test his divining ability, Chou Hsin brought King Wen a bowl of soup that was made of the flesh of his own son, who had been murdered. Realizing that it was his son's flesh, King Wen nevertheless took the soup in order to save his life. While imprisoned, King Wen was deeply involved in the study of lineal figures. According to tradition, he arranged the hexagrams and composed the Judgments based on visions that appeared to him on the wall of the prison.

Again, this is similar to the prophetic vision in the Book of Daniel and Revelation—and particularly of the handwriting on the wall at Belshazzar's feast (Dan. 5:5, 25).

Just as the vision of the River Map played an important part in Fu Hsi's discovery of the trigrams, the visions that King Wen saw on the prison wall became the basis for the present arrangement of sixty-four hexagrams in the *I Ching*.

The final authority of the *I Ching* comes from the visions of Fu Hsi and King Wen. The *I Ching* transcends the ordinary wisdom of the people because of the visions of these sages. *For the prophets of the Old and New Testaments, visions were understood as embodiments of divine truth. God spoke to them, especially in the so-called apocalyptic literature, through visions. Visions were, then, understood as expressions conveyed in divine language.* There are somewhat similar implications in the visions of Fu Hsi and King Wen in Chinese history. Visions were believed to be expressions of a higher intelligence. They convey spiritual meanings that are not directly accessible to ordinary people. The greatness of the East Asian mentality lies not in its logical reasoning, but in its intuitive insight that perceives the nature of spiritual reality. That is why the visions granted to the intuitive Chinese mentality are different from those presented in the rational mentality of Western people.

The final form of the *I Ching* that we have today is thought to have been completed by the duke of Chou, the son of King Wen. The duke of Chou—Tan, according to the tradition—was responsible for the formulation of the judgments on the individual lines of the hexagrams. He succeeded to the regency for his nephew when his brother, King Wu, died. Brilliant in his leadership, he was not only a great ruler but also a great philosopher. He succeeded his father also in the work on the *I Ching* and completed it as a tribute evincing his filial piety. His judgments for the individual lines of the hexagrams correspond with the Judgments on the hexagrams as a whole. This seems to indicate that the duke of Chou read the Judgments before appending the texts for the individual lines. Even if the duke did not have enough time to append every individual line, it is reasonable to believe that the whole work of the *I Ching* was completed in the Chou court under the leadership of the duke. The traditional name of the book, *Chou I,* also suggests the idea that it was originally a Chou manual on divination. It is, therefore, reasonable to conclude that the final form of the *I Ching* was completed sometime in the early Chou dynasty, about three thousand years ago.

This final stage of development of the I Ching *can be likened to the priestly writings in the Old Testament, as well as the final edition of the Gospels. The priestly writers were responsible for the refinement and editing of the Old Testament. They are the ones who brought various existing sources together to form the unified stories of the Old Testament. The final edition of the New Testament should be attributed to editors such as Matthew, Mark, Luke, and John, who finally brought together the existing stories and sources of documentation to form the Gospels. Some refinement and editing of existing materials seems to be indispensable for the completion of books such as the old classics and sacred scriptures.*

So far, I have attempted to reconstruct the origin and development of the *I Ching* according to Chinese tradition. As indicated, there is no way to make any truly definitive statement about the authorship of the *I Ching*. The *I Ching* is a unique creation of Chinese and East Asian civilization. Although tradition attributes the authorship of the book to certain individuals such as Fu Hsi, King Wen, and the duke of Chou, I doubt that they alone were responsible. Fu Hsi naturally became the symbol of the birth of Chinese culture, including the *I Ching,* just like the legendary Tan-kun came to represent the beginning of Korean civilization,

The text of the I Ching, *like that of the five books of Moses (or the Pentateuch) in the Scriptures, went through many years of oral transmission and revision before finally being written down and canonized. Moreover, the Gospels*

went through very much the same stages of development. Just as the Pentateuch was attributed to a great leader like Moses, and the Gospels were attributed to Matthew, Mark, Luke, and John, so also was the I Ching *attributed to great figures like Fu Hsi, King Wen, and the duke of Chou.*

Like any other great national epic, the *I Ching* probably went through revisions and refinements through centuries of experimentation in divination until it was finally completed and written down about the time of the early Chou dynasty. Thus, in the final analysis, the authorship of the *I Ching* belongs not to the several individuals whom I have mentioned, but to the corporate community of the early Chinese people. There is no evidence that men like King Wen and the duke of Chou, who are credited with the formulation of the book, were in any way separated from the community of those who shared the tradition of Chinese civilization, which is the real source of the book. Thus, even though it became the first book of the Confucian classics, it was never identified exclusively with the Confucian school. It has, in fact, become a source of wisdom to all people in the history of East Asian countries.

2

The Philosophy
of Change

The essence of the *I Ching* is the *I,* because *Ching* means simply "a book" or "classic." The *I Ching* is, then, a book about the *I,* which translates into English as "change" or "changes." In the Chinese character, there is no distinction between singular and plural. I personally prefer the use of the singular form when I translate *I* into English, because the idea of change in the *I Ching* is used in an absolute sense. Since change is known as the absolute or ultimate, it cannot take the plural form of expression. Change manifests itself, of course, in stages; and the stages of change comprise the process of change. I will make a distinction between change itself and the stages of change, or changes, when I need to differentiate the absolute meaning of change from its relative meaning. When I use change in a relative sense (the sense of its being a stage within the total process), I will use its plural form, "changes," throughout this chapter.

In the Judeo-Christian tradition, the absolute is known as God, who is one only. He cannot be expressed in the plural form because there is no one identical or co-equal with him. In this respect, God is always expressed in the singular form. When in other religions the plural form is used to describe God, God becomes gods, who are less than the God of Judeo-Christianity. In the Judeo-Christian faith, there is no continuum between God and gods. This idea is deeply rooted in the absolute monotheism of the Hebrews. Therefore, God in Judeo-Christianity cannot be identified with change, even though both of them are used in the absolute sense. Change can be understood as the absolute in nature, or the absolute principle of the cosmos. On the other hand, God in Judeo-Christianity is not only immanent but also transcendent. In this respect, change as the absolute principle of nature is then closely related with the immanent nature of God, the absolute principle of the cosmos. Since God in Judeo-Christianity also transcends nature, he cannot be totally identical with change in the I Ching. *This distinction between God and change should be kept in mind when we discuss the mutual understanding of the* I Ching *and the Christian faith. Because change is*

41

the absolute principle of nature, it is best characterized as the power of God in nature.

Change as the absolute principle of nature means that there is a continuum between change and changes, between the absolute and the relative, and between yang and yin. The *I Ching* and its philosophy are based upon the continuum that exists in all things. It is, therefore, important to be sensitive to this distinction between change and changes as we discuss the philosophy of change.

The Source of the Human Knowledge of Change

Where did the idea of change come from? Did this idea come from careful research conducted in laboratories or in libraries? Certainly not, since the early Chinese people did not have laboratories or libraries such as we now employ in our research. How did they discover the idea of change without these facilities? One of the most important things in research is precision of observation. Today, scientists attempt to comprehend the phenomena of the world through careful observation of various specimens and phenomena. Giant telescopes bring the universe into the laboratory and sophisticated microscopes reach down into the infinitesimal dimensions of the world and bring it to human eyes. Although the early Chinese did not have such elaborate tools for research, they discovered the idea of change through careful observation of nature. Nature itself was their laboratory. They used their finely honed intuition instead of machines to perceive the mystery of the world. The Great Commentary remarks, "The holy sages observed all the movements under heaven. They carefully surveyed how these movements were met and interpenetrated, in order to know the certain trends of movements" (1:8). The holy sages became one with nature in order to know the change that governs nature. They did not analyze small pieces of isolated material as a means of knowing the whole. Rather, they came to know the whole by becoming a part of the whole. They became part of the nature in order to understand what controlled nature.

This is similar to the humble country shepherds who knew about the birth of Christ while sophisticated city dwellers did not know about it. The wise men from the East knew about the birth of Christ by watching the stars, while the religious scholars of the day did not know about it even though they had prophesied it. The God who is in nature is understood by those who dwell in nature. Experiential knowledge seems more important than experimental knowledge for knowing the ultimate reality of nature. Knowledge of the immanent God has more to do with subjective reality than with objective reality. For the Chinese, the world has been thought of as alive; and therefore, to know the world is to live with the world and empathize with it.

If I define the approach of the *I Ching* to nature as subjective, then the contemporary Western approach to nature seems to be objective. This idea is deeply rooted in the Judeo-Christian notion that the world was made for human-kind. The world has often been regarded as a hostile object that must be con-quered. In this worldview, the world and humankind cannot exist harmoniously for mutual fulfillment. Human beings have the use of nature for their own ends. This desire to objectify the natural world seems to be the underlying force in the development of our technological civilization. Such a scientific and technologi-cal knowledge of nature is quite different from the *I Ching*'s understanding of nature. Moreover, the principle that governs natural phenomena as change seems to be poorly apprehended by today's scientific mind. I propose that the discovery of change through natural process by the early Chinese sages is as authentic as, and more ultimate than, the discoveries made by scientific methods in our time.

Modern science is interested in empirical analysis. It attempts to generalize the whole from observation of separate pieces, like the blind men who tried to visualize the elephant by touching different parts of its body. It is almost impossible to understand the whole from an analysis of different parts. The sum of the parts will never equal the whole. The holy sages who discovered the idea of absolute change not only were with nature, but became one with nature, so that they could observe nature as a whole. To perceive the reality of change required a holistic approach. Like the Taoist painter who does not paint without becoming one with what is to be painted, the sages could not understand what was natural until they became one with nature. The *I Ching,* therefore, is like a painting of nature depicted in hexagrams. The sages not only observed nature, but contemplated it so that nature and they were united. In this oneness, the inner essence of what was natural was understood. Nature herself was the source of their knowledge of change.

This discovery of ultimate reality through nature is like the task of natural theology. Many attempts have been made to understand the divinity of nature herself. For example, the Nineteenth Psalm describes vividly the manifestation of divine nature through Heaven and Earth:

> The heavens are telling the glory of God; and the firmament proclaims his handi-work. Day to day pours forth speech, and night to night declares knowledge. There is no speech, nor are there words; their voice is not heard; yet their voice goes out through all the earth, and their words to the end of the world. (Ps. 19:1–4)

The Meaning of Change

What is change? What does the *I Ching* say about change? Does it perceive change differently from the common understanding of change? As one of several possible approaches to understanding the idea, let me begin with the etymological understanding of *I*, or change. Since Chinese has its origin in symbols and images, etymology can provide us with the original connotations of change. The word *I* (易) can be analyzed from its representation as a pictogram. The archaic pictogram of this character was believed to be this: 易 It looks like a round head, a sinuous body, and a number of legs. Thus, it originally meant "chameleon" in an old Chinese dictionary. The peculiar characteristics of the chameleon are easy mobility and mutability. The chameleon is believed to change its color twelve times a day. Moreover, its sinuous body makes it easy for the chameleon to move around. It can also easily regenerate its tail if it is lost. Because of these easy and changeable qualities, the word *I* was believed to have been adopted for the *I Ching*.

A second etymological approach to understanding the meaning of change is to use the analytical method. The word *I* or 易 can be analyzed into two parts: 日, which means "the sun," and 勿, which means "to give up." However, the word 勿 is also understood as an old form of 月, which means "the moon." Therefore, an analysis of this word gives us the idea that it has to do with both the sun and the moon. (To give up the sun, then, is to expect the moon, or a transition from daytime to nighttime.) Further, the relationship between the sun and moon is implicit in the Great Commentary, which says, "Heaven (the sun) is above, and Earth (the moon) is below. Thus the first hexagram (Heaven) and the second hexagram (Earth) are determined. Because of this difference between below and above, inferior and superior positions are established" (1:1). Here, the relationship between Heaven and Earth is analogous to the relationship between the sun and the moon. Just as "Heaven is above," the sun is above the moon to make the word *I* (易). Just as "the Earth is below," the moon is below the sun. This relationship between the sun above and the moon below is fundamental to the word *I*. Since the sun and moon, like Heaven and Earth, are two fundamental forces that control the universe, the idea of yin and yang seems implicit in the idea of change. In other words, the idea of yin and yang had its origin in the idea of change, and these technical terms came later.

Finally, etymological study further complicates the understanding of change. According to the study of recently discovered material, it has been suggested that the word *I* could have been derived from the concept of the fixed and straight.[1] This study seems to contradict to some extent what was meant through the pictographic meaning of the chameleon as easiness and changeability. However, on a deeper level the contradiction points to something real. The paradox of change is that change contains within itself its own opposite meaning: fixedness or unchanging nature.

To summarize the etymological study of change, there are at least three different connotations of the word "change": easiness, transformation, and constancy. The idea of transformation comes from the pictogram of the chameleon, which signifies not only ease of change from one color to another, but ease of movement from one place to another. An analysis of the Chinese word *I* shows transformation is signified through the interaction between sun and moon, or yang and yin. Finally, the meaning of constancy comes from the idea of fixedness. These three characteristics of change are not exclusive; rather, they are mutually interdependent. According to a well-known apocryphal writing, the *I-wei Ch'ien-tsu-tu,* the *I,* or change, has three distinctive meanings: easy and simply (*I Chien*), transformation and change (*Pien I*), and changelessness (*Pu I*). By putting them together, one can arrive at the definition of change as easy, transforming, and constant. It is easy because it is simple; it is transforming because of the nature of change; and it is unchanging because of constancy. Everything involves the simply interplay of yin and yang. The process of transformation takes place through the transformation of the lines of the hexagram. It is unchanging because the constancy of change itself is, by definition, changeless.

One can also study the Bible etymologically. Studying the word "God" in Hebrew and Greek, for example, gives a deeper meaning, one originally associated with the early Hebraic and Christian civilizations. The study of the root meaning of the word "Yahweh," for example, is most helpful in understanding the meaning of "God" in the Old Testament. The word "Yahweh" is directly connected with the verb "Hayah," which means "to be" in an active and dynamic sense. Another name of God is El or Elohim, which means "to be strong" or "to be mighty." El was originally associated with the primitive notion of power.

What, then, is the significance of change? It is significant because everything is changing, and nothing is without change. Every moment is subject to and in the process of change. Nothing in the world can remain the same forever. Even time and space are subject to change. It is not time which effects change, but rather change which moves time. Change penetrates all existing things, whether internal or external in the dimensions of their existence. Change affects all. This is why change is the key to understanding all things in the universe.

The sages of China learned the idea of change through careful observation of nature. The very essence of nature was their teacher. In Heaven, the sun and the moon change their directions. When the sun reaches its zenith, it begins to decline. When the moon is full, it wanes again. When night reaches its peak, it begins to give way to dawn. On Earth, high mountains become valleys, valleys become hills, and hills become fields. Trees grow and die, flowers bloom and decay. Winter is followed by spring, just as decay is followed by new life. The human being cannot stop aging. Pride brings him down, and modesty wins love. Human thought-patterns change and patterns of behavior also change. Customs change just as fashions change from time to time. From the movements of the solar system to the motions of electrons in the electromagnetic field of atoms, change is at work. Attitudes and relationships also change. Order and disorder, success and failure, progress and decay, joy and sorrow, glory and tragedy—indeed, every moment of change is subject to change. Nothing can escape change. Contemporary composer John Cage tells us:

> That moment is always changing. (I was silent: Now I am speaking.) How can we possibly tell what contemporary music is, since now we're not listening to it, we're listening to a lecture about it. And that isn't it. This is "tongue-wagging." Removed as we are this moment from contemporary music (we are only thinking about it) each one of us is thinking his own thoughts, his own experience, and each experience is changing, and while we are thinking I am talking and contemporary music is changing. Like life, it changes. If it were not changing, it would be dead, and, of course, for some of us, sometimes it is dead, but at any moment it changes and is alive again.[2]

Besides contemporary music, art, education, and life are also changing. What I think of contemporary phenomena is only a static form in my thought. Even my thinking is changing. It is not the now which I possess but the moment which possesses me. The now-moment is also possessed by change. I am the slave of time, and time is the slave of change. Nothing is absolute but change itself, which is absolutely unchanging.

Both Eastern and Western thinkers have agreed that the best example of the changing process is running water. Confucius, who was standing by a river one day, said, "Like this river, everything is flowing on ceaselessly, day and night" (*Analects* 9:16). Heraclitus, the Greek process thinker, said that "it is not possible to step twice into the same river [for] they have different waters flowing ever upon them" (Diels 22:91, 12). Running water does not stand still. It moves always from the higher to the lower place. It moves constantly. It never repeats the same course. Everything can be compared with running water. The universe itself is in flux. It moves constantly to create the new from the old, and from the new, what is newer than the new. Just like water, everything is in transition. Nothing is permanent. Nothing is absolutely sure and right. Everything in the world is relative and is conditioned by change. Change affects everything but change itself, which is unchanging and absolute.

Change is more than mere movement. It moves to transfer from what was to what is, and from what is to what will be. It transfers things in order to create something new from the old, and create something old from what was new. The opposite of change is not the unchanging, but the illusion of change. Change is natural movement, and the opposite of change is a mere chimera, a fabrication of the mind. Moving according to nature is spontaneous. Thus, change is that spontaneous and natural movement that transforms and recreates all things in the universe. Production and reproduction, growth and decay, are signs of change in the world.

Everything is in a state of flux but never in a state of sheer chaos. Modern "chaos theory" has shown that even total randomness has a unique and predictable logic of its own, amenable to mathematical formulation.[3] All things are in order because change moves them according to definite trends. As the Great Commentary says, "Events are arranged according to their kinds. Things are classified into definite classes. . . . Symbols are formed in Heaven, and forms are shaped on Earth. In this way change takes place" (1:1). Change is the begetter of all begetting, for it is the procreative power of life. The procreation of life takes all kinds of things in order, because change operates in definite trends. Change is the essence of every procreative and recreative process. It is the power that renews itself and gives the strength of transformation to all. It gives life and takes away life. In respect of sheer change, life and death are one. From life to death and death to life, change renews and transforms all things according to their inclination.

The way of change is easy and simple. It is easy because it is simple; it is simple because it is easy. As the Great Commentary says:

Heaven (first hexagram) knows things through the easy. Earth (second hexagram) does things through the simple. It is easy, because it is easy to know. It is simple because it is simple to follow. He who is easy to know makes friends. He who is simple to follow performs good works. He who possesses friends can endure forever, and he who performs good works can become great. To endure is the power of the sage, and greatness is the affair of the sage. By means of easy and the simple, the laws of the whole world are known. When the laws of the whole world are known, the sage takes his position in the middle. (1:1)

The easy is the counterpart of the simple, just as Heaven is the counterpart of Earth. Heaven acts easily, and Earth responds simply. Just as Heaven and Earth are gates for all things in the universe, the easy and simple are the ways of change. The *I Ching* sustains the faith that at its ultimate roots (if we could only know them) change is easy and simple. The simplicity of change arises out of pure response, while the ease of change comes from direct action. What is natural is pure and direct, what is pure and direct is spontaneous, and what is spontaneous is simple and easy. Just as the emission or addition of a quantum changes the magnetic field, change, according to the *I Ching*, is simple and easy because it is simply the process of uniting divided lines and dividing united lines.

The process of change is also constant and invariable. Water never flows from lower to higher ground; the sun never rises from the west; the moon never shines during the day. The father is seated and the son bows before him. The ruler rules and the servant serves. Heaven acts and Earth responds. "The ways of Heaven and Earth are observed correctly, and the rays of the sun and moon emit their light. Thus all the movements under Heaven are constantly subject to this one and the same rule" (Great Commentary 2:1). This invariable and consistent process of change is possible because of the change that is unchangeable. The American idealist philosopher William Ernest Hocking once said, "As a first principle, the changeless is of course insufficient. Our Ultimate Reality must have qualities of both changelessness and change."[4] Change that is changeless is the way of Heaven and Earth. The Commentary on the Judgments says at hexagram 32:

> The way of Heaven and Earth is constant and unceasing. It is advantageous to turn in any direction. If there is an end, there must be a beginning. The sun and moon in heaven shine constantly. The four seasons are changed accordingly to produce all things. . . . When this constancy is understood, the nature of Heaven and Earth and all other things are also known.

This constancy is possible because change is unchangeable. This paradox presents the mystical meaning of change in the *I Ching.*

A favorite hymn, "Abide with Me," reflects on this same paradox in relation to God:

> *Abide with me; fast falls the eventide;*
> *The darkness deepens; Lord, with me abide!*
> *When other helpers fail and comforts flee,*
> *Help of the helpless, O abide with me.*
>
> *Swift to its close ebbs out life's little day;*
> *Earth's joys grow dim; its glories pass away;*
> *Change and decay in all around I see;*
> *O thou who changeth not, abide with me.*

In the midst of a changing world, God alone is changeless. This has been a profound affirmation of the Christian faith.

This idea, however, has often been misunderstood. It does not mean that God is unchangeable and is a fixed being. God is not the Unmoved Mover, as Aristotle attempted to define him. He is a living and dynamic and moving God. I define God as the Moving Mover rather than as an Unmoved Mover. In other words, God is the source of change and transformation; and, at the same time, he abides in the very process of the changing world. It is in this respect that Hocking said, "Our Ultimate Reality must have qualities of both changelessness and change." God is both changing and changeless. If God can be change itself that does not change, how do we justify Malachi's conviction: "I the Lord do not change" (Mal. 3:6)? Or Paul's statement in his letter to the Hebrews: "Jesus Christ is the same yesterday and today and forever" (Heb. 13:8)? I see God's unchangeableness as his unchanging fidelity to his promises and faithfulness to his people rather than as an existent that is utterly static and unchangeable. Can God be expressed in the paradoxical statement that he is "the change that is changeless?" This is a challenge that calls for the careful attention of contemporary theologians.[5] In fact, such issues are being addressed today by one of our major schools of current religious thought, that of the process philosophers and theologians.

The Basic Constitution of Change

How does change work? What makes change possible? The holy sages discovered the idea of change through careful observation of natural phenomena. Nature was their teacher and the world their laboratory. Society became the place in which to apply insights gained from nature. The sages observed that changes occurred through the interaction of two opposite poles. Everything changes because everything comprises a contrasting polarity; i.e., it is bipolar relationships that produce change. On Earth, day and night bring light and darkness. Summer and winter bring heat and cold. Solids and liquids are dry and wet. Everything has its opposite. There are male and female, negative and positive, creative and receptive, passive and active. Nothing can exist without its counterpart. Cause and effect, as well as rest and motion, are parts of the cosmic process. Even in the mind, love and hate, attraction and repulsion, faith and reason are necessary for creative thinking.

Without contraries, there is no progression. The eminent early nineteenth-century German idealist, G. W. F. Hegel, for example, using the bipolar relationship of thesis and antithesis, constructed a system of dialectic that produces progression. The bipolar relationship occurs even in human experience. The human experience of the sacred presupposes that of the secular. The experience of the ultimate is understood because of that of the penultimate. Painful experience cannot be apprehended without the experience of pleasure; sorrow is known only when joy is experienced. Goodness shines forth because of evil. The counterpoint of right is wrong, and that of pride is humility. If there is a master, there must be a servant, and if there is a parent, there must be a child. If there is a teacher, there must be a student.

Polarities are expressed in art and architecture as well. If there is light, then there must be shade. When there is form, there is content. There are polarities of symmetry and variation, unity and diversity, strength and delicacy. In sculpture and painting these contrasts are the basis of beauty. The greatness of music comes from the contrast of sounds. Drama and literature become alive through the contradictions, counterforces and paradoxes of expression and emotion of the characters. Dancing combines poise and movement. There is nothing that does not have its opposite. Even the invisible atomic structure consists of a polarity of positive and negative charges. The bipolar relationship is not only the basis for all things that exist (Being), but also the foundation of all the process of change (Becoming). This is the way of nature and change.

It is also the conviction of the Christian faith that God created everything to be in bipolar relationship: light and darkness, day and night, life and death, water and dry land, male and female. Everything comes in opposites, for God made it so.

Because of these oppositions, change is possible. However, this polarity is not possible without unity as well. As Chang Tsai said in his *Collected Works,* duality is impossible without unity and unity cannot exist without duality (2:1). Duality and unity are inseparable. The movement of duality toward union, as well as the movement of separation from that union, create change. The process of change is, therefore, merely the movement between union and separation. This idea is vividly illustrated in the yin and yang relationship in the *I Ching.* Yin (— —), the line that is separated, becomes yang (——), the line that is united. Through the movement of the yin line (separation) to the yang line (union), and the movement of the yang line (union) to the yin line (separation), change occurs. The movement between yin and yang, therefore, makes constant change possible. Again, this is why change is not only simple, but easy. We might liken this movement to the contemporary scientific assumption that everything in the world can be viewed as a manifestation of interaction between positive and negative forces.

Where did the concept of yin and yang come from? It is difficult to trace the origin of this concept, even though its technical use began around the third century B.C. During the Former Han dynasty, the relationship between yin and yang became prominent through the rise of the so-called Five Movements or Five Stages of Movement school. However, the concept of yin and yang was implicit long before the third century B.C. The idea can be traced all the way back to the most primitive idea of Heaven and Earth. As previously noted in my discussion of the River Map, the idea of yin and yang was expressed there in light and dark circles. Even if the map was a reconstruction of the Five Stages of Movement school, the eight trigrams, which existed long before, presuppose the relationship between Heaven and Earth. There, the trigrams Heaven (☰) and Earth (☷) serve as foundations for all the others. The existence of the eight trigrams was evident long before King Wen of the twelfth century B.C. In general, the relationship between Heaven and Earth is the most all-inclusive symbol of Chinese and East Asian civilization and represents the foundation of Eastern metaphysical speculation.

In Chinese, the word "Heaven" (*t'ien*) has an inclusive meaning. It includes both the concept of sky and that of a personal God. The concept of God in China came from the notion of a personified Heaven. That was why many national and social reforms took place in China under the mandate of Heaven. The concept of

Earth came to be used in China as a counterpart of Heaven. "Earth" was used to denote not only the soil, but the mother-god figure. The most primitive form of the Chinese word for Earth (*t'u*) also has the meaning of "soil." It may have been possible for the primitive people in China to personify the soil or the earth as the Great Mother who produced and raised trees, crops, and flowers through the reception of rain from the personified Heaven.

In this respect, the relationship between Heaven and Earth was analogous to that of father and mother, or male and female. In the Great Commentary it is said, "The way of Heaven produces the male, the way of the Earth produces the female" (1:1). The interaction between Heaven and Earth was compared with intercourse between male and female, resulting in the father/mother relationship. The polarity between what is above and what below is described in the relative position of male and female. The sexuality of male and female was also symbolized in the shapes of the lines. The straight or firm line (——) symbolizes the male sex organ, while the divided or yielding line (— —) symbolizes the female sex organ. Heaven, which is represented by the firm or yang line, moves forward, while the Earth, represented by the yielding or yin line, opens and receives Heaven. The Great Commentary says, "In a state of rest Heaven (the first hexagram) is concentrated, and it is straight in the state of motion. Thus it produces the great. Earth (the second hexagram) is closed in a state of rest, and it is open in a state of motion. Thus it produces the vast" (1:6).

The commentary illustrates the movement of yin and yang as analogous to sexual intercourse. Heaven, representing the male partner, is direct in movement and is at a standstill at rest. Earth, representing the female partner, opens up in movement and is closed in rest. The sexual union between Heaven and Earth—that is, between male and female—symbolizes the interaction between yin and yang. Just as the sexual union between male and female procreates, the interaction between yin and yang changes all things. Here, the symbols of yang and yin are implicit in Heaven and Earth; they are the most inclusive symbols in the process of change and transformation.

When the Israelites invaded Canaan, the Canaanites worshipped fertility gods. The worship of the mother-goddess, the personification of fertility, is regarded as one of the oldest forms of religion in the ancient Near East. In the Old Testament, the figure of Baal, whose rains brought fertility to the land, plays a prominent role in the story of Elijah on Mount Carmel. A characteristic feature of the fertility cult was the sacred ritual of sexual intercourse between priests and priestesses to stimulate the gods for fertilization of the land.

Similar fertility cults seem to have flourished in most parts of the world. Agricultural cults of this kind no doubt existed in early China when the initial personification of Heaven and Earth occurred.

Just as the interaction of yin and yang was the basis for Chinese cosmology, so also the interaction of male and female gods (*kami*) was the founding myth of Japanese cosmology. According to Japanese mythology, "Everything in this cosmos as well as all the deities were produced by the creative spirit of the two *kami*, namely the *kami* of High Generative Force and the *kami* of Divine Generative Force."[6] The *kami* of High Generative Force is analogous to the creative force of Heaven, and the *kami* of Divine Generative Force is compared with the receptive energy of Earth. The former is the male deity known as Izanagi, and the latter, the female deity, is known as Izanami. According to the creation myth of Shintoism, from the union of these two deities were born the Japanese islands and other things in the world. This story is leavened with a considerable amount of humor:

> The divine couple [Izanagi and Izanami] decided on to [*sic*] this island, where they built a sacred bower with a high, thick pillar at its center. Around this pillar the Female Deity turned from the right to the left, while the Male Deity turned from left to right. When they met in this way, she first addressed herself to him: "Oh, what a fine and handsome youth you are!" Whereupon he courteously responded to her amorous call, saying: "How pretty and lovely a maiden you are!" When they thus became united in marriage, they begot a misshapen leech, which they straightway placed in a reed boat and sent adrift to the sea.

This story seems to depict the procreative process occurring through the interaction of yin and yang, or the female and male energies. Again, the symbol of yin and yang plays a central role in conceptualizing cosmic change in Japan.

A similar idea is also found in Indian cosmology. In the later development of Hinduism, for example, the Samkhya school of thought speaks of *Prakriti,* the feminine creative power, and *Purusa,* the male creative power. The polarity of these two powers is implicit in the concept of male and female gods in India. Perhaps the most obvious example of this kind is found in the phallic worship that occurred in ancient India, even before the coming of the Aryans. The lingam, or the phallic emblem, in later Hinduism became the symbol of the god Siva. As its counterpart, the Earth is assimilated to the female organ of generation known as yoni. The idea of lingam-yoni in India is, then, almost identical with the yin-yang concept developed in early China.

It becomes quite clear, therefore, that the positing of polarity as the basis of cosmological production and reproduction is common to fertility cults. This seems to indicate that the idea of yin and yang is not unique. It is common to all agricultural and nature-oriented cults of the early days. What makes it distinctive is its preeminence in the cosmology of East Asia. When the bipolar relationship is conceived as implicit in the fertility cults, the world is then understood in terms of an organic whole and the idea of change is defined in terms of the procreative process. The symbols of yin and yang certainly encompass the organic worldview and the procreative process, but they also include the inorganic worldview and the creative process involved in change. Their inclusive character reflects a complementary relationship. They are opposite in character, but complementary in their relationship.

The idea of a complementarity between yin and yang can be easily understood from their root words. Literally, yin means "overshadowing," while yang means "brightness." The contrast between them originally came from the concept of the northern and southern slopes of a mountain. The southern slope where the sun shines is the yang side, while the northern slope that is in shadow is called the yin side. Yang thus represents what is bright or light, while yin represents what is dark and shadowy. In the Great Commentary, it is written:

> Heaven and Earth are the gateways to change. Heaven represents light things and Earth dark things. In the union of both dark and light, the firm and weak [lines] reveal themselves. In this way the phenomena of Heaven and Earth come to manifest themselves and the power of spirit is clearly perceived. (2:6)

Here, Heaven and Earth or yang and yin are none other than light and shadow. Shadow is the darkness of light, and light is the brightness of shadow.

In contrast, people in the West have thought in terms of the conflicting relationship of opposites. That is, Westerners envision the opposites in conflict rather than in complementary tension. This is, no doubt, a reflection of the Aristotelian logic of either/or which became an important part of Western thinking. In the "either this or that" approach, this cannot be that, and that cannot be this. Each is exclusive. Neither can complement the other, and no third alternative is allowed. What is good, for example, cannot complement evil, and what is evil cannot complement good. They are in conflict; one must win over the other. This kind of worldview seems to follow the Zoroastrian notion of the ultimate dichotomy between Good and Evil. This dichotomy is overcome only through the victory of one over the other.

Paul's description of the conflict between the flesh and the spirit, or between grace and the law, seems to illustrate this conflict relationship between opposites. The ultimate triumph of one over the other is considered the only answer. Despite the conflicting relationship view that has dominated Christian thinking in the past, the complementary relationship of opposites was suggested by Nicholas of Cusa. His theological method, the "coincidence of opposites" or coincidentia oppositorum, *is very similar to the complementary relationship of yin and yang in the* I Ching.

The complementarity of yin and yang also presupposes their mutual inclusiveness. In other words, yin includes yang, and yang includes yin. One cannot exist without the other. The existence of one presupposes the existence of the other. When yin exists, yang also exists within it because yin includes yang. When yang exists, yin exists within yang because yang includes yin. This mutually inclusive relationship is applicable in all aspects of change.

This kind of relationship is expressed in terms of the separation and union of the symbols of yin and yang in the *I Ching*. Union presupposes separation (what would be united but what was separate?), and separation presupposes union (what is separation but a parting of what was united?). Let me illustrate this principle from the lines of the hexagrams in the process of change. Change occurs because of the change of the lines. The undivided line (union) becomes the divided line (separation), and vice versa. The process of union and separation is merely the activity of change. This process in the *I Ching* can be described thusly: The undivided line pushes outward and becomes thin in the middle, and then breaks in two to form the divided line. The divided line, on the other hand, pushes inward and grows together to become the undivided line. Thus, the divided are not the same but are one in two different aspects. What makes the divided and undivided lines different is precisely their state of separation or union. The union and separation of these opposites are simultaneous and spontaneous. This process of union and separation continues without ceasing; it is the process of change itself.

The union and separation of yin and yang are similar to the opening and closing of the gates of Heaven and Earth. Just as everything in the universe is regarded as the creation of Heaven and Earth, so also all things are produced through the union and separation of the yin and yang forces.

Today, computer systems make use of the same process of union and separation. In the binary system, zero changes to one and one changes to zero. If we substitute zero for "union" and one for "separation," we will have no trouble seeing that the basic philosophy of change of the *I Ching* is almost identical with that of the binary system that is the basis of computer operations. Perhaps a simple analogy would be to compare union and separation with the "on" and "off" of a switch. "On" means union and "off" means separation. By on and off, or union and separation, all things change.

Paul also illustrates the renewal of life through union and separation. Union with Christ represents salvation, and separation from God is sin. The former represents life and the latter death. Through the process of death and resurrection, or separation and union, life is constantly renewed and change occurs.

The Way Amidst Change

If the constituents of change are yin and yang, the source of yin and yang should be the ultimate ground of all existence and of the process of change. In the Great Commentary, the source of yin and yang is called the *Tao*, the way or ultimate reality: "One yin and one yang owe their existence to Tao" (1:5). Yin becomes yang, and yang becomes yin. This alteration is possible because of Tao. Tao, therefore, is change itself. Ch'u Chai makes this clear when he says, "In the *I Ching*, the word *I* is used interchangeably with the word *Tao*, since *Tao* is life, spontaneity, evolution, or, in one word, change itself."[8] Tao, or the Way, and change are one and inseparable. In the *Tao te Ching* the Way accomplishes all things without action (chap. 63). This paradoxical concept of action is also known as the Taoist doctrine of *wu-wei* (action without action). In the Great Commentary, the same idea is expressed in the idea of change: "The change has no thought, no action. It is quiescent and still" (1:10). Change itself changes all things without action. The Way is then another name for change, and change is none other than the Way. The *Tao* and *I,* the Way and change, are not the same but are one. They can be used interchangeably because both of them signify the ultimate principle of the changing process. However, they are also—paradoxically—different.

The relationship between the Way and change is like the relationship between the humanity and the divinity of Christ. The humanity of Christ is also his divinity, for they are one. However, they are not identical. It cannot be said that the divinity of Christ is identical with his humanity, yet they are one. This relationship can be described in terms of "one in two" or "two in one." Two signifies the difference of one, and one signifies the oneness of two. The best way to describe their relationship is in terms of background and foreground: the divinity of Christ as the background of the humanity of Christ, and the humanity of Christ as the foreground of his divinity.

Using the same idea, I can say that the Way is the background of change, and change is the foreground of the Way. This distinction is made here simply for the sake of convenience; it is to say that the relationship between the Way and change is meaningfully understood in terms of background and foreground metaphors. The Way or *Tao* has a broad scope. It is, in fact, the most inclusive symbol of the ultimate reality. In this respect, it is somewhat unfair to make it the background of change. It can certainly act as change itself, as I have explained. However, for the sake of discerning a fine distinction between the Way and change, I have decided to use the Way as depicted in classical Taoism to assess its status as background. In the classical tradition, the Way is easily conceived in terms of principles, while change is perceived in terms of actions. That is why the Way can be known as the background of change, and change as the foreground of the Way. Using this idea, I can define the Way in terms of change: The Way is "the change that is changeless." In order to illustrate this relationship between the Way and change, let me use the idea of change in the Great Commentary, and the idea of the Way in the *Tao te Ching*. According to the Great Commentary, "The great ultimate is change. It produces the two primary forms, and the two primary forms produce the four images. The four images produce the eight trigrams" (1:11). According to the *Tao te Ching*, "The way begot one, and the one, two; then the two begot three and three all else" (chap. 42). Does the great ultimate or change in the Great Commentary correspond to the one in the *Tao te Ching?* Do the two primary forms correspond to the two? and the trigrams to three? If the one corresponds to change, the Way that begot the one can be easily understood as the background of change.

The Way as the background of change is unknowable. That is why Lao-tzu begins his *Tao te Ching* with the unspeakable reality: "The Way that can be told of is not the eternal Way." It is reminiscent of the statement of Ludwig Wittgenstein, the Austrian philosopher of language, that "unsayable things do indeed exist" and of the concluding line of his *Tractatus:* "Whereof one cannot speak, thereof one must be silent."[9]

This idea is also like the Hindu notion of the so-called Naguna Brahman, the attributeless divine being, who became the background of the Saguna Brahman, the divine being with attributes. They are one, but not identical. The attributeless divine being cannot be known to the human being. Thus, it is expressed in terms of *neti-neti,* "not this, not that." The Way as the background of change is, like the attributeless divine being, easily understood in terms of transcendence.

In Christianity, the God of transcendence is also the God of immanence. The transcending God is the background of the immanent God, just as the Way is the background of change. The Judeo-Christian concept of God includes both the transcendent and immanent characteristics of the divine being. Or to phrase it differently, the Christian concept of God is inclusive enough to accommodate both the background and foreground of the ultimate reality, that is, both the Way and change.

The relationship between the Way and change is clearly illustrated in the concept of principle (*li*) and vital energy (*ch'i*) in Neo-Confucian philosophy. The twelfth-century philosopher, Chu Hsi, a major figure in Neo-Confucianism, remarked that there is no vital energy without principle. The relationship between principle and vital energy is similar to the Aristotelian notion of form and matter, although the former is based on a dynamic and changing view of the universe. Because of this organic and dynamic worldview, the vital energy is not matter. It is more analogous to that more fundamental quantity in modern physics called "action," equal to energy times time. In fact, it is a process of change. As Carsun Chang explains it:

> The *ch'i* [vital energy] fills the Great Ether. It goes up, it comes down, or it flies high without cessation. This is what the *I Ching* refers to as the real secret of the change, or what is called by Chuang-tze the dust flying like a wild horse. *Ch'i,* which sometimes goes up and at other times comes down, is the beginning of motion or rest. What goes up is the light, *yang* part, what comes down is the heavy, *yin* part. It can consolidate or dissolve in the form of wind and rain, snow and frost, mountains and rivers, and myriad other things.[10]

While the vital energy (*ch'i*) is closely related to the active process of change, principle (*li*) is closely related to the Tao, the pattern or background of the changing process. Chu Hsi said, "Within the universe there are *li* and *ch'i*. *Li* constitutes the *Tao* that is 'above-shaped'; it is the source from which things are produced. *Ch'i* constitutes the 'instrument' that is 'within-shaped'; it is the means whereby things are produced."[11] If principle is "above-shaped" and vital energy is "within-shaped," the former is then best understood as the background and the latter as the foreground of the ultimate reality. The relationship between principle and vital energy is, then, analogous to the relationship between the Way and change.

According to Chu Hsi, "The principle and vital energy cannot be spoken of as prior or posterior. But if we must trace their origin, we are obliged to say that principle is prior. However, principle is not a separate entity. It exists with vital energy."[12] In the same manner, I am obliged to say that the Way is prior to change, if principle corresponds to the Way and vital energy to change. However, the Way is not a separate entity. It always exists with change. Because the Way is the background of change, it takes priority over change.

This is similar to the relationship between the covenant and creation in Christianity. The covenant is often understood as the divine self-communication which creates the community of divine-human participation. It is, therefore, more than the contract that God makes with his people. In covenant, God makes his decision to create the world in which he is going to participate. This decision is made in eternity. This community of divine participation is, according to Karl Barth, the internal basis of creation; and, at the same time, the creation becomes the external basis of the covenant.[13] In this respect, the covenant becomes the background of creation and creation the foreground of the covenant, just as the Way becomes the background of change, and change the foreground of the Way.

Nonbeing and Change

The priority of the Way over change implies that the Way existed even before the beginning of all things; that is, the Way is the source of all that exists. To exist means to change, for being is precisely the process of change. To be is to change, and to change is to be. Existence and change are simultaneous. Thus, being before existence implies nonbeing. The Way, as the background of change, can be regarded as nonbeing or void. However, despite the priority of nonbeing, nonbeing cannot exist without being. They are mutually inclusive, just as the Way and change are. Again, the limitations of human intellection must be invoked to justify this paradox. The priority of nonbeing does not deny the coexistence of nonbeing with being. Although nonbeing and being cannot be separated, nonbeing is prior to being. This idea can be conceived only in terms of nonspatial and nontemporal categories of thinking, for the priority in question is essentially logical. Perhaps the closest analogy for illustrating this is the relationship between potentiality and actuality as conceived by Aristotle. Just as actuality presupposes potentiality, the idea of being always presupposes the idea of nonbeing. Since being is none other than the process of change, change presupposes nonbeing. Nonbeing is, then, nonchange or the change that is changeless, the essence of change itself.

The idea of nonbeing, or the void, is deeply rooted in classical Taoism. However, the importance of this idea was fully appreciated only in the later development of Chinese philosophy. The Taoist concept of nonbeing was influenced by Buddhist scholars in the late Han era. Evidence for the concept of nonbeing in the early development of Buddhism is clearly apparent in the group of Buddhists known as the Six Houses and Seven Schools during the period of Disunity. They began to speculate about the word "emptiness" (*k'ung* or *sunyata*) as a substitute for nonbeing (*wu*). Tao-an (321–85), for example, expounded the concept of original nonbeing (*pen-wu*). He believed that *sunyata* or emptiness was identical with the origin of nonbeing. The concept of nonbeing became convenient for Neo-Confucian scholars as a means of reconstructing Chinese cosmology. The application of this idea was made by Chou Tun-yi, who was known as the forerunner of the intellectual movement in the Sung dynasty. He used the term "ultimateless" (*wu chi*) to express its priority to the supreme ultimate.

The application of nonbeing to the *I Ching* was made by Wang Pi in his commentary on the *I Ching:* "Though Heaven and Earth, in their greatness, are richly endowed with the myriad things; though their thunder moves and their winds circulate; though through their evolving operations the myriad transformations come to be—yet it is the silent and supreme nonbeing that is their origin."[14] In the process of manipulation of the fifty yarrow stalks for consultations of the *I Ching,* one stalk is set aside and never used. For this, Wang Pi derives a special meaning. The one which is set aside represents the nonbeing that is the source of the other forty-nine stalks. On the other hand, the forty-nine stalks represent being, or the changing process. The one which represents nonbeing is the basis from which all other numbers are manifested. Thus, setting the nonbeing aside signifies its priority over all the other numbers used for manipulation of stalks in the process of divination.

Perhaps the best illustration to help the Western mind understand the idea of nonbeing is the concept of zero. Both the Chinese word *k'ung* and the Sanskrit word *sunyata* mean "zero." We know that zero is more than a mere number. It is nonbeing or emptiness, because zero in itself is not a number, at least not in the sense of being the successor of anything. Actually, mathematicians differ as to whether to call it a number or not. The roman numeral system got along very well without it. In fact, it was not invented in the West until the ninth century. Although zero in itself is not a number, it can be understood as the potentiality of all numbers. In other words, it symbolizes the potentiality of both non-number and all numbers. It is both the positive and the negative. It can be regarded as the matrix of all and none. Zero transcends all of the differentiation between negative and positive, and between expansion or infinite contraction. It does not exhaust either infinite expansion or infinite contraction. It is like an embryo, the ever-swelling germ which contains all the possible forms of productive potentiality. No matter how many fractional numbers and diminutive numbers are added to it, it cannot be exhausted. No matter how many numbers are combined or multiplied, it is not possible to make zero. The invisible atom-like substance is still greater than zero. The productive potentiality of zero is beyond all arithmetical categories of addition, subtraction, division, and multiplication. As Heimann said, "Zero transcends all empirical data, all ciphers and forms, and yet, just because of this, it is the basis of all empirical data."[15] Because zero transcends all numbers, it is the background of all numbers, just as nonbeing is the background of being. Numbers are the foreground of zero, just as being is the foreground of nonbeing. Since being is none other than the process of change and nonbeing the Way, change is the foreground of the Way and the Way is the background of change.

The basic pattern of change confines itself within the two poles of yin and yang. Yin changes to yang, and yang changes to yin. When yin reaches its peak, it begins to change to yang. When yang reaches its peak, it changes to yin again. When yin is at its peak, it is called the old yin (══), which changes to young yang (══). Young yang is still growing and expanding toward its peak. When it is fully expanded and reaches its peak, it becomes old yang (══), which changes to young yin (══) again. In this way, change takes place through the expansion and contraction of yin and yang. When yin expands, yang contracts; and when yang expands, yin contracts. Expansion and contraction is the pattern of change occurring in the foreground of the Way. This pattern of change according to expansion and contraction, or growth and decay, was detected through the sages' careful observation of nature.

> When the sun goes, the moon comes. When the moon goes, the sun comes. The alteration of the sun and moon produces light. When cold goes, heat comes. When heat goes, cold comes. The alteration of cold and heat completes the year. What is gone contracts. What is to come expands. The alteration of contraction and expansion produces the advancement. (Great Commentary 2:5)

If there were no background of change, change would occur within the limited and would not produce advancement. It is the background that lends an infinite possibility to things. Thus, change expands indefinitely because of nonbeing or the Way.

The progress of human civilization is certainly limited when the sense of transcendence is not found in history. However much a human being wants to transform himself, he is confined within the limits of the givenness of creation.

Because God is still working through his spirit in the background of human civilization, the human being can find advancement beyond so-called human limitations. Just as, without the Way, change is limited, so also without God human potentiality of growth and expansion is limited. With God, human possibility can be beyond all hopes and dreams. God cannot be reduced to a creature, just as zero cannot be reduced to numbers. God transcends, but is at the same time totally immanent in the world of change and transformation. Because of God's presence in the world, change takes on multitudinous forms and manifestations. Without God, change is confined within the limits of creation.

When the background of change is not considered, change operates within a limited framework. Just as an astronaut can do only certain tasks within his space capsule, so also everything that changes must operate within the limitations of its own nature. Nothing within the universe can either expand or contract indefinitely. Everything has the limitation of its own expansion or contraction. As Whitrow has argued, "Advances in our understanding of natural phenomena have often been accompanied by the elimination of one *physical infinite* after another."[16] This limitation can be applied to both micro- and macrocosmic changes. "In microcosmic changes, expansion and contraction are limited within a unit of existence, and in the extreme, by the phenomenon of gravitational collapse."[17] In macrocosmic changes, the poles of expansion and contraction are extended to the entire cosmos where (according to one likely theory) they alternate with one another. Change, therefore, presupposes that everything, whether infinitesimally small or almost infinitely large, has to operate within the limitations of expansion and contraction.

This idea suggests that the traditional Western view of the cosmos as infinitude, championed especially by the Italian philosopher and astronomer Giordano Bruno, is not compatible with the cosmology of the *I Ching*—nor is it, in fact, any longer compatible with twentieth-century finitistic cosmology. If the cosmos were infinite, it could either expand or contract indefinitely. Because change is the process of expansion and contraction, however, neither expansion nor contraction can continue forever. It is, then, necessary to conclude that the universe is finite but infinitely bounded, like a circle, for it is in the process of change. But, in another sense, the change of the finite universe is infinite, because nonbeing is the background of change. The universe is finite when it is seen from the perspective of the changing process, but it is infinite when seen from the perspective of nonbeing or the Way. This finite dimension of the universe is constantly in the process of change, but its infinite dimension is unchangeable. This point is underscored by the fact of modern physics that at the core of a gravitationally collapsing body—and perhaps even in that of every particle—time stands still in its tracks.[18] What is changeable is, then, limited, but what is unchangeable is limitless. However, the limited and limitless are one in two different expressions, just as the foreground and background are united together. This idea reaffirms the classical definition of change as the change that is changeless. In the same manner, God changes all; but God himself is changeless in his essential nature.

The Pattern of Change and World Phenomena

Change occurs through expansion and contraction, or growth and decay. Expansion and contraction are confined within the limitations set by each unit of the changing process. Let me illustrate this basic pattern of change from the first hexagram, Heaven (*Ch'ien*):

This hexagram consists of six undivided lines. Expansion and contraction take place within the limitations set by this hexagram; that is, these processes transpire within these six undivided lines. The lines are counted from the bottom up, so the lowest line is to be taken first. According to the text or judgment on the line, the first (beginning) line designates a hidden dragon. This means that the dragon is not yet revealed. The second line depicts the dragon appearing in the field, and indicates that he begins to act. It is the expansion of power, the creative power of the dragon. The fifth line means a flying dragon in Heaven. Here, the dragon reaches the highest and fullest expansion of his power. Finally, the top or sixth line sets forth the repentance of the arrogant dragon. Here, the dragon exceeds the proper limit and, victimized by his own hubris, begins to lose his power. The top line, therefore, indicates the beginning of its reversion to the opposite, the beginning of contraction. Everything that reaches a certain peak must revert to its opposite. That is why the pattern of change presupposes the limitation of expansion and contraction. By mythologizing these principles, the *I Ching* succeeds in making them memorable.

Luther's famous doctrine of simul iustus et peccator *means that a just person is nonetheless a sinner at the same time. Like the dragon who grows in power, a person may increase in grace and develop a love for perfection. However, as soon as he is conscious of his justification and of his fellowship with God, he becomes at the same time increasingly aware of his sinfulness. No one can exceed his human limitations, go beyond his finiteness. However much one strives to exceed that limit, he must work within its bounds. Perhaps that limitation is the imperfection of humanity. Just as the dragon who exceeds his limit must repent, so also the human being needs to repent when he tries to become more than what he can become. Any change or transformation of humanity must be considered within the intrinsic limitations of creation.*

The pattern of change in terms of contradiction and expansion within given limitations presupposes that everything that changes is intimately related to all else. On the purely physical level, this is precisely the controversial point of Mach's Principle, according to which all inertia on the local level is a function of the influence of the entire starry heavens unto their most distant reaches. In the even broader sense of a biological metaphor, the interrelationships between things can be interpreted as illustrating organic unity. The universe which is in the process of continuous change can then be understood as an organic whole. In an organic whole, change occurs, as the Great Commentary tells us, in terms of "production and reproduction [which] is called the process of change" (1:5). The world conceived as a gigantic machine is incompatible with the worldview of the *I Ching*. Because the pattern of change takes place in terms of a continuous expansion and contraction or growth and decay, they are fittingly conceived as occurring within an organic whole. The Hindu concept of the cosmos is very similar to the cosmology of the *I Ching*. The world, for Hindus, is a living organism, the expression of a dynamic universe. For example, the Indian plant physiologist, Sr. Jagadis Chandra Bose, examined the beating pulse of a plant, in keeping with the Hindu idea that everything in the universe is a part of this living cosmic organism. Likewise, the Nobel Prize winner, Rabindranath Tagore, one of India's great poets and mystics, by adhering to the same idea of the intimate interwovenness of all cosmic forms, was able to express his ideas with a richness of imagery. Thus, the world that both the *I Ching* and Hinduism describe resembles a living organism.

In the West, the Jesuit paleontologist Pierre Teilhard de Chardin and the British metaphysician Alfred North Whitehead, for example, both conceive of the universe as a dynamic and organic whole. They apply the categories of becoming and process, rather than those of being and substance, to the interpretation of the changing world. The growing interest in process theology, following the philosophy of Whitehead, seems to indicate that their worldview of an organic and changing reality has been accepted by many Christians in the West.

Because the changing universe is an organic whole, what one does affects others. The pattern of change in terms of expansion and contraction presupposes a relationship between cause and effect. The process of change is, then, merely the process of transition from cause to effect and of inference from effect to cause. However, the cause and effect cannot be understood separately. They are correlative, mutually inclusive, and interdependent concepts. The cause/effect relationship is, therefore, possible because of the organic wholeness of things. Let me use a couple of examples to show that the cause/effect relationship of the *I Ching* is closely related to the pattern of changing process. Hexagram 14, Great

Possession (*Ta Yu*), is followed by hexagram 15, Modesty (*Ch'ien*). The Sequence of the Hexagrams (*Hsa Kua*) says, "Great possession cannot make it too full. Thus there follows modesty." Here, the great possession is the cause of modesty and modesty is the effect of great possession. According to the principle of expansion and contraction, when the great possession reaches its peak, it begins to revert to its opposite. When anything exceeds the proper limit, it has to come back. When it has too much, it must retrench. Thus, modesty follows after the great possession.

The last two hexagrams (hexagrams 63 and 64) will illustrate the mutual relationship between cause and effect in the changing process. Hexagram 63, After Completion (*Chi Chi*), is followed by the final hexagram, Before Completion (*Wei Chi*). After Completion is, surprisingly, the cause of Before Completion, and Before Completion is the effect of After Completion. One might at first suppose the opposite to be the case. Let us look, however, at the relationship between these two hexagrams, which can easily be discerned by observing the structure of the hexagrams:

After Completion   Before Completion

After Completion is the complete opposite of Before Completion. This indicates the reversal of movement that we noticed in the case of the arrogant dragon. When things are complete, based upon the pattern of change, they must revert to Before Completion. When things have expanded to completion, they then begin to contract to before completion. Here, the cause/effect relationship is, again, none other than the pattern of expansion and contraction.

In the organic and interdependent worldview, cause is not separable from effect. Cause is, in fact, a part of effect and effect is part of cause. They are mutually inclusive: cause is in effect, and effect in cause. It is not easy to understand this kind of interdependent relationship. Most of us think of cause as a movement separate from effect. We think that a certain thing causes something else to exhibit a certain distinct action or quality. Here, cause is conceived of independently of its effect. Moreover, in the West, the cause-and-effect relationship is understood linearly.

In the Christian understanding of history, God's promise is the cause of fulfillment, and the fulfillment is its effect. The history of salvation always moves from the promise to fulfillment; that is, from the cause to the effect. For most Christians, it is therefore quite unnatural to think of "after completion" preceding "before completion." In the I Ching, *however, cause and effect have a pattern of expansion and contraction. If we think of the history of salvation from the perspective of change, the fulfillment of the promise is not the end of time only but also the beginning of a new time. In this way, the old is renewed and the new becomes old. The promise is not a once-and-for-all event, but a continual process because of our sin and our limitations. God's promise is inclusive of his fulfillment and his fulfillment includes his promise to save the world. This reciprocity is, then, implicit in the pattern of change in the* I Ching.

The Center of the Changing Process

The pattern of change in terms of expansion and contraction also presupposes the importance of the center or the mean of the process of change. The most favorable position in a changing situation is known as the center, the mean between the two extremes. The word "center" (*chung*) appears thirty-six times in the Commentary on the Symbols. The center means the mean between the maximum degree of expansion and the maximum degree of contraction. For Asian thought, the center is also the most important position in the cosmos. In the hexagram, a human being occupies the center of three lines. The importance of human beings is affirmed in the Asian trinity because of their central position. In the hexagram, the second and fifth lines are, as a rule, regarded as the most important ones among the six lines because of their central positions in the constituting trigrams. We will grasp the significance of these central lines later when we come to discuss the interpretations of the hexagrams.

To illustrate the importance of the central positions, let us look at hexagrams 11 and 12. Hexagram 11, Peace (*T'ai*), consists of two trigrams: the trigrams Heaven below and the trigram Earth above. Hexagram 12, Stagnation (*P'i*) is the reverse of hexagram 11. In hexagram 12, the trigram Earth is below and the trigram Heaven is above.

Hexagram 11 is in a favorable position because both trigrams naturally move toward each other to the center. The trigram Heaven, which is below, moves upward because of its yang principle; and the trigram Earth, which is above, moves downward because of its yin principle. Thus, the symbol of this hexagram is "Heaven and Earth unite in peace. Thus the ruler fashions and completes the way of Heaven and Earth. He regulates the gifts of Heaven and Earth in order to aid the people."

In hexagram 12, however, both Heaven and Earth move away from the center: Heaven, as a light principle (yang), goes up, and Earth, as a heavy principle (yin), comes down. Thus the Commentary on the Symbols says, "Heaven and Earth do not unite in stagnation. Thus, the competent person falls into danger, but exercises his moral power, in order to escape the difficulties. Wealth cannot honor him."

One last example is sufficient to illustrate the importance of the center in the process of change. Hexagram 32, Endurance (*Hêng*), occupies the central position among all hexagrams in the *I Ching*. Because of its central position, it has the advantage of a capacity to move in both directions. The Judgment says, "Endurance has success. There is no mistake. It is advantageous to be correct and to move in any direction." The advantage of this hexagram lies in its correct position. Some of these illustrations suggest that the central position is closely related to the center of the changing process.

In the history of religions, the center has occupied an important position in religious life. In fact, the center is almost synonymous with the sacred place in religious usage. The *axis mundi*, or axis of the world, plays an important part in religious movement. In Judaism, Mount Zion is considered the sacred center. In Hinduism, Mount Meru, and in Shintoism, Mount Fuji, have been regarded as sacred centers. For Islam, the Black Stone in Mecca is the center of religious life. For Christians, Christ is the center of their faith and devotion. The closer we come to the center, the closer we become aware of the divine presence. If the center is the symbol of God's presence, it is certainly a sacred locus.

The center is also used as the norm for human affairs. The Doctrine of the Mean (*Chung Yung*) begins with the definition of center (*chung*): "Being without inclination to either side is called the center" (1:4). It is the state of harmony and equilibrium. When the mean or center is applied to personal life, it is the situation in which there are no stirrings of pleasure, anger, sorrow, or joy. This center is, then, the root from which all proper modes of human behavior arise. The center, or mean, is simply the middle way between extremes; it is the avoidance of any extreme. By such avoidance we can attain the mean that brings the harmony of opposites into our life. The *I Ching,* therefore, does not provide an ethical absolutism. A good life consists of the middle way. In a way, the *I Ching* seems to teach the golden mean, just as Aristotle did in the early history of the West.

Time and Change

Finally, time or timing also plays an important part in the process of change. The word "time" (*shih*) was originally meant to be sowing time and was related to the seasons of the year. Approaching the meaning of time from an etymological perspective, we find that the Chinese word 時 (time) may be derived from three different parts of the pictogram: 𝔞 or "the sun," �土 or "soil," and 寸 or "a small unit of measurement" (Korean inch). These three ideas are brought together to formulate the meaning of time. The sun has to do with the seasons, the soil with sowing and the small unit of measurement with the particular section or unit of the season. The word for "the small unit of measurement" was used in its early form as "sole of the foot" was used for measurement. Since the sole of the foot was also related to the planting of seeds in the field, the word "time" was used as a unit or portion of a season set apart for a certain activity. This idea later extended to the four seasons, and then to years. The concept of time, then, came from its foundation in these very concrete experiences. Time seems not to represent the abstract idea of progression. It means a segment or unit of a concrete event which takes place in the process of change.

This segment of an event is represented by the situation depicted in the hexagram as a whole. The situation that is signified by time changes according to expansion and contraction, increase and decrease, or fullness and emptiness. Since each situation changes differently, the time of that situation is also different. Each situation represents its own time. In the main text of the *I Ching,* the word "time" (*shih*) appears only once; it is found in the fifty-fourth hexagram, the Marrying Maiden (*Kuei Mei*). The symbol of this hexagram says:

The Marrying Maiden

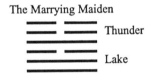

Thunder

Lake

"Thunder over the lake means the marrying maiden. Thus, the competent person comprehends the transitory in the eternal purpose." The concept of time is implicit here. However, the explicit word "time" appears in the fourth line of the hexagram. It says, "Maiden's marriage is delayed. There will be time for a late marriage." The literal translation of the last sentence, however, should be: "A later marriage possesses time." Here, time does not mean chronological time but "the opportune time" or "the appointed time." Time is an occasion rather than an abstract succession of movement. Time is a concrete event for fulfillment.

The concept of time in the I Ching *seems similar to the Christian concept of time as* kairos, *"the fulfilled time" or "the opportune time." It is certainly different from clock time, the* chronos, *which refers to the "succession of passing moments." The* kairos *is, then, "the appointed time" or "the proper time" (Luke 12:42). It is the decisive moment rather than a meaningless succession of moments. Time has to do with a decisive act. To act according to time is to be in accord with the proper situation for action. In fact, to be in a proper situation implies being at the proper time. The time for action and the situation for it appear to be inseparable.*

Let me illustrate the relationship between time and situation in the *I Ching*. For the thirty-third hexagram, Withdrawal (*Tun*), the Commentary on the Judgment says, "The firm (line) is in the proper place and is appropriately correlated with others. Thus it moves according to time." Also in the first hexagram, Heaven (*Ch'ien*), a similar expression for time is found. On the third line, the Commentary on the Words of the Text says, "The competent person advances in virtue and cultivates his duty. He does not make mistakes, because he intends to be at the time." In both instances, time signifies the idea of *kairos,* the decisive time and situation. In fact, to have the right time means to find oneself in the right situation for action. To have the right situation is to have the right time for change. Each situation has its own appointed time, the proper moment of its own action.

This idea is most clearly expressed in the Book of Ecclesiastes. The following passages illustrate time in relation to a particular situation for action:

> *For everything there is a season, a time for every matter under heaven: a time to be born, a time to die; a time to plant, and a time to pluck up what is planted; a time to kill, a time to heal; a time to break down and a time to build up; a time to weep and a time to laugh; a time to mourn, and a time to dance; a time to cast away stones, and a time to gather stones together; a time to embrace, and a time to refrain from embracing; a time to seek, and a time to lose; a time to keep and a time to cast away; a time to rend and a time to sew; a time to keep silence, and a time to love, and a time to hate; a time for war, and a time for peace. (3:1–8)*

These appointed times coincide with different situations in the process of change. According to the Great Commentary, change is correlated with the four seasons (1:6). Just as the relationship between yin and yang coincides with the relationship between the moon and the sun, change conforms to a definite time. As the Great Commentary says, "Changes and penetrations correspond to the time" (2:1). Because of this correlation, the competent person waits for a proper time for action. For the fortieth hexagram, Liberation (*Hsieh*), the Great Commentary reads: "The competent person maintains the mean [center] of his existence. He awaits his time for action" (2:5). The competent person, knowing the pattern of change, waits for the right time for action. For the forty-ninth hexagram, Revolution (*Ko*), the Commentary on the Symbols says, "Fire in the lake means revolution. Thus the competent person sets the calendar and makes the time clear." Missing the time brings misfortune. For the sixtieth hexagram, Regulation (*Chieh*), again the Commentary on the Symbols says concerning the second line: "Don't go out of the gate and the courtyard! It brings misfortune, because one misses the crucial time." Let me, finally, cite one more example of the meaning of time in the *I Ching*. For the forty-eighth hexagram, the Well (*Ching*), the Commentary on the Symbols says concerning the first line, "No animals can come to an old well, for time forsakes it." Here, time is not a mere succession of movements, but is filled with the potential energy of creativi-ty—which the well has lost. Time is, then, the decisive moment of change that affects the situation.

Time and the situation of the hexagram correspond with one another; they are mutually inclusive. Time does not exist in itself without the situation that changes. Each germinal situation symbolized in the hexagrams is, therefore, to be understood as a unit of time. Just as each situation is a part of the whole, time as a unit of a changing situation has to follow the process of changing situations. Time cannot be independent. It must follow the pattern of change, because time is a unit of the changing process. Change operates in terms of expansion and contraction so that time also follows the same pattern of movement. Time moves from past to future, just as change takes place in terms of contraction and expansion. When the past flows into the future, future again becomes past. The past then expands still more to become the future. In this way, time follows the pattern of change. Just as the pattern of change is discerned in all dimensions of existence, so also time is apprehended in all aspects of life. From microcosmic to macrocosmic dimensions, time operates in terms of expansion and contraction, or in terms of growth and decay. This never-ending process of growth and decay makes the past pass into the future, and the future lapse into the past. In this way, time occupies the dimension of the process of change.

In the background of time is eternity. Just as zero is the background of numbers, eternity is the background of time. Eternity is the infinite time that transcends the confinement of the temporal process. Because of eternity, time never comes to an end. It never repeats itself, but renews itself through recurrences of similar cyclic patterns of eternity. It is eternal time that opens up the infinite possibilities of becoming. The recurrence of the process of change can be a repetition of the same, but renewal of fulfilled time generates creative possibilities because of eternity. Time and eternity are inseparable. Time becomes infinite because of eternity, and eternity manifests itself because of time. As the Way is the background of change, and change the foreground of the Way, so the temporary and the eternal aspects of time are mutually interdepen-dent. Eternal time, therefore, is the background of time: that is, the "timeless-ness that is timely." On the other hand, time is the foreground of eternity; that is, "the time that is timeless."

In contrast to this complementary relationship that the I Ching *perceives between time and eternity, most Christians have a tendency to see a sharp contrast between time and eternity. For them, time belongs to this world and eternity belongs to heaven. Time belongs to the secular, while eternity pertains to the sacred. By sharply distinguishing the secular from the sacred, they exclude time from eternity and eternity from time. This exclusivist tendency can be surmounted, however, when we begin to see eternal time as the background of temporal time. By so treating eternity, we can realize its presence in every moment of life. However, if we think of eternity as separated from time, we will expect to have eternity when we are not in time. But, in fact, eternity does not come after time or even before time. Rather, eternity is here and now as the background of time. That is why we can say, "Now is the eternal." If eternity is none other than the presence of God, certainly eternity is present always and everywhere. To separate eternity from time is to do injustice to the continual presence of God in the world.*

3

The Symbolic Meaning
of Change

The *I Ching* is a book of symbols that display and demonstrate change. The sixty-four hexagrams in the *I Ching* represent the sixty-four germinal situations or archetypes that comprise the microcosm of the universe. Each hexagram in its totality is a symbolic unit or an archetype of a situation. However, the hexagram is composed of two trigrams, and the trigrams are constructed of lines. Since lines are the basic symbolic unit of which the trigrams and the hexagrams are composed, let us begin with the symbolic significance of lines.

The Symbolic Significance of Lines

There are two linear symbols in the *I Ching:* the undivided line and the divided line. These lines are combined in various ways to form the trigrams and hexagrams in the *I Ching.* The lines represent yin and yang forces in the world. Since these forces form the basis for all things in the world, the hexagrams—representing as they do every possible phenomenon of the world—must consist of the two lines, since no qualitatively diverse composite can be made of only one thing. As indicated previously, the origin of these two symbols may go back to the most primitive civilization of the Chinese people.

Yang represents the active principle and yin the passive principle in every situation. Although combinations of yin and yang forces symbolize every possible contrast in the world, it is helpful to see their primary meanings as reflecting the active and passive principles in each situation. Yang, as the active principle, is traditionally represented by the light, while yin, as the passive principle, is traditionally represented by the dark. If for the primitive mind the sun represented the day and the moon represented the night, then the sun and the moon thereby became the primordial symbols of yang and yin forces. Thus, the Great Commentary says, "The yin and yang are correlated with the sun and moon" (1:6). The sun represents the yang or light principle, and the moon the yin or dark principle. The sun was later known as the great yang (*t'ai-yang*) and the moon as the great yin (*t'ai-yin*). As the prototype of yin and yang, the character of change (*I*) consists of the sun and the moon.

If we look at the River Map (*Ho T'u*), the prototype of yin and yang were, indeed, the sun and the moon. As previously discussed, the River Map consisted of both light and dark circles. Circles having odd numbers were light, and those with even numbers were dark. The light circles represented the sunlike character of yang, and the dark circles represented the moonlike character of yin. The sun itself was, no doubt, symbolized by the light circle and the moon by the dark circle. Fu Hsi, considered to be the finder of the map, did not succeed in combining the circles to make trigrams and/or the sixty-four hexagrams. However, substituting lines for circles, he did succeed in constructing them. Fu Hsi substituted undivided lines for light circles, and divided lines for dark circles. Thus it is possible to see that the lines were originally circles, and the circles in turn were originally representative of the sun and the moon.

When the light principle is perfected, it possesses a heavenly character. When the dark principle is perfected, it possesses an earthly character. The perfection of the light principle, or yang, is symbolized in the first hexagram, Heaven; and the dark principle, or yin, is perfected in the second hexagram, called Earth. The first and second hexagrams (the great yang and great yin) form the foundations of the remaining sixty-two hexagrams. The first hexagram represents the complete yang because all of its six lines are undivided; the second hexagram represents the complete yin because all of its six lines are divided. It is quite clear why under the symbolic system of the *I Ching* the yang line is deemed to possess a heavenly character and the yin line an earthly character, for the divided line symbolizes Earth and the undivided line symbolizes Heaven. This idea will become important for understanding the symbolization of the trigrams and hexagrams when presented later in this chapter.

The conflicting forces dominating Christian thought embody moral categories: good and evil. The origin of good and evil is uncertain, but Christians believe they can be traced back to their anthropological origin in the human decision to revolt against God, who represents the source of all goodness, as expressed in the third chapter of Genesis. The first sin marks, then, the beginning of the conflict of forces between good and evil. A cosmological description of dualistic forces is later found in the Gospel according to John. The first chapter of John seems to depict the two forces of nature: the light principle in opposition to the dark principle. The light principle is symbolized by Christ's coming to the world, and the dark principle by the world's opposition to that light. These opposite forces of nature seem to coincide with the yin and yang forces of the I Ching. *However, the similarity ends here.*

In the New Testament, the power of darkness is the enemy of the power of light. They cannot permanently coexist. The eventual elimination of the darkness of the world and the victory of the light seem to form the dominant themes of the New Testament. Moreover, the origin of the conflicting forces lies not in the created order, but in moral order. The symbolic contrast of sun and moon does not play any significant role in the Christian understanding of the conflicting forces of good and evil in the world.

However, the Eastern concept of yin and yang, the divided and undivided lines, shows that the relationship between Earth and Heaven is more fundamental than that between good and evil. In other words, ontological relationships (relationships of existence) are more fundamental than axiological relationships (those of value). The former comprise a complementary relationship, while the latter form a conflicting dualism. Heaven is a symbolic expression of divine presence, while Earth is that of the presence of this world. Thus, the presences of God and Earth are not in conflict in an ultimate sense. Since God is in the world, and the world is God's creation, they are mutually inclusive. Although they are not equal, they are dependent upon one another. God intends the world to be his own, and the world, despite its rebellion against God, cannot possibly exist without God. This mutual inclusiveness comprises a notion more closely aligned with that of the relationship between yin and yang.

Just as Heaven and Earth are perfect forms of yang and yin, so also the divine presence in the world and the world's dependency upon God can be regarded as the bases for the Christ-events in history, which have come to be known as Heilsgeschichte. *In Christianity, then, I see the divine presence in the world as a form of yang, signifying the receptive activities of the Earth. In Christianity, the undivided yang line can be conceived of as a vertical dimension because of its divine transcendence in the world. The divided yin line, on the other hand, can be understood as a horizontal dimension because of its immanence in the world. When these two lines are united, they form the symbol of the cross (†). Just as the divided line (yin) and the undivided line (yang) are fundamental to all cosmic phenomena in the* I Ching, *so, too, the symbol of the cross is fundamental to our understanding of the Christian faith.*

These divided and undivided lines are significant first of all because of their simplicity. The line is, perhaps, the simplest form of symbol. Complex symbolism tends to distort the meaning of that which it signifies. The simpler the symbol is, the easier it is to understand its meaning. The lines which symbolize yin and yang are also the primary constituents of all other symbolic expressions. Just as yin and yang are the primary categories of all other existences in the world, so likewise undivided and divided lines can be understood as the primary units and bases of all other visual symbolic expressions. The words we use in our writing consist of lines, whether they shape Chinese or English characters. For example, the English word "change" is a combination of many lines. The lines used in this word are both straight and curved. The combination of many different lines makes the written word possible. The Chinese language consists of lines also. Without lines, we cannot communicate visually. The shapes and forms of all things consist of surfaces, which are in turn generated bylines. Thus, paintings, sculptures, and pictures are made of lines. Likewise, everything in the world can be understood as expressing yin and yang forces. Just as no graphic symbolism is adequately expressed without lines, no concept can be understood without thereby implying the contrast symbolized by yin and yang. The linear symbol of yin and yang is one of simplicity.

Truth is often best conveyed in simple symbols. We see, for example, that Einstein's simple formula $E = mc^2$ reveals a profound truth of cosmic metaphysics. I also believe that the profundity of Christian truth lies in its simplicity. The messages in the Gospels are simple and are written in language that most people can understand. The church fathers and theologians in the past made the simple message of Christ difficult for ordinary people to grasp. The German scholar Adolph von Harnack, one of the great church historians, once said that the simple message of Christianity became the complex metaphysical dogmas of the church through inordinate intellectual indulgence.[1] The message that the apostles preached was simple. Christ died for our sins and was raised from the dead for our salvation. This simple message inspired people to follow Christ. What we need today is to rediscover that simple truth of the Christian faith. The simpler the message, the more powerful it is.

The linear symbols of yin and yang also express the complementarity of opposites. The divided line, or yin, is the opposite of the undivided line, or yang. They are not in conflict, but are complementary. The divided is the opposite of the undivided, just as yin is the opposite of yang. Although they are opposite in character, they are essentially united. Both are lines. The divided line is none other than the division of the undivided line, and the undivided line is none other than the union of the divided line. What is not divided is undivided, and what is not undivided is divided. In this respect, the divided line (yin) and the undivided line (yang) are both different and the same at the same time. Their difference puts them in contrast to one another, but their sameness provides a complementary relationship. These symbols, the divided and undivided lines, help us to understand that yin and yang are opposite only in their character, and mutually complementary in their existence. The divided line is known as the divided line *because of* the undivided line, just as the undivided line is known as the undivided line *because of* the divided line. In this kind of relationship, we can easily conceive of the complementarity of opposites. We begin to see why the use of linear symbols has an advantage over the earlier use of dark and light circles.

In Christianity, the symbol of the cross seems similarly to represent the complementarity of opposites. The vertical line and the horizontal line are opposite but need one another to form the cross. The vertical line represents the divine presence symbolized by the incarnation of Christ, and the horizontal line represents the world that receives the coming of Christ. Their conflict of appearance and definition is resolved on the cross. At the cross of Christ, the reconciliation between God and the world takes place. The world is no longer hostile, but becomes a part of God's care; and God no longer judges the world. In this kind of relationship, God and the world work together for the eternal kingdom of Heaven. Just as the divided and undivided lines in the I Ching *are the best symbols for understanding the complementarity of opposites, the vertical line and the horizontal line of the cross help us to understand the complementarity of God and the world in the making of the eternal kingdom. In this respect, the cross does not represent a paradox, but rather symbolizes the complementarity of opposites.*

The symbolic significance of the divided and undivided lines in the *I Ching* must be understood from the standpoint of their historical origin. The *I Ching*, as indicated previously, originated as a book of divination. The most primitive method of consulting the oracles seems to have been the drawing of lots. In drawing lots, both long and short stalks were used. A long stalk represented a positive or affirmative answer to the question, and a short stalk represented a negative answer or denial of the inquiry. This kind of method is still used in Asia. Instead of using stalks, however, matchsticks are now often used to draw lots. It is probable that the long stalk, which represents the positive answer, came to be identified with the yang force, and the short stalk, which represented the negative answer, came to be recognized as the yin force. As Hellmut Wilhelm said:

> At the first the method seems to have been a sort of drawing of lots, wherein long stalks meant a positive answer and short stalks a negative. Then, because of the equality in rank of the two fundamental forces, and probably also because of the old conception that heaven is one and earth two, two short stalks were made equal to one long stalk and were used to symbolize the yin force.[2]

The divided and undivided lines also symbolize the distinctive characteristics of male and female. The distinctive characteristic of the divided (yin) line was softness, while that of the undivided (yang) line was hardness. Softness or tenderness is an attribute of female character, while hardness or firmness is an attribute of male character. It is the natural tendency of the male to be hard and firm, while it is natural for the female to be soft and tender. The undivided (male) line shows the double strength of the divided line (female); thus, it reflects firmness. In other words, a single, unbroken line (——) of yang is equal to the two halves of the broken line (— —) of yin. The divided (female) line shows double the strength of the undivided (male) line, however, in the quality of tenderness. The divided line, consisting of two short undivided lines, is thus twice as strong as the undivided single line in the characteristic of softness.[3] It is, therefore, impossible to say that yin, or the divided line, is superior to yang, or that yang, the undivided line, is superior to yin. They are equal in nature and quality. The divided line of yin excels in softness, and the undivided line of yang in hardness. In Chinese, the undivided line is known as *kang hsiao* or hard line; and the divided line is known as *jou hsiao* or soft line. The hard line is in contrast to the soft line. The former possesses inward strength. Its rigidity or inflexibility means that it can be broken, to become a divided yin line. The softer line of yin, like the tender shoot of a plant which bends easily in the face of adversity, is sufficiently malleable for its halves to be joined, thus forming an undivided yang line. In this way, the hard changes to the soft, and the soft to the hard.

This is, essentially, the process of change. The hard line pushes outward and becomes thin in the middle, and then breaks in two to form a divided line. The soft line, however, draws inward and grows together into an undivided line. In this manner, yang changes to yin and yin changes to yang through the process of change. There is no third alternative; yang must become yin if it is to change at all; and yin can only become yang in the process of change.

The Judeo-Christian faith in the past has stressed the importance of the male character over the female. The recent women's liberation movement attempts to restore the rights of women in the church. However, the movement errs in holding that women must compete with men. Using the yin and yang symbolism in the I Ching *as a helpful tool for understanding the complementary natures of male and female, it becomes apparent that neither need be in competition with the other, but that each should complement the other. The focus of competition is to offset one imbalance with another; one wins, one loses; one succeeds, one fails. Competition merely perpetuates lack of balance (disharmony). It does not address the true problem, which is the erroneous ascription of value to one category or characteristic at the expense of its complementary aspect. What is needed, then, is to develop an equal appreciation for the feminine qualities of softness and tenderness, and to recognize the limitations of the male characteristics of firmness and aggressiveness, which have been traditionally highly valued. I believe that the rediscovery of the feminine characteristics of the Christian faith is an important task. By rediscovering the feminine qualities in the Gospels, women may be restored to their proper place in the church. Human beings, male and female, are by nature equal since their respective qualities complement and complete one another.*

The Symbolic Significance of Duograms

Although the linear symbols of the duograms seem insignificant for the understanding of the *I Ching,* they do provide one important element that cannot be found anywhere else, and that is the element of time in the process of change. The duograms indicate the progressive evolvement of changes from yang to yin and from yin to yang. By ringing the changes on both the divided and undivided lines and taking them two at a time, we see that four duograms are possible. They are: young yin (☲), old yin (☷), young yang (☳), and old yang (☰). As we see, the young yin consists of a yang line above and a yin line below. When the yang line of the young yin changes to a yin line, the young yin becomes old yin. Conversely, when one of the yin lines of the old yin changes to a yang line, it becomes young yang. When the yin line of the young yang changes to a yang line, old yang emerges. Again, old yang changes to young yin when one of its lines changes to a yin line. In this way, the cycle of change takes place indefinitely. The pattern of the changing process is depicted in the following diagram:

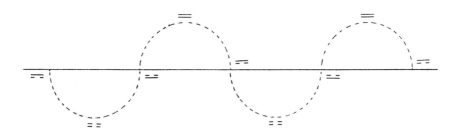

The changing pattern of the duograms can be easily understood in its relation to the four seasons of the year. When we relate the duograms to the changing seasons, we can clearly observe the principle of change in terms of expansion and contraction. Let us begin with the young yin, which represents autumn. When the young yin expands its yin power, it becomes old yin at the peak of the yin force. Old yin, thus, represents the winter season. When the yin force reaches its peak, it begins to lose its power. At the same time, the power of the yang force begins to grow. Thus, winter begins to lose its coldness and reverts toward warmth. It is followed by spring, which is represented by young yang. Young yang is between old yin and old yang, as spring is the season of moderation between cold and heat. As spring expands its warmth, the power of yang also expands. When the yang force reaches its peak, it becomes old yang, or summer. As old yang begins to lose its warmth, it must return to young yin, or autumn. In this way, the pattern of change repeats itself again and again, despite the fact that nothing is ever the same because eternal change is the background of the process of change.

Duograms serve to explain the change of yin to yang and of yang to yin. Yin (− −) always changes to yang (——) and yang always changes to yin. Yin changes to yang because yin has reached its peak, just as yang changes to yin because yang has reached its peak. The duograms illustrate this process. Yin

(− −), for example, includes both young yin (= =) and old yin (= =), just as yang (——) includes both young yang (= =) and old yang (=). When yin changes to yang, yin grows from the young yin (the minimum yin) to the old yin (the maximum yin), and has nowhere to go but to become young yang (the minimum yang). In the same manner, when yang grows from young yang (the minimum yang) to the old yang (maximum yang), it must then become young yin (= =).

This pattern of change in the *I Ching* is strikingly similar to that depicted by the pre-Socratic pluralist, Empedocles. For Empedocles there were six elements, reminiscent of the *I Ching*'s hexagrams: Earth, Air, Fire, Water, Love, and Strife. At the outset, the first four elements are thoroughly homogenized under the dominance of Love. Gradually, however, Strife begins to come into effect, tending to separate out the four elements. In due time, the process reaches its peak with all of the earth in one place, all the water in another, the fire in a third, etc. The ascendancy of Strife, however, cannot last; and Love soon begins to insinuate itself once more, mixing the elements more and more until they finally form again a complete amalgam. Here, in ancient Greek thought, we can discern in Love and Strife principles analogous to those of yang and yin in the *I Ching*.

The cyclic pattern of change in the I Ching *is very closely related to nature and her changes. Christianity seems to be less interested in nature and her cyclic change. Time for Christianity does not move cyclically. While time has an end and a beginning, it is not re-entrant to itself in total repetition. In Christianity, time moves from alpha to omega or from beginning to end. The beginning occurs as creation and the end is marked by the second coming of Christ. Thus, time moves from promise to fulfillment. The end of time is the time of fulfillment. In this respect, the* I Ching *seems to provide the Christian faith with very little insight concerning time and history.*

However, time does not in fact move linearly from beginning to end. The beginning is connected with the end after all, and the end with the beginning. The end of time, or eschaton, should not be understood as the ultimate end. It is the end of the old age, but also the beginning of the new age. As Jacob said, "Eschatology is a return to the beginning, but with something additional which was absent at the first creation."[4] When the Last Judgment is over, the new heaven and the new earth appear: "Then I saw a new heaven and a new earth, for the first heaven and the first earth had passed away, and the sea was no more. And I saw the holy city, the New Jerusalem, coming down out of heaven from God, prepared as a bride adorned for her husband" (Rev. 21:1–2). Here, the end is also the beginning but, in sharp opposition to the purely cyclic view of the Greeks as expressed by Empedocles, it is more than the beginning, for new things have been added to it. It is, therefore, not a meaningless cyclic change but a cyclic change with meaning, for newness always accompanies change. Even in

Empedocles, such meaning is implied when he calls the process "god"; he is a "sacred and unutterable mind flashing through the whole world with rapid thoughts" (Frag. 134). In Christian thought, everything changes; thus nothing remains the same in any particular. What is the same is the pattern of change. History moves toward its fulfillment, but fulfillment evolves through cycles of evolution. In this respect, the concept of time in the process of change as expressed in the duograms is helpful for the Christian understanding of time and salvation history.

The Symbolic Significance of the Trigrams

Just as the two divided and/or undivided lines combine producing the four duograms, when one rings the changes on combinations of three divided and/or undivided lines, one produces eight trigrams. Thus, the Great Commentary says, "The two primary forms (yin and yang) produce the four images (four duograms). The four images produce the eight trigrams" (1:2). These eight trigrams are the prototypes of the hexagrams, for the hexagrams are merely combinations of two trigrams. The eight trigrams are known in Chinese as the *pa kua* or the eight germinal situations; for *pa* means "eight" and *kua* means "germinal situation." The hexagram is often known as the *chung kua* or "double germinal situation." In other words, hexagrams are simply double trigrams. From an examination of these Chinese words, we can clearly grasp the fact that the trigrams are building blocks of hexagrams, which in turn represent the basic units of all possible situations in the universe. The trigrams are thus the keys to understanding the *I Ching.*

The trigrams, viewed as the basic units of existence, remind me of the trinitarian principle in Christianity. The Trinity can be understood as evincing the three prototypes of all existence, keeping in mind that the limitations of traditional patriarchal language exclude what is feminine, and thus appear to ignore the existence of the feminine nature. That is to say, the Godhead as the Father, the Son, and the Holy Spirit is not only the source of all things, but the fundamental unity of divine life. One of the basic themes that twentieth-century Swiss theologian Karl Barth attempted to convey was the priority of the Trinity. According to him, the trinitarian life of God is a blueprint for everything happening in the universe, the key to understanding all things. What distinguished the Christian idea of God from that of Islam and Judaism is certainly the notion of the Trinity. The classical affirmation that God exists in three persons seems to be fundamental to modern Christian faith. While this certainty does not imply that the Trinity of Christianity and the trigrams of the I Ching are identical, it is important for us to realize that a trinitarian principle is implicit to both the East Asian and Christian ways of thinking.

The Trigrams and the Yin-Yang Relationship

We have previously indicated that yin and yang are the bases for all procreations and transformations in the world. If this is the case, why do we need three lines (of yin and/or yang) to make the basic unit of existence? There is no doubt that the relationship between yin and yang constitutes the basic category of all existence. Nothing can exist without them, for they are the bases for all change. In Western thought, this fact was made clear by the pre-Socratic philosopher Parmenides, who showed that no change can occur in a world consisting only of "the One." Without yin and yang, there can be no process of change. Without change, there is nothing in existence or that can exist. In other words, according to the principle of change in the *I Ching,* change is prior to existence, just as the yin-yang relationship is prior to the eight trigrams. Yin and yang comprise a relational category, while the trigrams belong to the category of substance. Yin-yang deals with the process of becoming, while trigrams deal with units of being. Just as the yin-yang symbol is prior to the symbol of the trigrams, so also process is more fundamental than ontology in the *I Ching*. If we examine the duograms and trigrams together, it becomes clear why the yin-yang symbols represent process and the trigrams represent substance. As the reader will recall, the duograms—the combinations of two lines of yin and/or yang—are the symbolic representation of time. Time deals with processes, the processes of change. The trigrams, however, are basic units of being. Because the trigram is an evolution from the yin-yang relationship, its unit of being or substance is the evolutionary outgrowth of process.

This concept is very difficult for the Western mind to understand, because it is a reversal of the classical Western conviction that being is prior to change. In the very name for the discipline that studies reality—"ontology" (derived from the Greek word for being)—the West has prejudged the issue, intimating that being or substance is the essence of all things. According to the philosophy of change in the *I Ching,* however, change is more fundamental than existence; and therefore, process is more basic than being. In this respect, the process philosophy of Alfred North Whitehead is very closely related to the metaphysics of the *I Ching.*

Yin and yang are more relational symbols than symbols of existence. Let me illustrate this. I am yang in relation to my wife, but I am yin in relation to my father. Here, I can be both yin and yang depending upon the relationship at issue. It is my relationship, not my being, that decides whether I am yin or yang. The trigrams, however, are symbols of being or substance. They represent either actual things or potential beings, as we will see later when we discuss the various attributes of the trigrams. Again, what the *I Ching* tries to tell us is that relationship comes before substance. This idea is also expressed in Buddhist metaphysics. According to the Buddha's doctrine of *anatman* or "no soul," there is no such thing as a self or soul. What we think of as being or substance is process controlled by relationship. Process or karma becomes more important than substance. In this respect, Buddhist philosophy and the philosophy of the *I Ching* seem to converge.

The Trigrams and Family Life

The trigrams as complete units of existence were applicable to various aspects of personal and social life in early East Asia. The concept of family is very important in the Chinese and East Asian tradition and constitutes the core of social life. Because family life is the foundation of all other social and political life, it is easily described in terms of the trigram, the basic unit of all things. The close identification of human life with the cosmic process has also contributed to a better understanding of the relationship between the trigrams and family units. For the primitive peoples of East Asia, Heaven and Earth were regarded as macrocosmic symbols of father and mother. The idea that "the Heaven is my father and the Earth is my mother" is not strictly confined, however, to Eastern peoples. The conception of the Earth as a mother-god figure was almost universal in primitive thought. Moreover, Heaven and the father-god were often identified. In Christianity, we still use the phrase "Our Heavenly Father" to invoke the divine.

In the early days, Heaven and Earth were regarded as the sources of life. All things, therefore, including human beings, were understood to be the offspring of Heaven and Earth. Among creatures, human beings were given a special place in the universe. The uniqueness of persons in the *I Ching* lies not in their substance, however, but in their place in the universe. They occupy the center of the universe. Therefore, it is not the image of God that makes people different from animals, but their central position that makes them different. Because of this special position in the universe, human beings belong to the family of Heaven and Earth. Thus, the cosmic trinity—Heaven, Earth, and human beings—is the macrocosmic counterpart of the familial trinity: father, mother, and child.

We may ask whether the family is complete without children. In the West, the family often does appear to be complete when it is constituted of only the wife and husband. However, in East Asia, the family is not complete without children. The reason is precisely that the cosmos, including all family life, is conceived as a living organism. What makes it organic is its procreative ability. Without procreation, it cannot be a living organism. Thus, the male and female complete themselves by procreating offspring.

There is yet another reason why the family structure in the West is different from that of the East. In the West, the family life stresses the horizontal relationship between husband and wife. In the East, the family structure is based upon the vertical relationship between parents and children. *The Eastern way of family life is also expressed in the Old Testament. For example, Abraham's desire to have his own child was stronger than the ideal of monogamy. He, therefore, went to Hagar, his wife's maidservant, to conceive a son.* Just as the husband and the wife are insufficient without children, the relationship between Heaven and Earth, that is, between yin and yang, is incomplete without human beings, their offspring. Forke's remarks are quite appropriate in this regard: "One yin and one yang, that is the fundamental principle. The passionate union of yin and yang and the copulation of husband and wife is the eternal rule of the universe. If Heaven and Earth did not mingle, whence would all things receive life? When the wife comes to the man, she bears children. Bearing children is the way of propagation. Man and wife cohabit and produce offspring."[5]

The relationship between yin and yang becomes a complete unit of existence when it procreates either yin or yang. That is why threeness, or the trigram, is an inevitable outcome of twoness, or the yin-yang relationship. The trigrams, therefore, form the basic units of life, just as the mutuality of yin and yang is the basic relational category of all things. In the trigram, the bottom line is understood as the way of Earth, the middle line the way of human beings, and the upper line the way of Heaven. Thus, the human being occupies the center between Heaven and Earth. As the Great Commentary says, "The *I Ching* is a book which is vast and great and contains everything. It has the *Tao* of Heaven, the *Tao* of the Earth, and the *Tao* of Men. These three primal powers are doubled and make six lines. The six lines are nothing other than *Tao* of the three primal powers" (2:10).

The central position of man seems to be recognized by the physical sciences of our time. It is by no means a coincidence that a person's size is about 1,030 times the size of an atom, and that the total universe is about 1,030 times the size of a person. If the universe represents Heaven and the atom the Earth, man is certainly at the center, being halfway between them in size. Our interest, however, is not in the size but in the functional relationships among the three. The centrality of human existence in the universe has been a dominant theme throughout the history of human civilization.

In the trigrams, the central line which represents persons is similar to children surrounded by their parents. Perhaps, the life of the Oriental family would be best depicted in the trigram, where the central line, which represents children, becomes the center of attention. Children grow up with their mother's milk, that is, with the fertility of the Earth, and with their father's wisdom, that is, with the will of Heaven. If we examine the eight trigrams, we will observe that three sons—Chên (☳), K'an (☵), and Kên (☶)—and three daughters—Sun (☴), Li (☲), and Tui (☱)—are surrounded by their father

Ch'ien ($\equiv$) and mother K'un ($\equiv\equiv$). We will discuss their attributes more extensively in the last section of this chapter.

The Trigrams and Social Life

The trigrams not only represent the complete unit of family life but also that of social and political life. In every form of social structure, there are basically three groups of people. In the early days of East Asia, as in Plato's *Republic*, the upper class of people consisted of the sages, or the wise persons; the central position was occupied by the powerful knights and rulers; and the lower class or position was that of the mass of people, who were ruled by the others. In East Asia the class structure included a gentry group, the common people, and, at the bottom, the serfs and servants. The symbol of the trigrams thus reflects the social structure of the early days.

These three categories still exist in the West. Today, such divisions are generally made on the basis of wealth. The upper class is wealthier than the middle class; and the lower class usually lives in poverty and is poorly educated. The middle class is still a ruling class in the United States, even though a balance should be maintained. It is also important to notice that the branches of the power structure in our government—the executive, the judicial, and the legislative powers—also comprise a triadic structure. Thus, the trigram seems to serve as a useful symbol for the balance of these powers and, in general, for the unit of social and political life. Thus, the trinitarian principle seems to provide an archetype of human social and political behavior.

The Trigrams and Personality

Just as the trigram can serve as a model for the family, or as a social and political unit, so also it can become a basic unit of personality. The three distinctive levels of personality seem to be compatible with the structure of the trigram. As Culling said, "In the Western world is a prevailing tenet several centuries old: man is a threefold being, body, mind and soul. The *I Ching* said it a thousand years ago."[6] In the trigrams, the body occupies the bottom line. Since the mind is at the center, it characterizes the uniqueness of humanity. However, the body, occupying the lowest place, is more closely related with Earth and thus fundamental for survival. The soul, occupying the upper level of existence, becomes the subject of religious inquiry and possesses the heavenly character.

In a similar manner, the self can be classified in terms of three distinctive parts: passion, mind, and will. Passion occupies the bottom line of the trigram, the mind the central position, and the will the upper line. The relationship between passion, mind, and will symbolized in the trigram is not much different from Thomas Aquinas's idea that the mind controls the passions in order to attain a will that is essentially good. What makes the *I Ching*'s view different from that of Aquinas is that in Eastern thought, the mind does not control the passions. In the *I Ching,* the mind, which occupies the central position, always mediates and harmonizes both passion and will. Just as the Earth is the mother of humanity, so too the passions, inasmuch as they occupy the earthly realm, must be taken positively and reverently. The mind thus tries to understand passion and to fulfill the will.

It is also interesting to examine the psychic strata of personality in relation to the trigram. Since the *I Ching* has been used as an oracular book and because the oracles operate through disclosures from within the human consciousness, the trigram is very closely associated with the psychic structure of human personality, which we can easily understand by its means. If we appeal to Freudian psychology, the bottom line can represent our subconsciousness, the central line our consciousness, and the top line our superconsciousness. The stratum of the subconscious at the bottom is suppressed by that of consciousness, in the center of the trigram. The stratum of superconsciousness, represented by the upper line of the trigram, is revealed at the moment of enlightenment or liberation from the limitations of consciousness. The stratum of superconsciousness can then be compared with the heavenly realm, that of unconsciousness with the earthly realm, and that of consciousness with the human realm. Because of its central position, consciousness mediates between the subconscious and the superconscious in the oracle. The Great Commentary says, "It [the *I Ching*] receives one's fate like an echo, whether he is near or far, dark or deep. Thus he knows of the things that are coming" (1:10). Here, the subconscious is expressed in terms of the dark and deep in a person, and superconsciousness in spatial terms of far and near. Thus, consciousness enters into relationship with subconsciousness and superconsciousness.

The Trigrams and Cosmology

Since the *I Ching* is primarily a book of cosmology, there is no need to reiterate the cosmic significance of the trigrams. The trigram itself is a cosmic symbol and represents the structure of the cosmos. It is important to realize that cosmology as depicted in the *I Ching* is not unique. That there are three elements of the universe seems to have been held in many other civilizations. For example, in India the Samkhya school in particular teaches that there are three constituents of all worldly phenomena: the innate inertia (*tamas*), the driving force of tendency and passion (*rajas*), and the balance between the two, which is called the harmonizing medium (*sattya*). "In this way, the special importance of the number 'three' is philosophically interpreted: a union between the two opposites is finally established by a third harmonizing element."[7]

Thus, in the philosophy of the Samkhya school we can discern the idea of the balancing of the three forces in the trigram. The opposing forces of *tamas* and *rajas* are analogous to those of Heaven and Earth, or yang and yin; and the balancing force of *sattya* is analogous to that of the person who occupies the central position in the trigram.

The trigram is certainly an archetypal expression of cosmic symbolism that is also found in most folk religions in the world. In shamanism, which Mircea Eliade claims to be the most pervasive folk religion in the world, the cosmos is understood in terms of three levels of existence: heavenly paradise, hell, and the world. When a person dies, his soul goes either to hell or to paradise. it is the task of the shamans to rescue the souls of the dead from the clutches of the underground and take them to heavenly paradise. It is an almost universal scheme to envision the world of paradise as above and the place of hell as below. Between them is the present world.

We also find the same kind of worldview depicted in the New Testament. Rudolph Bultmann's demythologizing task began with the cosmological myth in the New Testament. Bultmann noticed that, to the scientifically minded people of our time, the primitive cosmology of the New Testament based upon the idea of a three-story structure is obsolete and irrelevant. His attempt to eliminate this cosmological myth was nonetheless a failure, because he failed to recognize the archetypal symbol of the trigram, which is deeply rooted in the unconscious stratum of human existence.

Many of us still think and behave as though the world consists of three levels of existence. Most of us unconsciously believe that the good belongs to above, and bad belongs to below. We tend to value the qualities of things in terms of high and low. Thus, even intellectuals and scientists cannot dismiss the symbolic significance of the tripartite structure of the cosmos. The trigram itself is a cosmic symbol, and its symbolic significance is perhaps more powerful, and even older, than human consciousness. The symbolic significance of the trigram lies in its expression of a principle deeply rooted in the Trinity. This is, perhaps, why the trigram should be regarded as an archetypal symbol of the cosmic drama.

The Eight Trigrams and Natural Images

When the lines of yin and/or yang are taken three at a time, and combined in all possible ways to make trigrams, these three-line units comprise eight trigrams. In other words, 2 x 2 x 2 equals eight (from the general formula $N = 2n$, where n is the number of variables). The eight trigrams can be easily constructed upon the duograms. We can recall that the old yang (☰) changes to young yin (☳), the young yin then changes to old yin (☷), and the old yin to young yang (☱), which then changes to old yang (☰). In this way, the four images or four duograms are completed. The addition of either a yin or a yang line to these duograms—an operation that is equivalent to adding another variable—makes the eight trigrams possible. Following the same order of the duograms that we have formed, we can add a yang line to the old yang line to make the trigram *Ch'ien,* or Heaven (☰). By adding a yin line to the old yang, we attain the trigram *Tui,* or Lake (☱). Using the same procedure for the rest of the duograms, we can obtain the following trigrams: *Sun* or Wind (☴) and *K'an* or Water (☵) are obtained from the young yin. Trigrams *Kên* or Mountain (☶) and *K'un* or Earth (☷) are formed from old yin. Trigrams *Li* or Fire (☲) and *Chên* or Thunder (☳) are derived from young yang.

These eight trigrams can be correlated with everything, especially with natural phenomena and the seasons of the year. The primitive view of the natural world is reflected in these eight objects: they are Heaven, Earth, Mountain, Lake, Thunder, Wind, Water, and Fire. If we observe the early landscapes in East Asian art work, we see that almost all of them are primarily based upon a combination of these eight objects. If I were to construct a landscape out of these eight objects, I might put them together in the following way: Between Heaven (*Ch'ien*) and Earth (*K'un*), a Wind (*Sun*) gathers over the mountain (*Kên*), the dark clouds produce Thunder (*Chên*) and Lightning (*Li*), and then the Rain (*K'an*) fills the Lake (*Tui*). Despite the Thunder and Lightning, the Mountain is still and the Lake is calm. In this landscape, these images correspond to the trinity of world principles. Wind and Thunder arise in Heaven, the Mountain and the Lake are of the Earth, and Fire and Water are most commonly used by human beings. Heaven, therefore, is on top, Earth is on the bottom, and human beings are in the middle of the trigram.

The Sequence of the Eight Trigrams

The order of the eight trigrams is best expressed when the trigrams are correlated with seasonal changes. According to the Discussion of the Trigrams (*Shou Kua Chuan*), "Heaven and Earth determine the position. The powers of Mountain and Lake are correlated. Thunder and Wind meet each other. Water and Fire do not meet each other. Thus the eight trigrams are mutually intermingled" (chap. 2). The above sequence of arrangement in pairs is often known as the Primal Arrangement or the Sequence of Earlier Heaven. This arrangement, based on the natural change of seasons, is, the reader will recall, believed to have been made by Fu Hsi himself.

The Sequence of Earlier Heaven (or Before the World) is as follows:

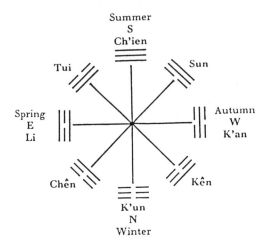

According to this diagram, Heaven (*Ch'ien*) and Earth (*K'un*) determine the directions of north and south, or the seasons of winter and summer. They represent the poles or axis of the universe. They correspond to the direction of the old yang and the old yin of the duograms. Wind (*Sun*) and Thunder (*Chên*) arise from each other in Heaven. Both of them are situated in the east, that is, the heavenly realm of yang domination. The Mountain (*Kên*) and Lake (*Tui*) bring cosmic harmony to the Earth. They are situated in the west, dominated by the early realm of yin influence. Water (*K'an*) and Fire (*Li*) balance one another in their opposite directions. They point to the east and west as well as to autumn and spring. The west corresponds to the young yin, while the east corresponds to the young yang. They belong to the human realm, occupying the center between the heavenly and earthly realms.

The Sequence of Earlier Heaven is an *a priori* or mathematical order which is not dependent on the immediate experience of time and situation. This arrangement is practically identical to that of the duograms. The seasons of the year correspond to the relative intensities of the yin and yang forces as represented by the trigrams. When yang forces are at their peak, they indicate summer, while when yin forces peak, it becomes winter. In the autumn, there is more yin than yang, and in the spring, more yang than yin. Moreover, each season has a direction. Autumn is correlated with the west and spring with the east, just as summer is correlated with the south and winter with the north. It is, therefore, a logical and mathematical arrangement, with modes and quantities proportional to the yin and yang forces.

The sequence of movement in this arrangement begins with Heaven (south) and moves in a counterclockwise direction. Thus, Heaven moves to Lake (southeast), from Lake to Fire (east) and from Fire to Thunder (northeast). These counterclockwise movements belong to the heavenly realm or to yang domination. From Thunder, the sequence moves to Wind (southwest). From Wind, the sequence moves to Water (west); Water moves to Mountain (northwest) and finally to Earth (north). When we observe the sequence of movement carefully from Heaven (Ch'ien) to Earth (K'un), we begin to notice the binary change from the upper lines of the trigrams. Heaven, consisting of all unbroken lines, changes to Lake by changing its upper line to a broken line. Lake then changes to Fire by changing its upper line to an unbroken line, which change feeds a change in the middle line. In this way, the binary change takes place from Heaven to Earth. The mathematical sequence of movements is carried out according to the binary system. That is why this arrangement evinces a logical and intrinsic order of the universe.

This is reminiscent of the original order of creation in Judeo-Christianity. When God first created the world, the world must have been in perfect order, with everything in harmony and all things complementary to one another. The life depicted in the Garden of Eden in Genesis is reminiscent of the Sequence of Earlier Heaven. In other words, the world before the Fall can be conceived as the perfect order of God's creation. Because of the Fall, the relationship between God and human beings was distorted, and because of this distortion the world as a whole became distorted as well. As a consequence, we lost the perfect order of the world that provides harmony and tranquility. In contrast to this logical and perfect order is the Sequence of Later Heaven, which became the basis for the order of the world in which we actually live.

A new arrangement of the eight trigrams, or the Sequence of Later Heaven, is believed to have been devised by King Wen, the founder of the Chou dynasty. King Wen put the eight trigrams in order according to the temporal progression of the cyclic year. This arrangement, therefore, follows the immediately experienced situations of natural phenomena. According to the Discussion of the Trigrams, "The ruler comes forth in Thunder (Chên) and completes everything in the Wind (Sun). He causes things to see one another in the Fire (Li), and causes them to serve one another in the Earth (K'un). He gives them joy in the Lake (Tui) and battles for perfection in the Mountain (Kên) (chap. 5). The illustration on the next page attempts to show the Sequence of Later Heaven.

As we see, the arrangement according to the Sequence of Later Heaven is not in a logical sequence as was the case in the preceding arrangement. It does not correspond with the forces of yin and yang, but with the attributes of the trigrams. In this sequence, everything begins with Thunder (Chên) because thunder symbolizes electricity and sound that awakens all things under Heaven and over the Earth. All living things arise in the sign of Thunder because it means awakening and stands in the east, the symbolic location of new life. The day breaks in the east, and because of this, the east also symbolizes spring. That is why the Chinese calendar starts the New Year with the beginning of spring.

Spring means not only new life, but also the new age. All living things begin with the sign of awakening and move to the sign of Wind (*Sun*).

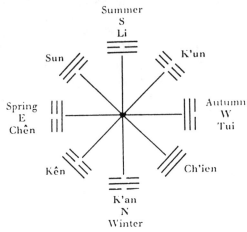

The Wind, which is characterized by gentleness, can be compared with midmorning and with the transition between spring and summer. In this season of the year, all living things are completely formed and the seeds change into plants. Midmorning is the time of renewal and refreshment, for the wind blows gently. Further, it represents the transition from spring to summer.

Wind is then followed by Fire (*Li*). The attribute of Fire is light and brightness. It is, therefore, situated in the south. Because of this location, it corresponds to the noontime of the day and the summer of the year. It symbolizes midsummer, the hottest time of the year. Since south is always warmer than north, summer is correlated with the south. In political and social life, the brightness of Fire represents the shining seal of power and glory. The holy sages thus turned their faces to the south.

The trigram *Li* is followed by Earth (*K'un*). Earth represents mid-afternoon, the transition from summer to autumn. This is the time when all living things begin to bear fruit, which signifies the essence of the Earth. Like the womb, the Earth is always receptive. Bearing fruit is followed by nourishment. Earth is the symbol of mother, who not only gives birth to a child but also nourishes it by her milk and, prepartum, from her body. In other words, in this season the fruit grows through the nourishment of the Earth Mother.

The receptive symbol of Earth is followed by Lake (*Tui*). Lake symbolizes joy. It represents mid-autumn and the westerly direction. It is also the time of sunset. It is the season of harvest, for the fruit is ripe. Harvest is a joyous time. It is, however, the time when darkness begins to expand its power.

Lake is followed by Heaven (*Ch'ien*), which symbolizes creativity. It is located in the northwest and moves toward deeper darkness. The victory of the yin power is certain, but the final effort of yang is desperate. In the moment of the final battle, the creative energy of Heaven is radically manifested.

Heaven is followed by the trigram Water (*K'an*). Water is the abyss, for it represents the depths. It is situated in the north, symbolizing the cold of winter as well as midnight. It is the time of rest. After toil and struggle comes comfort. Winter is also the time of quiescence. Everything ceases its work. It is the time when the yin force expands to its maximum extent, and the yang force contracts to its minimum.

Water is followed by Mountain (*Kên*). The trigram *Kên* symbolizes the transition between winter and spring. Mountain signifies stillness and is, therefore, the posture of meditation. Through meditation, the beginning of new birth takes place. It is, therefore, a symbol of dawn, the beginning of the new day. Hidden rest and comfort join with the new year. It is the place where the beginning of the new and the end of the old join.

Mountain is followed by Thunder (*Chên*), the symbol of awakening. In this way, the Sequence of Later Heaven reflects the cyclic recurrence of things. In this cycle of changes, the old and the new are linked together inseparably.

What, then, are the distinctions between the Sequence of Earlier Heaven and the Sequence of Later Heaven? The characteristic difference between them is illustrated in terms of the distinction drawn by the epoch-making German philosopher, Immanuel Kant, between "noumena" and "phenomena." Just as noumena represent things in themselves, the Sequence of Earlier Heaven depicts an *a priori* order that is not conditioned by the sensory experience of human beings. It represents a logical and mathematical order that serves as the background of the phenomenal world. Likewise, the Sequence of Later Heaven is analogous to Kant's notion of "phenomena," which are conditioned by our sensory data. This is the order of immediately experienced reality. It, therefore, represents the *a posteriori* order that deals with the empirical world. The Sequence of Earlier Heaven is, then, the background of the Sequence of Later Heaven. Not only are they inseparable, but they are complementary. In fact, their relationship can be compared with the yin and yang relationship. Just as yin presupposes yang and yang presupposes yin, the Sequence of Earlier Heaven presupposes the Sequence of Later Heaven and vice versa. "To understand fully, one must visualize the Inner World Arrangement (the Sequence of Later Heaven) as transparent, with the Primal Arrangement (the Sequence of Earlier Heaven) shining through it."[8]

Historically speaking, the Sequence of Earlier Heaven seems to represent the old eon, and the Sequence of Later Heaven to represent the new eon. However, the new age becomes the old and the old becomes new. In this way, the cyclic change of eons takes place. In this way, also, the Sequence of Later Heaven becomes the Sequence of Earlier Heaven.

This idea is clearly expressed in the Revelation of John: "Then I saw a new

*heaven and a new earth; for the first heaven and the first earth had passed away,
and the sea was no more. And I saw the holy city, the New Jerusalem, coming
down out of heaven from God, prepared as a bride adorned for her husband" (Rev.
21:1–2). Here, the new heaven and the new earth, which seem to correspond to
the Sequence of Earlier Heaven, or the perfect order, are merely the renewal of the
old heaven and earth, which correspond to the Sequence of Later Heaven, or the
order of the present world. According to the Korean Book of Change, the*
Chongyok *(literally, "The Book of Correct Change"), the Sequence of Later
Heaven is ready to be replaced by the Sequence of Earlier Heaven.*[9] *In the
Christian counterpart, the Kingdom of God is at hand.*

The Attributes of the Eight Trigrams

Since the trigrams are the basic constituents of the hexagrams in the *I Ching,* it
is important to know the basic attributes of the trigrams in order to understand
the hexagrams. Using the pair of opposites, Heaven (*Ch'ien*) and Earth (*K'un*),
we note that Heaven (☰) consists of three undivided lines, while Earth (☷)
consists of three divided lines. *Ch'ien* (☰) originally meant "dry," while *K'un*
(☷) meant "moist." The concepts of Heaven and Earth may have come out of
the original meanings of dry and moist. "What is pure and light rises up and
becomes Heaven; what is turbid and heavy sinks down and becomes Earth." Dry
corresponds to the pure and light, and moist corresponds to what is turbid and
heavy. Purity and light are attributes of Heaven, and the turbid and heavy are
attributes of Earth.

In the Sequence of Earlier Heaven, the trigram Heaven stands for the south
and summer, the time of heat that dries everything. The trigram Earth stands for
the north and winter, which is the time of coolness that preserves moisture from
evaporation. Heat symbolizes the active force and coolness is the sign of rest and
calm. The active force is the natural endowment of the male character, while the
passive force is the natural expression of the female character. In this way, the
trigram Heaven becomes the archetype of yang forces, while the trigram Earth
becomes the archetype of yin forces.

Heaven is represented by the symbol of a dragon, often associated with
storms with their thunder and lightning. The image of thunder and lightning in
Heaven means power, creative energy, and active movement. In contrast to the
dragon, a mare belongs to the Earth. The dragon gives rain to make the pasture
green, while the mare eats the green pasture. The mare, therefore, stands in
apposition to the dragon, just as Earth stands in apposition to Heaven. The mare
is the symbol of the vast expanse of the Earth, because she can run tirelessly
over the green pastures. The mare is also the symbol of a certain gentleness and
submissiveness. Thus, she is receptive while the dragon is creative.

The trigram Heaven is the symbol of prince and father, while the trigram Earth is the symbol of mother and the masses who are ruled from above. Heaven is symbolized by the head, for the power of creativity manifests itself in the head; and Earth is symbolized by the abdominal cavity, for receptivity takes place in the belly. Heaven is round because it looks round; Earth is square and flat because it appears to be so. Heaven is symbolized by metal, for it is strong and solid, while Earth is symbolized by fragility, for it is tender and soft. Heaven is jade, while Earth is cloth. Heaven is content, while Earth is form. Heaven is fruit, while Earth is the tree trunk. The color of Heaven is deep red, which is the intensified color of the light principle; the color of Earth is black, which is intensified darkness. Red activates people's minds and emotions, while black receives them. The combination of Heaven and Earth procreates all things, for Heaven and Earth are archetypes of yang and yin. In terms of family life, Heaven represents father and Earth represents mother. The union of father and mother procreates three sons and three daughters.

The trigram *Chên* or Thunder (☳), the first son, resembles his mother because the female searches first for the power of the male and receives a son. On the other hand, the trigram *Sun* or Wind (☴) is the first daughter, who resembles her father, because this time the male searches first for the power of the female and receives a daughter. It is because of this that the son generally resembles his mother while the daughter resembles her father. As we notice, the first son consists of two yin lines and one yang line; thus, he has more yin than yang. On the other hand, the first daughter consists of two yang lines and one yin line.

Before dealing with the other four children, let us note that the character of Thunder is arousal, which also signifies movement. The character of Wind is gentleness, which also signifies penetration. Thunder is compared with the foot of the body, for it moves along the ground. Wind, on the other hand, belongs to the thigh of the body, for it separates downward. Thunder takes from his father the signs of the dragon and the horse, both of which are noted for their swiftness. Wind is symbolized by the cock, whose voice penetrates and pierces the stillness. Thunder is decisive and vehement, while Wind is yielding and retiring, or indecisive. Thunder is bamboo that is green and youthful, while the Wind is wood, which grows long and high. The bamboo that grows fast represents autumn. The color of thunder is dark yellow, which is the mixture of dark heaven and yellow earth, while the color of Wind is white, which is the texture of the yin principle.

The trigram *K'an* or Water (☵) is the second son, who resembles his mother because she seeks the power of the male a second time and receives the son. The trigram *Li* or Fire (☲) is the second daughter, who resembles her father because he seeks the female power a second time and receives a daughter. Since the structure of *K'an* in its old form is the pictogram 氺, which later came to be written as 水 or "water," it is plausible to believe that the Chinese word "water" originally derived from the symbol of *K'an*. The trigram *Li* stands in apposition to *K'an* and symbolizes Fire. Water and fire do not go together. Thus, the place of *K'an* is the north and winter, for it is the counterpart to fire, while the place of *Li* is the south and summer.

K'an or Water symbolizes the abysmal, for water forms the abyss. *Li* or Fire signifies clinging, for fire clings to the fuel it consumes. Water, the abyss, is like the ear, for the ear is deep inside the body. Fire, however, signifies the brightness of the eye, for the eye is a shining part of the body. Water also represents ditches, ambush, bending, straightening out, the bow and the wheel, which are all analogous in one way or another to the abysmal. Especially, "bending and straightening out" is characteristic of flowing water. The uneasy flow of water signifies in man melancholy, sick hearts, and earaches, however, while *Li* signifies flaming, the sun, and lightning. Because of the shape of the trigram *Li,* it also symbolizes the big-bellied person. The color of *K'an* is red and symbolizes blood. Its animal is the pig, which lives in mud and water. The animal of *Li* is the pheasant, which is like a firebird. *Li*'s sign is aridity because of fire. It also represents shell-bearing creatures, such as the tortoise, the crab, the snail, the mussel, and so on. Among trees, *Li* symbolizes those which dry out in the upper part of the trunk. The sign of *K'an,* on the contrary, is penetration, for water easily penetrates. Among woods, it represents those that are firm and durable, textures that result from the constant penetration of water.

The trigram *Kên* or Mountain (☶) is the third son, who resembles his mother because she seeks male power for a third time and receives a son. The trigram *Tui* or Lake (☱) is the third daughter, who resembles her father because he seeks female power for the third time and receives a girl. *Kên* is the symbol of keeping still, not only because it is the attribute of the immovable mountain but also because in the structure of the trigram, the upper line is firmly supported by the two lower lines. When the upper line, which represents the will of heaven, is strong and both human beings and Earth are receptive to it, it is steady and remains at a standstill. However, in the trigram *Tui* or Lake the structure is reversed. The upper line, the will of heaven, is receptive to the strength of both the middle and bottom lines. Thus, it signifies the joy that comes from the immediate satisfaction of the desires of passion and worldliness. It is the joy of the mouth, for it shows interest in communication. In the human body, therefore, *Tui* would be symbolized by the mouth and tongue. *Kên*, on the other hand, is symbolized by the hand that holds firm. Its animal symbol is a dog that stands at the door to protect the house. The animal of *Tui*, in contrast, is the sheep, because the two parts of the divided line at the top of the trigram correspond to the horns of the sheep. *Kên* is the bypath, the mountain path with little stones along the road. *Tui* is the symbol of dropping off and bursting open, because its structure has an opening above. Because *Kên* is the door or the gate, it also means the doorkeeper and watchman who guards the street and protects the people. *Tui,* however, is the concubine or wastrel who is led by the joy of immediate satisfaction and regrets it in later life. Thus, joy is short-lived.

These attributes of the eight trigrams are taken mostly from the Discussion of the Trigrams. Clearly, they reflect the conditions of the early days in China. Theoretically, the eight trigrams represent everything in the world; they are, as indicated, the basic units of existence. In the early days, people thought of the world as consisting of a few basic elements, such as water, wood, fire, metals, and so on. In general, such ideas as the "four elements" in ancient Greece or the "five elements" in China were common among primitive peoples.

Representative of everything in the world, the trigrams can be compared with the original units of existence in the Creation story of Genesis. We are told that God created Heaven and Earth, light and darkness, water and other creatures according to their kind. These original forms of creation can be regarded as the archetypes of all other forms of existence in the world. From these basic units of existence, all other things evolved or were produced, just as occurs in the I Ching.

The Trigrams and Gender

Before concluding the discussion of the symbolic significance of the eight trigrams, let me explain more carefully the relationship between children and parents. As noted, the combination of Heaven as father and Earth as mother generates three sons and three daughters. The sex of a child is opposite to that of the one who seeks after it. The sons, therefore, have a strong resemblance to their mother and the daughters to their father, which is a reflection of the fact that, according to the Great Commentary, "the yang (light) trigrams have more yin (dark) lines; the yin (dark) trigrams have more yang (light) lines." The Great Commentary explains it further: "What are they and how do they act? The yang (light) trigrams have two rulers and one subject. This indicates the way of the inferior person" (2:4). The notion of differentiating between the superior person and the inferior person is a common Confucian notion. More important here is the fact that sons can have two yin lines and one yang line, while daughters can have two yang lines and one yin line. The uniqueness of the male is that one yang can balance two yin forces. According to the Confucian interpretation, one master (one yang line) has two subjects (two yin lines). The uniqueness of the female is that one yin force can balance two yang forces. Here, the strength of woman lies in the power of yin, while that of man is in the power of yang. In this respect, the sons and daughters are complementary to one another.

My comments so far have been based on King Wen's Sequence of Later Heaven, which became the basis for understanding the present world as expressed in the sixty-four hexagrams of the *I Ching*. However, according to Fu Hsi's Sequence of Earlier Heaven, the sex determinant is based upon the first, or bottom, line of each trigram, rather than the single line as King Wen's interpretation requires. According to the Sequence of Earlier Heaven, the sons are *Chên* or Thunder (☳), *Li* or Fire (☲), and *Tui* or Lake (☱). Here, both Fire and Lake differ from King Wen's understanding. The daughters, according to the Sequence of Earlier Heaven, are *Sun* or Wind (☴), *K'an* or Water (☵), and *Kên* or Mountain (☶). Here again, the alteration of sex occurs with both Water and Mountain. Thunder and Wind, the first son and first daughter, are the only ones whose gender identities remain the same in both sequences. Except for these two trigrams, the rest then are sexually interchangeable. For example, the second son, *K'an* in the Sequence of Later Heaven, is Water, which is also Lake, the youngest daughter, *Tui*. *K'an*, therefore, changes to the second daughter, and *Tui* to the youngest son in the Sequence of Earlier Heaven. According to the Sequence of Later Heaven, *Li* is the second daughter and symbolizes Fire, the Sun, and Lightning. These attributes are parts of the male or yang characteristics. *Li*, therefore, changes to the second son in the Sequence of Earlier Heaven.

From the gender designation of the trigrams, it is obvious that the Sequences of Earlier and Later Heaven must be viewed together: the Sequence of Earlier Heaven is to be understood in terms of the Sequence of Later Heaven, and vice versa. As I noted previously, the Sequence of Later Heaven becomes the foreground of the Sequence of Earlier Heaven.

One important observation to be made about gender in the I Ching *is the interchangeability of male and female. Male can become female and female can become male. Like yin and yang, they can be transformed from one to the other. This idea is explicitly upheld in the biblical story of Creation. God's creation of woman out of man is a metaphorical description of the interchangeability of the sexes: "And Adam said, 'This at last is bone of my bones and flesh of my flesh; she shall be called Woman, because she was taken out of Man'" (Gen. 2:23). The story has been interpreted to mean that woman should be subservient to man because she was taken from man. Just as the Confucian tradition in the commentaries of the* I Ching *attempted to elevate man and subject women, so likewise did the Judeo-Christian tradition. In both cultures, men were regarded as superior to women. These historical remnants should not hinder us from drawing the profound implication of the mutual and complementary relationship between men and women.*

The Relation between the Trigrams and Hexagrams

What is the relationship between the trigrams and the hexagrams? "Hexagram" simply means "a diagram consisting of six variables." In the *I Ching,* these variables are the lines. The Chinese word *kua* is used to designate both the trigram and the hexagram. In order to distinguish the hexagram from the trigram, the word *chung kua* is generally used for the hexagram. *Chung kua* means "the double *kua*" or "the double trigram." Sometimes, the term *ta sheng kua* is used to distinguish the hexagram from the trigram. This means "the great *kua*." For its part, the trigram is often known as the *hsiao sheng kua,* which means "the small *kua*." However, there is no qualitative distinction between them. The hexagram is, according to its etymology, merely an expansion of the trigram.

For example, the first and second hexagrams, *Ch'ien* and *K'un,* are expansions respectively of the trigrams *Ch'ien* and *K'un*. The hexagram *Ch'ien* is simply the trigram *Ch'ien* (☰) doubled, and the hexagram *K'un* is the trigram *K'un* (☷) doubled.

It is therefore evident that a hexagram is a doubled trigram. The sixty-four hexagrams, then, consist of various combinations of the eight trigrams, taken two at a time. When the eight trigrams are doubled in every possible way, sixty-four hexagrams result. Thus, the hexagram is a great trigram, and the trigram is a small hexagram. The hexagram can be reduced to its component trigrams, and the trigram expanded into a hexagram. They are not, however, identical. Just as the whole and parts of the whole are different, so, too, the hexagram and the trigram are different. The distinction between them is more than qualitative, and therefore the etymological approach must be modified.

The relationship between the trigram and the hexagram is comparable to that between yin and yang. Just as the duogram is the combination of yin and yang forces, the hexagram is the combination of two trigrams. Just as yang does not exist without yin, one trigram alone cannot make a hexagram. It is the complementary relationship between yin and yang lines which makes the duogram possible, and likewise, it is the complementary relationship between the upper and lower trigrams that makes the hexagram possible. Just as yin and yang together comprise an inseparable whole, the hexagram too must be understood as an inseparable whole. The two trigrams of a hexagram cannot be compartmentalized; the hexagram must be seen as a whole. It is complete in itself, just as the trigram alone is a complete unit. The uniqueness of the hexagram lies in its totality. It is, in fact, different from a mere juxtaposition of two trigrams. Just as the whole is greater than the sum of its parts, the hexagram is greater than the sum of two trigrams.

The trigram consists of three lines, each representing a different variable; the hexagram has six lines, each representing a different variable. In the trigram, the upper line represents Heaven, the middle line represents a person, and the lower lines represents the Earth. In the hexagram, however, the lines are taken two at a time, and thus the two upper lines (the fifth and sixth lines from the bottom) represent Heaven; the two middle lines (the third and fourth lines from the bottom) represent persons, and the two lower lines (the first and second lines) represent the Earth.

To illustrate this, let me quote from a familiar passage of the Great Commentary: "The *I* is a book which is vast and contains everything. It has the *Tao* of Heaven, the *Tao* of the Earth, and the *Tao* of a person. These three primal powers are doubled and make six lines. The six lines are nothing more than the *Tao* of the three primal powers" (2:10). Since each force in the hexagram is represented by two lines, or double forces, the hexagram is called the great *kua*. Being more than the sum of two trigrams, it is unique unto itself.

The complementary relationship between the two constituting trigrams, like the relationship between yin and yang, can be illustrated in our life experience. For example, the power of electricity is different from either the positive or the negative current. However, the combination of the positive and negative makes electricity possible.

In the same manner, the combination of vertical and horizontal lines makes the form of the cross possible. The cross, however, has a unique meaning in itself. It is more than the complementary relationship between the vertical and horizontal lines. An analogy will help: existence is often described in terms of space and time, indeed of space-time. But while the combination of space and time makes our existence possible, existence itself is distinct from both space and time and is, in fact, unique. Likewise, the cross consists of both the vertical and the horizontal lines, but it is also more than those lines. It is distinct from both of them. According to the traditional Christian confession, the cross is a symbol of Christ, who is both God and human being at the same time. In the same manner as with space-time, Christ is not a simple mixture of both of them. He is unique. He is God, but a human being, and is a human being but God.

Likewise, the hexagram is unique in itself, even though it is the combination of two trigrams. It has its own identity as its own unit of existence. Like atoms, the hexagrams are germinal units of all possible situations in the universe; they are microcosms of the universe. Everything and every possible predicament in the universe can be expressed with these sixty-four hexagrams. That is precisely why the Great Commentary says, "The *I* contains the measure of Heaven and Earth. Thus it enables us to perceive the Tao of Heaven and Earth" (1:4).

The Sixty-Four Hexagrams

Why the hexagrams? Why sixty-four of them? It seems possible to expand the germinal situations indefinitely by adding an indefinite number of yin and yang lines. As we have seen, the formula (in Western terms) for the number of *kua* is simply $N = 2n$, where n (the number of yin and yang lines) equals 1, 2, 3, 4, or (for hexagrams) 6. For the original combination of yin and yang lines, where $n = 2$, the formula ($N = 2^2$) makes four duograms possible. With the addition of one more line to the duograms, making $n = 3$, the formula becomes $N = 2^3$ and eight trigrams are produced. Again, by adding another line to the eight trigrams, $N = 2^4$ makes sixteen quartagrams. In this way it is possible to expand the germinal situations indefinitely. In fact, as previously detailed, Eddington did so almost indefinitely—up to the formula 2^{256}, which yields, however, the total number of particles in the universe, not the total number of *kinds* of particles. Why does the *I Ching* stop with the formula $N = 2^6$, which yields the number 64? Why do sixty-four hexagrams complete all of the possible situations in the universe? The *I Ching,* perhaps in the spirit of Ockam's razor ("entities are not to be multiplied beyond necessity"), simply stops with $N = 2^6$ (i.e., with hexagrams), a restraint that would be appreciated in modern high-energy particle physics, now embarrassed with many dozens of particles as yet irreducible to simpler terms. But given the limitations to hexagrams, the question "Why sixty-four?" is answerable in relation to the trigrams. Since the eight trigrams are archetypal units of every possible situation in the universe, every possible combination of those eight produces the sixty-four hexagrams. If the first trigram is taken paired with itself, and then with each of the other seven, and so also with the second trigram, and with the third, and so on to the eighth, then there must be eight times eight hexagrams.

It would be helpful, perhaps, to our understanding of why the number sixty-four represents all of the possible situations if we study the Chinese word *kua,* which means "the germinal situations." Since the hexagram is known as the great *kua,* the trigram or the small *kua* cannot be expanded into more than its own intrinsic potentials will allow. Thus, no small *kua* or trigram can expand into more than the number eight. For if the bottom two lines are yang, the top can be either yin or yang (two choices); and so also, if the bottom two are yin (two more choices). Then, if the bottom is yang and the middle yin, this can combine with either yin or yang (two choices); and finally, for a bottom yin and yang (two choices). In other words, the small *kua* cannot go beyond its intrinsic limit of things which could be chosen, which add up to eight. Then the small *kua* can be expanded into the great *kua* by every possible multiplication of eight. Thus sixty-four, or eight times eight, is the maximum possible number. The great *kua* cannot expand indefinitely because of the intrinsic limitations of the small *kua*.

The analysis of the word *kua* (圭卜) yields still more enlightenment on the limitation to the number sixty-four. The word *kua* comes from the practice of prognostication (divination). The Chinese character can be separated into two parts: *kuei* ('圭) and *pu* ('卜). *Pu* means prognostication, especially the method of prognostication by use of a tortoise shell as done in the early days, before the more convenient use of stalks became prevalent. *Pu,* therefore, came to imply all forms of prognostication. Let us then look at the other part of the word *kua* or "general situation." The word *kuei* ('圭) is the combination of two identical uses of the word *t'u* (土). Although *t'u* means "the soil," the structure of the word is similar to that of the trigram. The pictogram for *t'u* consists of three lines, two horizontal and one vertical. By doubling the *t'u,* just as in doubling the trigrams, the word *kuei* (圭) is attained. *Kuei* is, then, analogous to the hexagram. It may be stretching things to illustrate the relationship between the trigram and the hexagram through an analysis of the word *kua.* However, it seems to be more than a coincidence that some early Chinese thinker chose the word *kuei* (圭) as having some relation to the hexagrams. The word actually signifies "a sundial," which enabled the measurement of seasons and changing situations. *Kuei,* therefore, is also the name of a measurement that is divided into sixty-four degrees. The sixty-four divisions of *kuei* appear to correspond to the sixty-four hexagrams. Just as all the changing phenomena in the course of a day are measured by the sixty-four degrees of *kuei,* so also the sixty-four hexagrams represent all the possible germinal situations in the universe. Thus, the number sixty-four completes the sequence of numbers expressing the whole.

Limiting the germinal situations to sixty-four seems problematic, however, to many people. Life appears to be more complex than anything reducible to sixty-four categories. Especially with the development of technology and modernization, it seems that new situations are being created all the time. It would seem, therefore, impossible to deal with today's life situations through the use of only sixty-four hexagrams. However, it is a grave mistake to identify the sixty-four hexagrams with sixty-four actual situations. The hexagrams do not represent actual or phenomenal situations (in Kantian terms), but germinal situations, each of which might be actualized in many different ways.

The hexagrams are analogous to seeds that have the potential for growth. The Great Commentary says,

> To know the seeds is to know the mystery. In his dealing with those above him, the superior person does not flatter. In his dealing with those beneath him, he is not arrogant, for he knows the seeds. The seeds are the slight beginnings of movement and the first indication of good fortune and misfortune. The superior person realizes the seeds and acts immediately without any delay of a single day. (2:5)

Here, the seeds, or the hexagrams, are identical with embryonic stages. They can be understood as the undifferentiated forms from which all kinds of actual situations will eventually evolve. They are pure potentialities that are not yet actualized in human experience. If we believe that a single cell can evolve in its multiple dimensions into all of the living creatures of our time, it should not be difficult to believe that sixty-four germinal situations or sixty-four undifferentiated continuums are sufficient to summarize all the possible phenomena of the universe. The illustration is, in fact, remarkably apt inasmuch as we know today that the genetic code of DNA common to all evolving life is composed of only four "letters"—two purines (guanine and adenine) and two pyrimidines (cytosine and thymine)—analogous to the four duograms of the *I Ching*.

This is rather like the traditional Protestant affirmation that the Scriptures alone contain sufficient wisdom for the salvation of humankind. It is certainly difficult for non-Protestant believers to accept this premiss, for the Bible is only one book among millions of books in the world. Nevertheless, the Bible contains all of the seeds required in order to transform our lives in all human situations. In this respect, the I Ching *and the Bible seem to have something in common.*

The Structure of the Hexagrams

The hexagram is the combination of two trigrams. The two constituting trigrams are known as the primary trigrams. The lower primary trigram consists of the first three lines (reading from the bottom of the hexagram), while the upper primary trigram consists of the fourth, fifth, and sixth lines of the hexagram. For example, hexagram 11, *T'ai* or Peace, is the combination of the primary trigrams *Ch'ien* or Heaven (☰) and *K'un* or Earth (☷).

T'ai

The trigram Heaven is the lower primary trigram, while the trigram Earth is the upper primary trigram.

Besides the two primary trigrams, the hexagram Peace can also be divided into two nuclear trigrams. The lower nuclear trigram of Peace consists of the second, third, and fourth lines (the trigram *Tui* or Lake [☱]). The upper nuclear trigram consists of the third, fourth, and fifth lines (the trigram *Chên* or Thunder [☳]). They are called "nuclear" because they are situated (in part) within the primary trigrams. The function of the nuclear trigrams is rather limited within the function of the primary trigrams, just as the function of the primary trigrams is limited within the function of the hexagram as a whole.

The relationship between nuclear trigrams and primary trigrams can be compared with that between children and parents. The relationship between the mother and father is analogous to that between the lower and upper primary trigrams in the hexagram; the relationship between daughters and sons is analogous to that between the lower and upper nuclear trigrams. Just as the parents delimit the function of their children, the two primary trigrams also restrict the function of the nuclear trigrams. The relationship between the mother and father establishes a norm of family life for the children. This does not mean, however, that the children are unimportant. Many major crises of family life, such as the destruction of harmony and the separation of parents, can result from an unfortunate relationship among the children. Likewise, the relationship between the two nuclear trigrams can have a destructive effect within the hexagram. Just as the function of the parents is conditioned by the welfare of the whole family, the function of the two primary trigrams is confined within the hexagram as a whole.

The Hexagrams and the Attributes
of the Constituting Trigrams

The attributes of the constituting trigrams affect the nature of the hexagram. Let me revert to hexagram 11, *T'ai* or Peace, and its two primary trigrams: *Ch'ien* or Heaven below, and *K'un* or Earth above. Some of the main attributes of Heaven are the creative, strong, and fatherly, while those of Earth are the receptive, weak, and motherly. It is not difficult to observe that they are favorably correlated. The relationships between the creative and the receptive, between the strong and the weak, and between the fatherly and the motherly show the harmonious coexistence of opposites. The correlation of these attributes is also relative to their positions. The lower trigram always occupies the "below," "within," and "behind." The upper trigram occupies the "above," "without," and "in front." The lower trigram, therefore, stresses the idea of coming in, while the upper trigram stresses the concept of going out. Thus, the lower trigram is inner-directed, while the upper trigram is outer-directed. Because of their opposite movements, the center between the two trigrams becomes an important factor in understanding their relationship. The trigrams either move closer to the center or away from it.

With these preliminary remarks, let us now return to the hexagram *T'ai* or Peace. The lower primary trigram, Heaven, is in the position of below, within, and behind the upper trigram Earth. The upper trigram Earth is in the reverse position: that is, above, without, and in front of the trigram Heaven. The relationship between these two trigrams is relative to the direction of their movement. The trigram Heaven moves upward, because it is a light principle. The trigram Earth moves downward because it is a heavy and inactive principle. Thus, the primary trigram, Heaven, being lower, moves up toward the center, just as the upper primary trigram, Earth, being higher, moves down toward the center of the hexagram. These impulses are good because both of them move closer together toward the center. The commentary on this hexagram, therefore, says, "The Receptive (Earth), which moves downward, stands above; the Creative (Heaven), which moves upwards, is below. Hence their influences meet and are in harmony, so that all living things bloom and prosper."[10] This is why the hexagram is named T'ai or Peace.

The significance of the position of the trigrams becomes clear from one more example. In hexagram 12, P'i or Stagnation, which is the reversal of hexagram 11, we find that the primary trigram Heaven (☰) is above, and the primary trigram Earth (☷) is below.

P'i

The attributes of Heaven and Earth are opposite to one another. What makes this hexagram different from hexagram 12 is the positions of the constituting trigrams. In this hexagram, the light principle (the trigram Heaven) is above and moves upward. The heavy principle (the trigram Earth) is below and moves downward. Both trigrams, therefore, move away from the center. The commentary on this hexagram says, "Heaven is above, drawing farther and farther away, while the Earth below sinks farther into the depths. The creative powers are not in relation. It is a time for standstill and decline."[11] The importance of the position of the constituting trigrams here becomes evident: when the trigram Heaven is above and Earth is below, as is the case in the hexagram Stagnation, it is a time of standstill. When the trigram Heaven is below and Earth above, as in the hexagram Peace, it is a time of harmony and prosperity. Let me now focus on the nuclear trigrams within the hexagram Peace. As noted, the constituting nuclear trigrams of Peace are Lake (☱) below and Thunder (☳) above. Some of the main attributes of the trigram Thunder are awakening, movement, wood, and the elder son. The attributes of Lake are joy, pleasure, and the youngest daughter. The trigram Thunder, as the awakening, moves upwards in the manner of his father, Heaven; and Lake, as joy, also tends upward because of its light principle. Both of them, therefore, move upward from the center. Their influences do not impact each other. This unhealthy circumstance, created by the relationship between the two nuclear trigrams, is not strong enough, however, to upset the harmonious correlation between the two primary trigrams. The Judgment on this hexagram points out the side effect arising from the two nuclear trigrams: "Peace. The small departs and the great approaches. It is good fortune and success." Here, "the small departs" is an unfavorable effect created by the relationship between the nuclear trigrams. However, "the great approaches" is a favorable situation created by the relationship between the primary trigrams. The significance of the relationship between the nuclear trigrams is delimited by that of the primary trigrams.

If one compares the hexagram or the germinal situation with the Christ-event in history, the primary trigrams are compared with the act of God in Christ, while the nuclear trigrams evince the human response to this act. Both God's act and the human response are necessary for the efficacy of salvation. Just as the center is important for the hexagram, the center in the Christ-event is Christ himself, who draws both God and humanity together. When this center is lost, disharmony arises and order and peace are no longer possible. Because Christ himself occupies the center of salvific efficacy, he becomes the Mediator between God and humanity. Just as the nuclear trigrams are conditioned by the primary trigrams, so also all human response is conditioned by the divine act of redemption. Nevertheless, God's redemptive act suffers owing to human revolt. Peace between God and humanity is possible, however, through Christ, who occupies the center. That is why the centrality of Christ is the core of the Christian faith.

The Revealed and Hidden Hexagrams

In order to understand the hexagram as a whole, one must also acknowledge the existence of the hidden hexagram as the counterpart of the revealed hexagram. For every visible hexagram also contains an invisible hexagram. This idea is based on the basic philosophy of change, in which yin and yang complement each other. Yin presupposes the existence of yang, and yang presupposes the existence of yin. Since the hexagram is constantly in the process of change and transformation, it is subject to the laws of such change and transformation. For example, the hexagram *Ch'ien*, or Heaven, presupposes the existence of its opposite, *K'un,* or Earth, as the hidden hexagram of Heaven. In the same manner, the hexagram Earth presupposes the existence of Heaven as its hidden hexagram.

Let me illustrate the existence of the hidden hexagrams using the Diagram of the Great Ultimate (*T'ai Ch'i T'u*), where the two opposing symbols of the primal monad are intertwined together ( ). In this symbol, what is light includes dark, because of the dark dot in it; and what is dark includes light, because of the light dot in it. Just as the light principle presupposes the existence of the dark, each hexagram presupposes the existence of its opposite. What is revealed includes what is not revealed, just as what is hidden also includes what is revealed.

The relationship between the revealed and hidden hexagrams can be compared with the relationship between yin and yang. Yin changes to yang, and yang changes to yin. In a similar manner, the revealed hexagram changes to the hidden hexagram; and the hidden hexagram manifests itself and becomes the revealed hexagram. For example, when the hexagram Heaven changes every one of its lines, it then becomes the hexagram Earth. Also, when the hexagram Earth changes completely, it becomes the hexagram Heaven. In this way, the revealed hexagram becomes the hidden hexagram and the hidden hexagram becomes the revealed one. They are one in two different aspects of existence. Just as the yang line presupposes the existence of the yin line as its background and the yin presupposes the existence of the yang, the revealed hexagram always presupposes the existence of a hidden hexagram as its background. Because the hexagrams are germinal situations of everything in the world, everything has to be seen in terms of both the revealed and the hidden, or the foreground and the background existence. Everything has its hidden element within it. This idea is illustrated in the relationship between matter and energy expressed in Einstein's formula $E = mc^2$. Matter is the revealed aspect of energy and energy is the hidden aspect of matter. In the same manner, wherever energy is, the potential of matter always exists. Thus, matter and energy illustrate the coexistence of the revealed and hidden aspects in all things. In the ultimate sense, existence presupposes non-existence, just as *Yu* (thing) presupposes *Wu* (nothing). This gives us the simple formula that one and two are the same but different. In other words, any revealed hexagram is ultimately a hexagram that is both revealed and hidden. On the other hand, the revealed hexagram is different from the hidden hexagram. There is here an identity-in-difference similar to that of some forms of panentheism. In this respect, the hexagram is one, but two at the same time.

The relationship between the revealed and the hidden hexagrams is like Paul's idea of the relationship of the physical body to the spiritual body in First Corinthians. In the fifteenth chapter, he attempts to explain the Resurrection of Christ, alluding to the spiritual body as the counterpart of the physical body. According to Paul, the physical body and the spiritual body are not totally independent. They seem to complement each other, just as the revealed and the hidden hexagrams, or yin and yang, are complementary. He says, "If there is a physical body, there is also a spiritual body" (1 Cor. 15:44). This seems to imply that the two are inseparable. This analogy can be extended further. The physical body corresponds to the world of manifestation, which we can sense; but the spiritual body would then correspond to the spiritual world which we cannot see. The spirit can then be understood as the background of our existence.

If God is spirit, He is then present everywhere. This leads me to consider the idea of panentheism—that is, that God is in all things. This makes us take the idea of panentheism seriously in our understanding of the God who is truly present in the world.

Another consideration is that Christians believe that God revealed himself through Christ. If we apply the idea of the revealed and the hidden hexagrams, God's revelation in Christ presupposes his mystery which is hidden from us. When the divine mystery is not taken seriously, God becomes an idol, because he is replaced by the human idea of God. Behind God's love is his wrath, behind his grace is his justice, and behind his joy is his suffering. This dialectical unity accommodates the divine mystery. The paradox of divine and human unity makes sense if we apply the idea of the revealed and the hidden hexagrams. The revealed hexagram is analogous to Jesus of Nazareth, the complete and perfect human. The hidden hexagram is, then, analogous to the Christ, the Son of God, who is perfectly divine. Just as the revealed hexagram presupposes the hidden hexagram, Jesus of Nazareth presupposes the Son of God. In other words, Jesus' humanity presupposes his divinity. They are mutually dependent yet complete in themselves. They are one, but two at the same time. Besides such christological questions, other theological issues, such as that of the relating between the written words of God and the Word, can also be seen as congruent with the idea of the revealed and hidden hexagrams.

The Hexagrams and the Process of Change

Understanding the changing process of the hexagram requires a careful observation of the lines of the hexagram, for these lines represent the process of change. "The lines," the Great Commentary remarks, "are imitations of movements under Heaven" (2:3). The hexagram expresses the opportune time, and the line expresses the change of time. Time flows through the situation of the hexagram, for a situation occurs in time. The situation that is expressed in the hexagram changes all through time, just as the lines of the hexagram transform from the divided to the undivided. The lines change within the changing hexagram. Again, the Great Commentary says, "The *I* is the book which is not far away. Its way is forever changing and transforming everything. It flows through the six empty places of above and below. The firm [the undivided line] and yielding [the divided line] transform each other. They do not have to be confined within a rule, because the change is at work here" (2:8). Although there are no definite rules for changing lines, there are certain fixed rhythms: e.g., the movement from inward to outward implies the movement of the lower trigram, which represents the position of the inward, to the upper trigram, which represents the position of the outward. In this movement from inward to outward, or from the bottom to the upper portion of the hexagram, change is in progress. In the Great Commentary, it is said that the book begins with the first line and is summed up in the last line (2:9).

The process of change within the hexagram may be compared with the process of building something, which begins with the foundation and moves upward. The beginning line or the bottom line is the foundation of the hexagram. This line, however, is difficult to comprehend because it represents the depth of the unconscious. In contrast, the top line or the last line is easy to comprehend, for it begins to reveal the unconscious. That is why judgment on the first line is tentative, while the judgment on the last line is certain. The first line and the last line do not belong to the nuclear trigrams; instead, they set the limitations of the hexagram.

The real evolution occurs in the lines of the two nuclear trigrams. The four lines in the middle are active in the process of evolution. Since the beginning and the ending lines do not participate in the active process of evolution, they represent the unconscious and the conscious in the personal psyches of the masses and the sage in society. The masses represented the lower class and the sage the highest class of society in the early days. They set the minimum and maximum degrees of evolvement. That is why they are regarded as the limits of the hexagram. The fifth line represents the most active position in the process of change. The fourth line represents activity which supports the fifth line. The third line is the continuing evolution of the second line, which makes the evolution apparent. Among them, the fifth and second lines are the most active, because they occupy the central positions in the primary trigrams. The fifth line is the central position of the upper primary trigram, and the second line is that of the lower primary trigram of the hexagram.

From the above, it should be clear that the activity of each line is based on its position in the hexagram. All six lines are dependent on one another and work together for the whole hexagram. The fixed rhythm is a gradual evolution from the bottom line to the top line.

Let me again use hexagram 1, *Ch'ien* or Heaven, this time in more detail, to illustrate this evolution. The first (beginning) line is: "The dragon is hidden. It is no use to act." Here, the beginning line symbolizes the hidden dragon, the deep unconsciousness or the ground of strength. It is the state of non-action, a line that shows no apparent evolution. The second line is: "The dragon is seen in the field. It is advantageous to see the great person." The hidden dragon is now manifested in the field. Thus, the dragon evolves from the underground to the ground. It makes the evolvement of this hexagram now apparent. The third line is: "The superior person is creative and creative all day long, but he rests with care in the evening. It is dangerous but no mistake." The dragon is analogous to the creative power resident in this line. He is active and creative all of the time. It marks the evolution of appearance into the active engagement of creativity.

The fourth line is: "Leaping over the depths. There is no mistake." Here, active work has evolved into the activity of leaping. This marks an evolution from activities on the ground to those in the air. The fifth line is: "Flying dragon in the sky. It is advantageous to see the great person." Here, the limit of the dragon's activity is defined. To go beyond the limit precipitates remorse. When all of the six lines are put together, it says: "There is a herd of dragons without a head. It is good fortune." Here, the limit is surpassed and the dragon loses its head. It is the end of creative power in the hexagram Heaven. The humiliation and destruction are followed by the birth of a new situation. In this way the process of change and transformation occurs within the hexagram, and then from one hexagram to another in the *I Ching*.

What is interesting in this evolutionary process is the limitations that the hexagram has set between the first and last lines. When the limitation is exceeded, the hexagram cannot maintain its own nature. When the dragon, for example, exceeds its limitation, it becomes remorseful or repentant. What this impresses upon us is the importance of knowing one's own limitations—whether they be in individual or sociohistorical life.

This process of change is exemplified in the Judeo-Christian tradition in the story of Adam and Eve. The sin that they committed, according to the Genesis story, was their attempt to exceed their own human limitations. Because they wanted to become like God or because they wanted to become more than what they were, they disobeyed God. This was the beginning of humiliation. Each of us must act within the givenness—that is, within the limits—set by the intrinsic nature of our own existence. A human being is a human being. He cannot become more than what he is. To go beyond his own essence is to humiliate himself.

The Hexagrams and the
Positions of the Lines

The lines of the hexagram are either yin or yang, or divided or undivided lines, but their positions in the hexagram condition their characteristics. The positions of the lines can be either correct (or central) or incorrect (not central) depending upon circumstances. A line is correct when it stands in an appropriate place. For example, as a rule, a firm or undivided line occupies the first, third, or fifth place, while a tender or divided line occupies the second, fourth, or sixth place. That is, the proper positions of the yang lines are the odd places, while those of the yin lines are the even places. However, this kind of general rule does not always work. When the opportune time comes for receptiveness, for example, the yin line is regarded as favorable irrespective of its position. Likewise, when the time calls for firmness, the yang line is judged favorable irrespective of its position.

In hexagram 19, *Lin* or Approach, the line in the second place ought to be divided according to the rule. However, at this particular time it calls for a firm line in the second place.

Lin

The second line, therefore, says: "Approach together will bring good fortune. Everything is advantageous." The fifth place, as a rule, must take a yang line. However, in this particular instance, the yin line is appropriate. Thus, the fifth line says: "To know the approach is the duty of a great prince. It brings good fortune."

Let me take another example to illustrate the propriety of the rules applicable in most places. In hexagram 16, *Yü* or Eagerness, for the yin line to be in the first place is not correct or central.

Yü

The first line, therefore, means: "Proclaiming eagerness. It brings misfortune." Because it is an odd place, the yang line should be appropriate. However, the yin line in the second place is correct because it is an even place. The judgment on the second line, therefore, says: "It is firm as a rock, but it does not last all day. Correctness brings good fortune." The Commentary on the Symbols says concerning this line: "It is not a whole day. Correctness brings good fortune, because it is central and right." The yin line in the third place is not correct, because it is an odd place. Thus, the judgment on this line says: "Eagerness looks upward. If it is delayed, it brings remorse." The Commentary on the Symbols remarks: "Eagerness that looks upward brings remorse, because the place is not appropriate." As in the case of hexagram 16, the rules of correlation seem to work in most cases, although some exceptions are made.

There is also a certain rule of correspondence. Generally, yang lines correspond to yin lines only, and vice versa. The first, third, and fifth places are correct for the yang line, and the second, fourth, and sixth places are correct for the yin line. Since a yang line corresponds to a yin line, and the hexagram consists of two primary trigrams, the first place (yang line position) corresponds to the fourth place (yin line position). The second place (yin line position) corresponds to the fifth place (yang line position), and so on.

To summarize, the first and fourth, second and fifth, and third and sixth lines are correlated. Among them, the correlation between the second and fifth places is the most important. Their relationship is analogous to the relationship between the official and the ruler, the son and the father, or the wife and the husband. The firmness of the official corresponds to the yielding of the ruler, and vice versa. In the case of hexagram 4, *Meng* or Immature Youth, the second line, or the official, is firm, while the fifth line, or the ruler, is yielding.

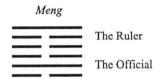

Meng

The Ruler

The Official

As the Judgment says, "Difficulty is originating, penetrating, advantageous, and correct." A similar relationship is also found in hexagrams 8, 25, 42, 45, 49, and 53. It is, therefore, important to observe that the correlation between the second place and the fifth place—regardless of whether the yang line is in the second place and the yin line is in the fifth place, or whether the yin is in the second place and the yang line is in the fifth—plays a decisive role for the hexagram as a whole. In contrast, the correlation between the first and the fourth, or the third and the sixth place, appears to be rather insignificant to the total hexagram.

Both "the ruler" and "the official" are political symbols conditioned by the early governmental structure in China. In America, the official could be thought of as the governor of a state, while the ruler could be regarded as the president of the country. Thus, the lower primary trigram would represent the local government, while the upper primary trigram would be the federal government. They can also symbolize nonpolitical entities. However, what makes both the third and fifth lines important for the hexagram as a whole is that they occupy the central place in the two primary trigrams which constitute the hexagram. The importance of correlating the centers seems to make them the keys to success and tranquility.

Finally, there is a rule of mutual dependence. This idea is well illustrated in hexagram 8, *Pi* or United Together. Mutual dependence is possible because of unity. This rule is applicable to any pair of adjacent lines in the hexagram. The relationship between adjacent lines is such that the lower line receives the upper line and the upper line rests upon the lower line. In this mutual dependency, the relationship between the fourth and fifth lines is the most important, for it represents the relationship between the minister and the ruler. The mutual cooperation between the ruler and the minister is a key to understanding the function of the traditional Chinese government. Likewise, in the family situation the relationship between the husband and the wife is most important. The fourth place represents the wife, and the fifth, the husband.

Let me illustrate the importance of mutual dependence between the fourth and fifth lines through the use of the hexagram 8, *Pi* or Uniting Together:

Pi

The fourth line of the hexagram is yielding, representing the minister or wife. The fifth line is firm, representing the ruler or husband. The fourth place means: "Uniting together with others." Here, "others" can be understood as the ruler(s) or king(s). The fifth line says: "It expresses the most illustrious instance of uniting together." Thus, the fourth and fifth lines are illustriously held together in unity. Similarly, in hexagrams 9, 20, 37, 42, 48, 55, 59, 60, and 61, the firm ruler (the yang line in the fifth place) and the yielding minister (the yin line in the fourth place) are mutually dependent and the outcome is favorable. However, if the relationship is altered—that is, with a yielding ruler (yin line in the fifth place) and a firm minister (yang line in the fourth place)—it usually results in an unfavorable interaction. One can illustrate this altered relationship with hexagram 32, *Hêng* or Endurance:

Hêng

In this hexagram, the fourth line is yang, or firm, and the fifth line is yin, or yielding. The fourth line says: "No game in the field." The fifth line says: "Endurance maintains right virtues. It is good fortune for a wife, but misfortune for a husband." Misfortune comes to the husband because the position of husband (fifth place) is here occupied by his wife, symbolized in the yin line. It is good fortune for the wife because the fourth place (the wife's position) is occupied by a yang line. Other hexagrams having this altered relationship between the fourth and fifth lines are hexagrams 30, 35, 50, 51, 56, and 62.

There are some exceptions to this ruling position. The fifth place is not always the position of the ruler or the ruling line. Such an exception is found, for example, in hexagram 16, *Yü* or Eagerness, where the fourth place is the ruling line because it alone is the firm line or yang line of the hexagram.

Yü

In hexagram 23, *Po* or Breaking Apart, the top line is the ruler for the same reason:

Po

The same principle can be applied, too, to hexagram 24, *Fu* or Returning:

Fu

Here, the first line acts as the ruler, for it alone is the yang line in the hexagram.

Sometimes a distinction is made between the governing ruler and the constituting ruler. Their relationship is analogous in the United States to that between the executive and judicial branches of our government. The governing ruler often acts as the constituting ruler, and at other times the position of the constituting ruler carries the prerogatives of the governing ruler. The governing ruler is, as a rule, in the fifth place of the hexagram, but there is no definite rule to determine the place of the constituting ruler. In order to find out the position of the constituting ruler, we have to rely on the Commentary on the Judgments. The function of the constituting ruler, we learn, is to explain the structure of the hexagram. The constituting ruler may then be compared to a justice of the U.S. Supreme Court, who is responsible for the correct interpretation of the constitution of the government. In hexagram 12, *P'i* or Stagnation, for example, the constituting ruler is in the second place. It reads, "Bearing endurance, the small person receives good fortune. The great person also attains success in stagnation." This line seems to correctly interpret the hexagram as a whole.

There is no single rule which can be made applicable to all situations. There are many exceptions to the rules, for rules are arbitrary devices that human beings have made. Because the hexagram represents the germinal situation, which is not fully actualized in the present, it cannot be fit into the situation our logical thinking may create. The hexagram expresses the unconscious stratum and is unknown to our conscious mind. Because the reality involved is hidden, the lines in the hexagram serve as symbols pointing to the unseen.

It is thus similar to the Word of God, which cannot be apprehended by our logical systems and is therefore beyond our understanding. Therefore, the written words of the Bible can serve as symbols pointing to the incomprehensible reality of God. There is no way for us to apply any definite category or rule to fathom the word of God. Likewise, we fool ourselves if we think we possess a methodology or rule by which to interpret the words of Scripture. All we can do is find some reliable guidelines, such as those offered long ago by Milton Terry,[12] to help us interpret the symbolic expressions of the Word.

4

Guidelines for Interpretation

The *I Ching* is more than a book of hexagrams; it is also a literary work. The hexagrams are symbols of germinal situations and are, therefore, known as primary symbols. The secondary symbols that surround the hexagrams are the written words, or literary expressions, of the judgments. The hexagrams are the lineal interpretations of germinal situations, and the judgments are the literary interpretations of the hexagrams.

In the Christian faith, the germinal situations are the Christ-events in history. Just as in the I Ching *the germinal situations are expressed by the lineal symbols of the hexagrams, so also the Christ-events in history are expressed by the symbol of the cross. In the Christian faith, therefore, the cross is the primary symbol of Christ and his works. The written words in the Bible are comparable to the judgments in the* I Ching. *Just like the judgments, the Bible texts are secondary symbols of Christ-events in history. Failure to distinguish between the primary and secondary symbolism results in a serious fallacy of interpretation. This distinction, therefore, serves as an important hermeneutical guideline.*

Understanding the Hierarchy of Symbolism

The distinction between the primary and secondary symbols is based on the hierarchy of symbolism in the *I Ching*. Secondary symbols are always relative to primary symbols. To illustrate this relationship, let me cite the example of an art student who takes notes on paintings in the art museum. The student looks at the paintings and interprets them in words. In this case, the paintings are the primary symbols, while the student's notes are secondary symbols. Just as the written notes of this student interpret the paintings, the judgments in the *I Ching* are interpretations of the hexagrams. The hexagrams are analogous to the paintings, which depict reality. However, in the strict sense, the hexagrams and paintings are quite different. The hexagrams never become objects in themselves, for they always serve as symbols pointing beyond themselves. However, the paintings are not only images but also objects to the viewers. In spite of this difference the example is useful for helping us understand the hierarchy of symbolisms in the process of interpretation. The primary symbols of the paintings are more authentic than the student's notes regarding them. The hexagrams are more authentic than the judgments in the *I Ching*. In the interpretation of the *I Ching*, it is very important to keep this distinction of symbols in mind.

Among the secondary symbols, or judgments, there is yet another level of symbolism. Judgments on the hexagrams are prior to the judgments on the lines. Because the judgments on the lines are secondary to those on the hexagrams, the former are interpretations of the latter. In other words, the judgments on the lines are ancillary to the Judgments on the hexagrams. Just as the lines are dependent on the hexagram as a whole, the judgments on the lines cannot be understood independently of the Judgments on the hexagrams.

The relationship between the Judgments on the hexagrams and the judgments on the lines can be compared to that between descriptions of the paintings as a whole, and analytical descriptions of the paintings. The art student is not only interested in his impressions of the paintings as a whole, but also in his analytical understanding of them. Just as the analytical understanding of the paintings is relative to understanding the paintings as a whole, so also the judgments on the lines are relative to the Judgments on the hexagrams as a whole. The judgments on the lines cannot be understood independently of the Judgments on the hexagrams.

This is like interpreting the Bible. The written words of the Bible must be understood as a whole before they are understood analytically. In other words, the story as a whole is primary compared to the parts of the story. Any particular sayings or quotations cannot be read or properly interpreted out of context. Just as the judgments on the lines are relative to the Judgments on the hexagrams as a whole, the understanding of particular passages in the Bible must be a function of the understanding of the biblical story as a whole.

If we regard the judgments on the lines as symbols ancillary to the Judgments on the hexagram, we can then distinguish three hierarchical orders: the hexagrams as symbols of germinal situations, the Judgments on the hexagrams as symbols of the hexagrams, and the judgments on the lines as supplementary symbols of the lines. The hexagrams, as lineal interpretations of reality, comprise the primary symbols; the Judgments on the hexagrams, being verbal interpretations, make up the secondary symbols, and the judgments on the lines, as analytical interpretations, constitute the tertiary or supplementary symbols. To sum up, the main text of the *I Ching* contains a tripartite symbolism: the primary, the secondary, and the supplementary symbolisms. The correlation of these different symbolisms in their proper hierarchical order is necessary for the interpretation of the *I Ching*. Let me take hexagram 46, *Shêng* or

Moving Upward, to illustrate. This hexagram is the combination of the trigrams *Sun* (Wind) below and *K'un* (Earth) above. The primary symbol of this hexagram is the hexagram itself, that is, the set of six lines, either broken or unbroken, as depicted in the following diagram:

Shêng

The interpretation of this primary symbol is the Judgment on the hexagram. The Judgment says, "Moving upward has supreme success. It is necessary to see the great person. Fear not. Going toward the south will bring good fortune." This then explains the hexagram itself. The supplementary symbols are the judgments on the lines of the hexagram. Since the lines are always counted from the bottom up, the lowest is the beginning line, which reads, "Moving upward is welcome. It will be great fortune." The judgment on the second line says, "If you are sincere, it is advantageous to bring a small offering. There is no mistake." The third line says, "Moving upward in an empty city." The fourth line says, "The king must offer sacrifice to Mount Ch'i [located in western China, the homeland of King Wen, the founder of the Chou dynasty]. It will bring good fortune and no mistake." The fifth line means, "Correctness will bring good fortune. One moves upward by steps." The top line means, "Moving upward blindly. It is advantageous to be correct ceaselessly." In all cases the lines indicate their gradual evolvement to complete the Judgment on the hexagram, i.e., "Moving upward has supreme success." Thus, the judgments on the lines are supplementary symbols. Here is evident the hierarchical symbolism: the lineal symbol of hexagram *Shêng,* the Judgment on the hexagram, and the judgments on the lines of the hexagram. The lineal symbol is primary, the Judgment on the hexagram is secondary, and the judgments on the lines are supplementary. Any interpretation of the hexagram has to presuppose this hierarchical order and keep it in mind.

In addition to gaining an understanding of the hierarchical order of symbolizations, it is also important to know the nature and function of the symbols themselves. Symbols, or *hsiang* in Chinese, should not be understood as images, for images do not point beyond themselves. The symbol never becomes its own object, while the image does. The symbol always points beyond itself, just as the hexagram points to the invisible potential, or the germinal situation. The hexagram as the primary symbol points to the invisible realities of the universe. The secondary symbols, the judgments, are translations of the primary symbols into meaningful expressions of human experience. The judgments are, in a strict sense, the symbolizations of the primary symbols. The judgments also point beyond themselves, for they represent the hidden realities of the hexagrams. The judgments on the lines are also symbols pointing beyond the words, for they point to the lines. Thus, in order to interpret hexagrams, we need to know the nature of symbols.

Symbols are not something that can be arbitrarily created or destroyed, for they grow out of the community or out of its self-conscious elements. That is why symbols bear the characteristics of the civilization in which they have been formed. Because symbols are not fully understood apart from the context in which they have been formed, the nature of the symbols in the *I Ching* cannot be comprehended without knowing the Chinese or Far Eastern civilizations. Symbols are analogous to trees that grow only in certain kinds of soil. They also can adapt themselves to given circumstances.

These principles are also true of Christian symbols. It is impossible to understand the significance of these symbols without knowing the circumstances in which they originated. That is why any interpretation of Christian symbols presupposes an understanding of the Greco-Roman civilization in which they were generated. Such religious symbols as the cross, star, dove, fish, and shepherd were deeply rooted in the historical circumstances of that time. That is why no interpretation of these symbols can be cut free from their cultural and historical contexts. To interpret them without their context is to distort the real meaning they convey.

The symbols of the *I Ching* were generated at the beginning of Chinese civilization. According to tradition, the origin of the symbolic expression through hexagrams goes back as far as the period of King Fu Hsi, the founder of Chinese civilization. The Great Commentary stresses that the civilization of China was the by-product of these symbols. In other words, these symbols constituted the archetypical ideas from which the new civilization arose.

For example, the development of fishing and hunting came from hexagram 30, or *Li*. According to the Great Commentary, "Knotted cords were used for nets and baskets in hunting and fishing. They were perhaps taken from the hexagram of *Li*" (2:2). What this commentary tries to tell us is that the invention of fishing and hunting tools came from the idea symbolized in this hexagram. As we see from the structure of the hexagram, it displays a form like that of nets and baskets for fishing and hunting.

Li

Agriculture was developed from hexagram 42, *I,* or Gain. The Great Commentary says, "He split wood to form a plowshare and bent it to make the plow handle, and taught the whole world the advantage of plowing and weeding. This idea was probably taken from hexagram *I"* (2:20). As we see from its structure, the primary trigrams that constitute *I* are *Sun* and *Chên. Sun,* or Wind, means also "wood," and *Chên,* or Thunder, means "movement." The nuclear trigram, *K'un* and *Kên* are associated with earth.

I

The combination of the primary and nuclear trigrams gives us the idea of cultivating the land for planting.

In a like manner, the Great Commentary attempts to demonstrate that all other aspects of early Chinese civilization were based on the hexagrams, the archetypal ideas of all things. The origin of commerce and market, for example, was based on hexagram 21, *Shih Ho,* or Chewing. The invention of the upper and lower garments was based both on hexagram 1, *Ch'ien* or Heaven, and hexagram 2, *K'un* or Earth; that of marine life was based on hexagram 59, *Sui* or Following; that of transportation on hexagram 16, *Yü* or Eagerness; that of the mill on hexagram 62, *Hsia Ku,* or the Small Excess, and so on. What is implied in these passages from the Great Commentary is that the symbols or hexagrams are not only the by-product of an incipient civilization but also the origin of civilization's flowering. In other words, the symbols provide archetypal ideas for the invention of new levels of civilization. And if they are, in fact, the archetypes of civilization, this means that the hexagrams have universal implications.

The same idea is implicit in Christian symbolism as well. For example, the symbol of the cross was not only the product of the particular historical event of the Crucifixion, but also became the basis for the creation of a new culture, that of Christian civilization. Because of this, the cross has universal implications for all people. While the hexagrams are firmly rooted in primitive cosmology, the cross is deeply rooted in the primitive Christian community. Understanding this symbolic significance is an essential aspect of interpretation.

The judgments, on the other hand, are always relative to the civilization or historical context from which they emerged. Since the judgments of the *I Ching,* or the secondary symbols, are traditionally attributed to King Wen and his son, the duke of Chou, they must be understood in relation to the civilization of the early Chou dynasty about three thousand years ago. The Chou civilization is, in fact, clearly reflected in the Judgments on the hexagrams and on the lines.

Unfortunately, the materials that are available from the period are not sufficient to give a very accurate picture. The Book of Songs, to be sure, reflects the mood of that time; but it does not give enough evidence to paint a real picture of the civilization prior to the Ch'un Ch'iu period (722–481 B.C.). It is clear, however, that the literary character of the appended judgments assumed the primitive form of lyrics, proverbs, omen sayings, and oracles. We know, too, that the early Chou dynasty was ruled by a feudal aristocracy. In each feudal state, all members of the ruling houses held their offices in perpetuity through heredity and the common people were completely denied a share in political power. The governments of the feudal states not only consisted of hereditary officers, but were also elaborately graded into a hierarchy of offices. The hierarchical system of feudal government is well expressed in the Judgment on hexagram 7, *Shih* or the Army, which describes the hierarchical order from the masses of people at the bottom to the great prince at the top. Clearly, unless we consider the political system of that time, we cannot understand the meaning of the judgments. Thus, in general, any attempt to proffer a faithful interpretation of the text requires some prior understanding of the political, economic, and cultural background in which the text was written.

The same principle is also applicable to the interpretation of Scripture. When the Christian message is interpreted in today's world, the political and social situations of New Testament times must be considered. Unless we know what kind of political situation the Jewish people lived under at the time of Jesus, it is difficult to transpose the message to the situation of our time. Some of the common terms, such as king, messiah, prince, etc., reflect the political and religious thinking of that time. Without understanding the historical context, a meaningful interpretation of the text is impossible.

In the *I Ching*, there are only two judgments that are related to man-made objects. They are the cauldron in the Judgment on hexagram 50 and the well in the Judgment on hexagram 48. These objects represent the most primitive symbols of early Chinese civilization and are, in fact, quite fundamental to all civilizations. Hexagram 48, *Ching* (The Well), consists of the trigram *Sun,* or Wind, which also means "wood," and the trigram *K'an* or water. This image derives from the pole-and-bucket well of the early Chou period.

Ching

The handle of the bucket is still a wooden pole which is connected to a rope. The Judgment on this hexagram describes the types of pole-and-bucket symbolism prevailing in the early civilization: "The well changes the town, but the well cannot be changed. It neither decays nor grows. People come and go and draw the water from the well. When the drawing is almost accomplished and the rope does not go all the way, the bucket is broken. Thus it brings misfortune." The Judgment gives us not only the picture of bucket and well, but also the function of the well for early civilization, which was not only to supply water but also to provide people with social intercourse. It is still true in many villages of Oriental and Third World countries that the well serves, particularly for women, as a social gathering place.

This also is reminiscent of the well of Jacob, and especially of the Samaritan woman at the well. Unless we understand the type of well that existed in those days, one from which the water was drawn by a bucket, it is difficult to grasp the real meaning and spirit of Jesus' message to the Samaritan woman. Our interpretation must include our reflection on the historical conditions behind the text that we interpret.

Another man-made object, the Cauldron, is drawn from hexagram 50, *Ting.* The concept of the cauldron may come from the trigram *Sun* below and the trigram *Li* above.

Ting

Sun represents wind and wood, while *Li* represents fire and flame. The combination of *Sun* and *Li* brings out the image of the cauldron which is used for cooking food. The shape of the cauldron is rather well graphed in the lines of the hexagram. The cauldron possesses legs to stand by itself (the first line), and handles (the third line). Moreover, the handles are yellow with golden carrying rings (the fifth line), and the cauldron has jade rings (the top line). The judgments on these lines elaborate upon the form of the cauldron used in the early days. Those who live in Asia can easily identify the cauldron as depicted in the hexagram. However, for Westerners, this kind of cauldron is unfamiliar and not easily understood. Even more problematical is that the reading of its form in the hexagram reflects an alien mode of thought. This is why some understanding of the early civilization of East Asia is helpful if we are interested in the *I Ching,* for without such knowledge the *I Ching* cannot be properly interpreted. Many other expressions, such as the "flying dragon," "sagging the ridgepole," or "treading upon the tail of the tiger" are similarly products of the early civilization of East Asia, and are not understood without some background knowledge of Asian history and civilization.

Another issue in the interpretation of the secondary symbols or the judgments is that of language. Since the original text of the *I Ching* was written in

Chinese, knowing Chinese is almost essential to understanding the original meaning of the text itself. Let me summarize, then, the salient characteristics of the Chinese language. First of all, Chinese is pictographic; secondly, it is simple; and finally, it is intuitive. Every Chinese character is an integrated visual symbol of lines or strokes expressing a single concept or idea. By studying the original forms of a few Chinese characters, we can gain some idea about the nature of the Chinese language. The pictographic characters can be classified into three groups: simple, complex, and compound characters.

Let us examine first the origin of the simple characters, taking the word "person" (人) as an example. This character may be described in the beginning as that of a human form (大), which then evolved to the present pictographic symbol. The word for water in Chinese (水) was originally written in the form of flowing water (水). The origin of complex characters is similar to the preceding. For example, the word "stand" in Chinese (立) may come from the form of a person standing (立), which is a combination of "person" (大) and place (−). The word for "fruit" in Chinese (果) is a combination of "tree" (木) and "field" (田). Originally, the field (田) was shaped like a fruit (⊛). Since fruit comes from the tree, the combination of these two characters makes sense.

The compound characters are more complicated than the preceding ones. For example, the word "tree" (木) is combined with another tree (木) to make "forest" (林). When one more word, "tree," is added to the forest, it becomes "jungle" (森). Thus, the language has its own evolutionary history.

The structure of the Chinese characters evolved from one stage to another through history. Perhaps the earliest form of such characters was that found during the Shang dynasty, about 1300 B.C. According to archaeological evidence, the Shang inscriptions were originally written in oracle bones and shells, and preceded the *I Ching*. These were therefore called *Chia ku wen*, which literally means "the writings of shells and bones." The Shang inscriptions were discovered at Anyang in Honan Province in China. The second stage in the evolution of Chinese characters came in the Chou dynasty (1122–221 B.C). The Chou inscriptions are known as *Chung ting wen*, or "the writings of the bronze cauldron," for the characters were written on a bronze cauldron. The original copy of the *I Ching* was probably written in Chou-type inscription, which is quite different from the inscriptions used in China today. After the Chou inscriptions, the so-called *Hsiao chuan* style developed during the Ch'in dynasty (221–207 B.C.). Then, during the Han dynasty (202 B.C.–A.D. 220) the *Ni shu* style came into being. This style is very similar to the current style, known as *K'ai shu*. This style has been used in China since the Chin dynasty (A.D. 280–420). For nearly two thousand years, Chinese characters have not changed, with the exception of the simplification of certain characters in recent years.

What I have tried to explain by these illustrations is the complexity of interpreting the original text. If the *I Ching* was originally written in a Chou-type inscription, the evolution of the Chinese characters makes it almost impossible to recover the original meaning of the text. When a new style of writing develops, a new interpretation of the old style is necessary. Thus, the evolution of language necessitates reinterpretation.

This idea is applicable to the Christian tradition as well. Originally, the New Testament was written in Greek. However, when the use of Latin became widespread, translations of the text into Latin were necessary. Again, the Latin Bible was translated into English and other languages. Although most English translations today are based on the original Greek text, the cultural and linguistic gaps are so enormous that it is difficult to recover the original meaning of the text. Among the English translations, there are many different versions. It is clear, however, that any translation of a text from one language to another can be merely interpretation. Even within the Greek language, a certain evolution occurred down through history. For example, New Testament Greek is quite different from modern Greek, and even a bit different from that of the Greek classics. In order to understand New Testament Greek when knowing only modern Greek, we have to make certain interpretations. We begin to realize, then, what a complexity of issues is involved in the interpretation and translation of a language.

As noted earlier, one of the characteristics of Chinese is the simplicity of its structure. Like Hebrew, Chinese is almost without grammar. Because Chinese has no inflection, it is often called the language of isolation. There are no tenses, cases, genders, or numbers (singular or plural). The Judgment on hexagram 1, *Ch'ien* or Heaven, illustrates the difficulty of translating the text into English. According to Wilhelm's translation, the Judgment reads: "The Creative works sublime success, furthering through perseverance." However, Legge translates: "*Khien* [represents] what is great and originating, penetrating, advantageous, correct, and firm." Both translations come from the same Chinese text, but have different meanings. In a strict sense, they are not translations, but interpretations. There is no way to translate anything from Chinese to English without interpretation. Finally, the characteristic feature of the Chinese language is that it is aesthetic and intuitive. It is excellent for poetry and art. The lack of grammatical features makes it a difficult medium for precise expression, but it is an effective medium for creative and intuitive expression. The simplicity of sentence structure and the possibility of rich metaphor help the Chinese language to be more poetic and aesthetic. When employing only the English translation of the *I Ching,* we fail to comprehend the richness of the aesthetic and emotive expressions found in the original Chinese text. For those students who do not read or write Chinese, this is a reminder how limited we are when we interpret the *I Ching.*

The same limitation is applicable to those Christians who do not read or understand New Testament Greek. Many fine, rich textures of meaning that are found in the Greek of the New Testament may be lost when we read an English translation. When we realize this limitation, we can become less literalistic and more open to various interpretations.

Practical Suggestions for Interpretation

There are several useful ways in which to proceed with the interpretation of the *I Ching*. First, one should deal with the hexagrams alone, without reference to the secondary symbols. Since the hexagrams are primary symbols and more authentic than any of the other symbols, it is important to deal with the hexagrams before treating any of the other symbols. Moreover, the hexagrams are made up of lines which, since linear expression is universal, transcend cultural and linguistic differences. Wang Pi, a great commentator on the *I Ching,* achieved much insight by contemplating the hexagrams alone, without any reference to the written words or the judgments. Like an art student who wants to understand a painting and goes directly to the painting before reading reviews or commentaries about it, the student of the *I Ching* should take up the primary symbols, the hexagrams, before consulting the secondary or supplementary symbols.

In approaching the primary symbols alone, we need to be aware of some general guidelines for interpreting them. Let me, therefore, arbitrarily select three different hexagrams—11, 21, and 31—as models by which to illustrate some of the practical steps for interpretation. Hexagram 11, *T'ai* or Peace, consists of the trigram *Ch'ien* below and *K'un* above.

T'ai

Since the attribute of *Ch'ien* or Heaven is a creative and active energy, it seeks to unite with the other pole, *K'un* or Earth, which is receptive and passive. These trigrams in combination, therefore, bring harmony and unity that result in good fortune. The uniting of the sexes is fundamental to prosperity and reproduction. Thus, it is related to the spring season and to the beginning of new life. Some of these ideas are suggested in the bare structure of hexagram 11.

Hexagram 21, *Shih Ho* or Chewing, has the strange shape of an open mouth, chewing the bar (the fourth line) between the upper and lower jaws (the first and sixth lines). Undoubtedly the name of this hexagram derives from its external shape:

Shih Ho

However, instead of looking at it externally, we can analyze the attributes of the constituting trigrams. The trigram *Chên* is below and *Li* above. Since *Chên* signifies "arousing," like Thunder, it tends to move upward. However, *Li,* being Fire, moves upward also. Since they both move upward, they neither meet nor conflict with one another. Since Thunder (*Chên*) is accompanied by Lightning, which is Fire (*Li*), the two trigrams can coexist without interference.

Let us now look at the constituting nuclear trigrams: *Kên* is below and *K'an* above. The trigram *Kên,* or Mountain, means "stillness," while the trigram *K'an* or Water means "abyss" or "the abyss of water." Both nuclear trigrams move downward and coexist with one another. Just as the mountain and water are harmonious in Chinese landscape, the combination of these two trigrams is favorable. The upward movement of the two primary trigrams and the downward movement of the two nuclear trigrams are well balanced. Therefore, the concepts of justice and equilibrium are suggested by this hexagram.

In hexagram 31, *Hsien* or Influence, it appears that its center is closely knitted together.

Hsien

The concentration of yang lines in the center signifies firm unity and togetherness. The constituting primary trigrams are *Kên* below and *Tui* above. *Kên,* the symbol of Mountain, is "stillness" while *Tui,* the symbol of Lake, is "joy." As previously noted, lake and mountain go together. They are mutually attractive. Furthermore, *Kên* represents youngest son, and *Tui* represents youngest daughter. They are, thus, young people of opposite sexes. This seems to suggest the union of vitality and joy. The constituting nuclear trigrams are *Sun* below and *Ch'ien* above. *Sun,* or Wind, means "penetrating," while *Ch'ien,* or Heaven, means "creative." Both the penetrating and the creative are qualities of achievement. This hexagram therefore suggests penetrating creativity, which can influence every possible situation. As a whole, hexagram 31, is very favorable.

A careful observation of these hexagrams alone, without reference to the written words or the judgements, gives us some clues to understanding the germinal situation. Because the primary symbols, the hexagrams, are lineal symbols with universal implications, their interpretations are not strictly limited within the context of certain civilizations or languages. What is needed for meaningful interpretation of the symbols is merely to acquire a sufficient background knowledge of symbolic significances and attributes. It is also important to have some intuitive and creative insights to facilitate reflection on the hexagrams.

This kind of direct interpretation seems to be unknown in the ·Christian faith. If we were to contemplate the cross and reflect upon the various Christ-events in history, we would receive rich spiritual resources because our strong theological background would provide adequate guidelines for reflection. For those who have no theological foundation, this kind of contemplation without any scriptural guidance could lead to religious fanaticism or some cultic phenomenon. Just as the hexagrams themselves are not helpful without some background knowledge of their symbolic significance, so also our contemplation on religious symbols alone is not helpful without an appreciation of some of the theological implications of the symbols. A strong spiritual growth can emerge from our reflection upon and contemplation of religious symbols. When we rely solely on the words of the Bible, we become less spiritual and less creative. The lack of spirituality in our Christian life may reflect our lack of contemplation of our religious symbolism, and thus, our study of the written words of the Bible may not help much toward the spiritual nurture of our Christian faith.

The second step toward effective interpretation of the *I Ching* deals with the words or the judgments alone, without reference to the structure of the hexa-grams. In other words, the secondary symbols are taken into consideration without the primary symbols. Wang Pi found great wisdom by reading the words in the *I Ching* without reference to the shape of the hexagrams. Although this is a difficult task for those who cannot read Chinese, it is still worthwhile to read the translation alone. The advantage of reading the judgments alone, without reference to the hexagrams, is that it provides an opportunity to think deeply about the meaning of the words. It can help us to concentrate on the deeper connotations of the words. Just as the reading of the notes taken on a painting can stimulate the creative imagination, the reading of the judgments alone can provide new insights and ideas that we have not received from the primary symbols. The individual characters and the creative insights emerging from the written words may help us perceive an extra dimension of rich cultural heritage.

Let's return to hexagram 11 again and read the written words, the Judgments, without reference to the hexagram itself. The Judgment on hexagram 11 says, "Peace. The small departs, and the great approaches. It is good fortune and success." It is useful to reflect on these words, for they cast many shades of meaning on the concept of peace. We can make some personal conjectures when we read these words. We can, for example, concentrate on specific words, such as "the small departs" or "the great approaches." Does "the small" signify small fortune or advantage? Does it imply small wealth or knowledge? What does the word "depart" mean in this text? Clearly, the judgments are more metaphorical than descriptive. Because these cryptic sayings are pregnant with many meanings, it is not possible to precipitate any literal interpretations out of the *I Ching*. For an understanding of the judgments, we need to project our own creative imaginations beyond the written words.

Now let's look at the Judgment on hexagram 21, which says: "Chewing brings success. It is advantageous to use the punishment." The concept of "chewing" is a metaphor. What does it mean? When the word is considered without looking at the hexagram, we can project many meanings onto this word. What does the word "punishment" imply? How does it relate to the Judgment as a whole? Many questions can be asked regarding the Judgment on this hexagram.

The Judgment for hexagram 31 says, "Influence brings success. It is advantageous to be correct. To take a maiden will bring good fortune." What does the word "influence" mean to us? What does it mean "to be correct"? Who is the maiden? As we ponder some of these questions, we may be able to project our unconscious feelings in the search for the deeper meaning of the words in relation to our own situations. The Judgments are quite similar to koans, the paradoxical word puzzles of Zen Buddhism. They do not, in fact, have any meaning at all independent of those who read them. They are not objective; they are always relative to those who interpret them. Through contemplation on these words, new insights emerge. Thus, the Great Commentary says, "First take up the judgments, and see the principles to which they point. Then the rules reveal themselves" (2:8).

The third step is a correlative of the first and second steps, putting them together in a meaningful way. The point is to see both the primary and secondary symbols simultaneously. Sound interpretation of a Judgment is possible when it is understood in light of the hexagram itself. Thus, it is essential to integrate the interpretations of the hexagrams and the Judgments. The correlation of these two independent interpretations facilitates a deeper and sounder understanding of the hexagrams as a whole.

Returning once more to hexagram 11, *T'ai* or Peace, we recall that the hexagram consists of the trigram Heaven below and the trigram Earth above. As we have seen, the Judgment says, "Peace. The small departs, and the great approaches. It is good fortune and success." If the structure of the hexagram and the Judgment are seen together, a much more reliable interpretation is possible. Since both of the primary trigrams, Heaven and Earth, despite (or perhaps because of) their opposite character, move toward each other, from a structural point of view this results in harmony and unity. The concept of peace in the Judgment likely comes from the idea of harmony and unity as expressed in the structure of the hexagram. We can also observe from the structure of this hexagram that the union of opposite sexes signifies the beginning of new life, i.e., spring. "The small departs, and the great approaches" in the Judgment may imply that the force of cold winter is ready to depart and the force of spring to appear. Winter is dominated by yin forces, which begin to diminish. It, therefore, represents the small. On the other hand, spring comes by the domination of yang forces, which increase and become great. It, therefore, represents the great. Yang is the symbol of strength and greatness, and yin symbolizes weakness and smallness. Thus spring comes when the small departs and the great approaches. This is one of many different interpretations available for hexagram 11.

Let me next examine hexagram 21, *Shih Ho* or Chewing, together with its Judgment. Again, the Judgment says, "Chewing brings success. It is advantageous to use the punishment." As previously noted, the name of the hexagram probably derived from its external appearance. It certainly resembles an open mouth (which is also the shape of hexagram 27, *I,* or Jaws).

Shih Ho   *I*

When hexagram 21 is compared with hexagram 27, the former has an undivided line in the fourth place. The open mouth (hexagram 27) is, therefore, obstructed because of the fourth line in hexagram 21. This obstructing line must be bitten through or chewed up, for it comes between the jaws. This is, perhaps, why this hexagram is designated as "Chewing." What is the meaning of "chewing" from the point of view of justice? Justice here is, no doubt, used in connection with law and order. This hexagram is meaningful to our generation because of various revolts and obstructions in society. The trigram *Chên* below means "awakening" and the trigram *Li* above means "flaming." The awakening thunder and the flaming fire seem to depict the breaking out of violence in the cities owing to revolt against the government. This obstruction is represented by the yang line in the fourth place of the hexagram. It is a powerful revolt, which stops the functioning of the bureaucratic machine. According to the Judgment, the government must use legal constraints or penitentiaries to eliminate this obstruction. The law should not yield to any revolutionary demands that obstruct the function of government. That is why "it is advantageous to use the punishment."

The Judgment for hexagram 31, *Hsien* or Influence, reads, "Influence brings success. It is advantageous to be correct. To take a maiden will bring good fortune." The idea of influence could be derived from the attributes of the constituting trigrams. As previously indicated, the trigram *Kên* (Mountain) means "stillness"; the trigram *Tui* (Lake) means "joy." The mountain below and the lake above, stillness with joy, attract one another. Moreover, the nuclear trigrams, *Sun* below and *Ch'ien* above, actively influence one another. The trigram *Sun* means "to penetrate like the wind," while *Ch'ien* means "an active energy," like a dragon in heaven. Combining the attributes of both penetration and active energy, the idea of influence is possible. The compatibility of the mountain with the lake, and of penetration with active energy, makes success possible. The idea of taking a maiden to wife may be derived from the two primary trigrams: *Kên*, "the youngest and most youthful son," and *Tui*, "the youngest and most youthful daughter." The union of the youngest male and the youngest female, therefore, produces the image of their marriage. Of course, this results in good fortune. Some of these illustrations have been made to correlate the approaches of both the structure of the hexagrams and the meaning of the Judgments. One of the advantages of bringing them together into a coherent system is to understand them as a unity.

The correlation of the symbols of hexagrams and the written words of the Judgments is helpful to the interpretation of Scripture in Christianity. In the past, especially in Reformation tradition, justification by grace through faith has been adopted as a norm for the interpretation of the biblical message. Everything in the Bible has been understood in terms of faith and grace. I think that this paradigmatic interpretation creates some problems, because in many places in the Gospel, human deeds are also stressed as a means of salvation. Especially in Matt. 25:31–46, divine judgment at the end of time is based on deeds. As Jesus said to those who are on his right side (those who are saved), "Truly I say to you, as you did it to one of the least of these my brethren, you did it to me" (v. 40). A hermeneutical method based upon a doctrinal affirmation such as justification by grace through faith alone has many shortcomings.

What I would like to suggest, following the third step in the interpretation in the I Ching, *is the correlative method, the method of correlating the central symbol of Christianity with the written words of Scripture. In other words, the correlation of the cross with the biblical message can provide a sound interpretation. Everything in the Bible can be seen in light of the cross, which points to the actual events of Christ in history. Just as the hexagram, the primary symbol, is to be related to the Judgment as the secondary symbol in the interpretation of the* I Ching, *so also the symbol of the cross, the primary source of Christianity, should be correlated with the written words of Scripture, the secondary symbol of the Christian faith. When our contemplating of the cross and our reflection on the words of Scripture are brought together in a coherent manner, we will then have a sound hermeneutical method.*

The fourth step in the interpretation of the *I Ching* is to relate the meaning of the judgment on the lines to the Judgment on the hexagram. This time, it is essential to observe each line of the hexagram rather than to examine the hexagram as a whole, in order to correlate each line of the hexagram with the total effect. When we look at the judgments on individual lines together with the Judgment on the hexagram as a whole, they are found to be coherent, just as the structure of the hexagram is coherent with the Judgment on the hexagram. One thing that should be remembered here is the hierarchy of symbolisms. The lines, which are supplementary symbols, are always relative to the hexagram. Likewise, the judgments on the lines are always relative to the Judgment on the hexagram. The judgments on the lines must, therefore, be understood in light of the Judgment on the hexagram. Keeping this in mind, let us take up the same hexagrams previously considered.

Hexagram 11 is the symbol of Peace. Its Judgment is, as we have already examined, "Peace. The small departs and the great approaches. It is good fortune and success." The lines of the hexagram move from the bottom up. Since the judgment on the line is always on the moving line, let us look at the moving line. It says, "When ribbon grass is pulled up, it brings the sod with it. Advance will bring good fortune." What is said here is always relative to the Judgment on the hexagram. It has to do with peacetime, for the Judgment on the hexagram deals with peace. Since the first line represents the masses of the people, who are led by officials, it deals with the common people, who also constitute the roots of the social structure. It indicates that all kinds of common people work together in the peaceful community. A harmony and unity of action prevail in peacetime. This kind of cooperation is the sure foundation of peace.

The judgment on the second line says, "One who embraces the unsophisticated can cross the river without a boat. He does not neglect those who are far away because of his friendship. Thus he can walk in the middle." The second place of the hexagram is an official position, indicating the caution of the official in time of peace. His ability to practice his leadership in the middle way in respect to his action reflects his nobility and wisdom. This line is also relative to peace, as it is in the Judgment.

The judgment on the third line says, "There is no evenness that is not liable to be disrupted. There is no going that is not followed by a return. It is difficult to maintain righteousness without mistake. Do not complain about this truth: Enjoy the blessings which you still possess." The third place of the hexagram is a transitory position, for this is where it adjoins the upper trigram. Thus, it deals with the transitoriness of all things in peace. Here, "evenness" implies an aspect of peace. Everything is subject to change. Even peace and prosperity can change to chaos and poverty. This line certainly depicts the mood when a transition takes place from a time of peace to a time of turbulence.

The judgment on the fourth line states, "One flutters down and does not boast of his wealth. He calls his neighbors in sincerity." The fourth place is also a position where two trigrams adjoin. It belongs to the upper trigram, occupying a higher rank than the third place. But the characteristic feature of peaceful society is that the people of higher rank come closer to the lowly people. The accommodation of the wealthy with the poor forms a sound basis for the mutual trust and confidence which maintains peace.

The judgment on the fifth line says, "The King I gives his daughter in marriage. By doing this there will be blessing and supreme good fortune." Since the fifth place is the position of the ruler, it has to do with the sovereign ruler, I, which may mean here the first ruler of the Shang dynasty. Moreover, the marriage is a symbol of supreme harmony and unity, which is the foundation for peace and prosperity. It is the crowning event of the peaceful situation symbolized in this hexagram.

The judgment on the top line reads, "The wall [town] returns into the moat. Do not use the army. Announce your orders to the people of your own city. Correctness will bring humiliation." The height of peace and prosperity that is expressed in the fifth place begins to decline at the top place, which represents a transitory situation, just as the third place does. The transition from peace to turbulence was alluded to at the third place, and is actually transpiring at the top place. The lines evolve, therefore, from the inner to the outer, from the least to the most, and from the bottom to the top within the delimitation of the hexagram. All of the judgments on the lines are relative to the Judgment on the hexagram, for their movements and changes confine themselves within the limitations of the hexagrams. Thus the judgments on the lines are symbols ancillary to the Judgment on the hexagrams, just as the Judgments are secondary to the hexagrams themselves.

We can now look at hexagram 21, *Shih Ho,* or Chewing. Let us restate the Judgment on the hexagram: "Chewing brings success. It is advantageous to use the punishment." The judgments on the lines are all relative to this Judgment on the hexagram. The judgment on the first line says, "One's feet are in the stocks, and his toes are cut off. It is no mistake." Since the Judgment on the hexagram deals with a time of unrest and disturbance, the individual lines must be seen in the light of this unfortunate circumstance. If we look at the structure of the hexagram, we notice that the beginning line corresponds to the top line. The beginning line deals with the foundation of the situation represented by the hexagram, while the top line deals with the head of a hierarchical structure of society. The beginning line, therefore, is fixed at the bottom—that is, the feet—of society. In contrast, the top line is fixed at the top—at the neck of society. The judgment on the top line therefore says, "He wears the cangue, and his ears are cut off. There will be misfortune." At the bottom, the toes are in the stocks and immobile, but at the top, the ears are restricted. Both of them represent yang energy, which is obstructed by the presence of the fourth line. They are, therefore, fixed and do not move. The rest of the lines of the hexagrams deal with the punishment for crimes.

In the second line, he chews up the skin and the nose, which means that he bites tender meat. In the third line, he chews on old dried meat and meets with poison. This seems to indicate that in times of waxing turbulence, punishments meted out for crimes evolve into more severe forms. The old dried meat is harder to chew, so it represents a heavy punishment decreed for a greater crime. In the fourth place, he chews on dried gristly meat. From the structure of the hexagram, the fourth place is represented by a strong obstacle. It is, therefore, the most difficult to bite through. "He," therefore, "gets metal arrows. It is advantageous to be firm at the time of difficulties." With the yang line in the fourth place, the analogy is that of metal arrows, which are almost impossible to chew. This is the most difficult obstacle to be overcome by law and order.

The judgment in the fifth place says, "He chews on dried meat. He gets yellow gold. Correctness brings danger, but there is no mistake." The dried meat is less difficult to chew than the dried gristly meat of the fourth line. Also, the yellow gold in the fifth line is tenderer than the metal arrows of the fourth line. From the structure of the hexagram, the most intensive trouble has been caused by the fourth line, the yang line, which poses the most obstruction for peace. The fifth line, therefore, signifies the overcoming of the most difficult time. As we have seen, the judgments on the lines are relative to the Judgment on the hexagram as a whole. Lines support the hexagram and express the movement of each position within the structure, which is delimited by the Judgment on the hexagram. In this way, the judgments on the lines act as supplementary symbols, subordinate to the Judgment on the hexagram, which is precisely the secondary symbol of the hexagram itself.

Let's now discuss the judgments on the lines of hexagram 31, *Hsien* or Influence. The Judgment on the hexagram says, "Influence brings success. It is advantageous to be correct. To take a maiden will bring good fortune." Since the lines show the movement of the changes occurring within the given situation of the hexagram, we can observe how the power of influence moves from the bottom to the top. The moving line at the bottom says, "The influence affects his big toe." As an instance of synecdoche, a metaphor in which a part stands for the whole, the judgment uses "big toe" to refer to the lower end of the body. Since the position of the line is at the bottom of the hexagram, its correspondence with the lower end of the body is confirmed. It then moves upward and comes to the second place, where the second line says, "The influence affects the calves of your legs." The calves, however, belong to those parts of the body that are farther up than the toes. The third line says, "The influence affects the thighs." Here, the movement of influence reaches a part of the body that is higher yet. The influence then moves from the thighs to the heart, in the fourth place. The fourth line, therefore, says, "Correctness brings good fortune. Remorse disappears." What is strange in this line is that the judgment on the line begins with "correctness," while all the other lines begin with "influence." What, then, does the idea of correctness suggest in this hexagram? It seems to suggest that the lower part of the stomach is the correct place, for it is regarded as the center of the body. In meditation, for example, this part of the body becomes the most important because of its central location. The correct position is, then, the stomach. Thus, influence reaches the stomach from the thighs. The judgment on the fifth line says, "The influence affects the nipples." Again, the influence reaches a part that is higher up. Finally, at the top line, the influence reaches its height. Thus, the judgment on the top line says, "The influence affects the jaws, cheeks, and tongue." Here, the influence extends to the highest part of the body. The movement of influence that begins with the lowest finally attains the highest part of the body. These lines, therefore, express their movement within the limits of the hexagram. What we learn from this analysis is that the idea of influence, although here used in a broad sense, is closely related to the idea of sensation in the body. In fact, the Chinese word "influence" (咸) becomes "sensation" (感) by adding the word "mind" or "heart" (心). This explains why the lines suggest a more explicit meaning of influence.

The fifth step for interpretation of the *I Ching* is to consult the Ten Wings. The Ten Wings, the appended commentaries on the *I Ching,* should not be used side by side with the main text. They are material supplementary to the text, and should be used to support it. Among the Ten Wings, the most reliable and helpful materials are those of the Great Commentary and the Discussion of the Trigrams. Both of them deal with the general philosophy of the *I Ching.* These commentaries can serve as background knowledge against which to interpret the hexagrams. The rest of the Ten Wings may be used to illuminate our interpretation of the main text. Because they are supplementary to our interpretation, they cannot be the ultimate basis for our interpretation. They can merely enrich our understanding of the main text. Sometimes, however, commentaries confuse rather than clarify that which we seek through interpretation. Therefore, it is important not to rely on the commentaries too heavily. In interpreting the hexagrams, the Commentary on the Judgments and the Commentary on the Symbols are the most helpful aids.

Returning to hexagram 11 once more, let me illustrate why the Commentary on the Judgments is the most helpful for our understanding of the hexagram. The Commentary on the Judgment of hexagram 11 says:

> The small departs, and the great approaches. It is good fortune and success. Heaven and Earth, therefore, unite, and all things come into harmony. The unity of above and below makes one will. The yang [light principle] is without. Strength is within, and devotion is without. The superior person is within, and the inferior person is without. The way of the superior person is growing, while the way of the inferior person is decaying.

As we see, this is a good commentary, for it illuminates our understanding of the hexagram. Various attributes of both trigrams, Heaven and Earth, help us to apprehend the rich meaning in this hexagram. Applying the principle that the concepts of "within" and "without" are relative to the positions of the constituting trigrams, we see that the trigram Heaven (*Ch'ien*) represents the inner nature of the hexagram, because it is located below, and the trigram Earth (*K'un*) represents the outward or external aspect of the hexagram because it is above the trigram Heaven. The attributes of Heaven and Earth are opposite: light versus shadow, strength versus devotion, superior versus inferior. The commentary specifically points out that the small represents the inferior person and the great represents the superior person. In this way, the commentary enriches our understanding of the hexagram.

We can now appreciate what the commentary tries to say regarding this hexagram. This commentary is divided into two parts: the Commentary on the Great Symbols and the Commentary on the Small Symbols. The Great Symbols commentary deals with the totality of each individual hexagram, while the Small Symbols commentary deals with each individual line of the hexagram. The Commentary on the Great Symbols for hexagram 11 says: "The unity of Heaven and Earth signifies peace. The ruler, therefore, fashions and completes the course of Heaven and Earth. He advances and regulates the wills of Heaven and Earth. Thereby he aids his people." This commentary is helpful for the illumination of the judgment. It suggests, moreover, the idea that spring may come through the unity of Heaven and Earth.

The Commentary on the Small Symbols says about the first line of hexagram 11: "When ribbon grass is pulled up, it brings the sod with it. Advancement will bring good fortune. His will is external to himself." The will that is directed outward can be understood as the direction of the movement from the inward, the bottom line, to the outward, the upper lines. Since the lower trigram represents the inner nature of the hexagram, the movement from the bottom line is directed to the outward, or the upper trigram. Here, the commentary stresses something that is not important, i.e., that "his will is external to himself." The commentary says, concerning the second line, "'One who embraces the unsophisticated . . . walk[s] in the middle,' because the light is great." The greatness of light, or the yang line, is clear because it occupies the central position within the lower trigram. It is great because it occupies a ruling position. However, this commentary does not explain the importance of the reference to walking in the middle. On the third line, the commentary remarks, "There is no evenness that is not liable to be disrupted. 'There is no going that is not followed by a return,' because it is the boundary of Heaven and Earth." The third line marks, indeed, the boundary between the trigram Earth and the trigram Heaven. This is self-evident. But the commentary does not amplify its message regarding the boundary. On the fourth line, the commentary says, "'One flutters down and does not boast of his wealth,' because he and his friends lost what is real. There is no warning, because he desires it in the depths of his heart." "What is real" can be understood as spiritual reality. However, this passage is vague and it is difficult to make sense of these comments. Regarding the fifth line, the commentary says, "This [marriage] brings blessings and supreme good fortune, because he is central in carrying out his wishes." Here, the reference is to King I, who gives his daughter in marriage. Because he is in the fifth, or ruling, position, he can carry out his wishes. For the top line, the commentary remarks, "'The wall [town] returns into the moat' shows that society has been ruled by injustice." The cause for the fall of the city is identified as the disorder that disrupts the community. It is followed, however, by prosperity and peace, for even these are subject to change and transition.

From what we have observed, these commentaries, although they suggest some new insights, are inadequate and insufficient to explain some of the basic issues raised in the judgments on the lines. In this respect, these commentaries will never substitute for the creative insights coming directly from the observation of the lines and the hexagrams. They can only serve as supplementary aids to one's own interpretation.

The Commentary on the Judgments regarding hexagram 21, *Shih Ho* or Chewing, is quite helpful in explaining why it is called "chewing." The reason is that "there is something between the jaws." From the structure of the hexagram, we have already determined that the fourth line represents that "something between the jaws." The idea of jaws is based on hexagram 27, *I* or Jaws, where the top and bottom lines are yang, forming jaws. Moreover, hexagram 21 is similar to hexagram 27, except for the fourth line. Because the fourth line is yang in hexagram 21, the presence of an obstruction between the jaws calls for the caption "Chewing." The commentary further remarks, "Thunder and lightning are united together and make lines. The yin lines receive the place of honor and advance." The trigram *Chên,* which is below, signifies thunder; the trigram *Li,* which is above, signifies lightning and fire. The yin lines receive the honor because the yang line, which occupies the fourth place, is the obstacle to be chewed up and removed. They advance because both thunder and lightning are light and move upwardly. The result of such advancement is a successful outcome owing to the enforcement of law and order. The commentary is helpful, therefore, for our understanding of the Judgment on the hexagram.

The Commentary on the Great Symbols is also helpful here. It establishes the firm stand on law and order to be taken by the government: "The former kings made the law effective through clearly defined penalties." Thus, a turbulent society can be successfully governed through the firmness of laws and clearly defined sanctions of the penal system.

The Commentary on the Small Symbols remarks, regarding the first line, "One's feet are in the stocks, so his toes are immobilized. Thus he cannot walk [to do evil]." The commentary on the top lines says, "He wears the cangue, so that his ears are restricted. Thus he does not hear clearly." In neither instance does the commentary offer an explanation or background for the situation shown in the line. The commentary on the second line says, "He chews on the skin and bites off the nose. Thus he rides on a hard line." From the structure of this hexagram, we notice that the second, or yin, line rests upon the yang line (a hard line), which is also the beginning line. Thus the commentary speaks of a hard line. Regarding the third line, the commentary remarks, "He meets with poisons. The place is not the right one." The place is inappropriate because the third line is the yang position rather than the yin. For the fourth line, the commentary tells us, "It is advantageous to be firm at the time of difficulties. It is good fortune. His light is not yet manifested." This ambiguous statement seems to suggest that light is not reflected even though the trigram *Li,* or Light, begins with this line. The fourth line is the object between the jaws of the mouth, the "dried gristly meat." For the fifth place, the commentary states, "Be aware of danger. There is no mistake. It has found an appropriate place." This is also an ambiguous statement. From what we have observed regarding hexagram 21, we can conclude that the most helpful commentaries are the Commentary on the Judgments and the Commentary on the Small Symbols, although the second is less valuable than the first.

Hexagram 31, *Hsien* or Influence, is clearly expounded in the Commentary on the Judgments. "Influence brings stimulation. The weak is above, and the strong is below. The two forces stimulate and respond to each other." The weak means the trigram *Tui,* "the youngest daughter," while the strong is trigram *Kên,* "the youngest son." The female is representative of the weak, and the male of the strong. The combination of the sexes, therefore, makes the stimulation and attraction possible. The commentary further stresses the relationship between these two primary trigrams: "The Mountain and Lake. The male subordinates himself to the female. Hence it brings success. It is advantageous to be firm. To take a maiden brings good fortune." The attribute of the trigram Mountain is stillness, and that of Lake is joy. The male, the trigram Mountain, is subordinated to the female, the trigram Lake. However, the commentary does not explain further why this kind of relationship produces good fortune. The rest of its exposition is inclined to be exaggerative, describing the relationship between *Tui* and *Kên* as having universal significance and analogizing *Tui* with her yin parallel, Earth, and *Kên* with his yang parallel, Heaven. The relationship between *Tui* and *Kên,* therefore, is identical with the relationship between Heaven and Earth. "Heaven and Earth stimulate each other and produce all things. The holy sages stimulate the hearts of the people to attain the peace of the world. If the place of influence is known, the attributes of all things are to be understood." The commentary thus makes the relationship between male and female—that is, the relationship between yang and yin—the basis of all things in the world. This exposition provides a philosophical foundation by which to interpret the hexagrams.

As to the Commentary on the Symbols, it is not as comprehensive as the preceding one. The Commentary on the Great Symbols on this hexagrams says: "A lake on the mountain is influence. The superior person, therefore, makes ready to receive people." The mountain, *Kên,* takes the initiative, for it is male. However, the statement is not comprehensive for the understanding of the hexagram as a whole. The Commentary on the Small Symbols stresses the will as power to exert influence. On the first line, the commentary says, "The influence affects the big toe, for his will is external to himself." Here, the will is directed from inside out, as previously noted. The commentary regarding the third line says that the will is firmly set toward greater influence. It says, "When the will is external to things that one's friends desire, it is very low." In the fifth place, the will reaches its final destination. The commentary says, "The influence affects the nipples. The will is going to reach to the end." The second and fourth lines are too insignificant to be examined, and, indeed, the commentary says little about them. Regarding the top line, the commentary remarks, "The influence [finally] affects his jaws, cheeks, and tongue. He opens his mouth and talks." *Tui* here signifies the mouth, as the jaws, cheeks, and tongue have to do with talking. *Tui,* the youngest daughter, is also known as the talkative girl. The divided line on the top is analogous to the open mouth. Therefore, the Commentary on the Small Symbols makes sense.

As previously indicated, the Commentary on the Small Symbols is not always reliable. It often stresses something unimportant. Sometimes, it misleads or confuses us in our attempt to understand the meaning of the hexagram as a whole. It is, therefore, unwise to read the commentaries side by side with the main text of the *I Ching.* My suggestion is to read the main text first, and then receive assistance from the commentaries for further enrichment and illumination. The commentaries are always to be consulted after the main text has been studies and reflected upon.

The sixth and final step is to adapt the meaning of the hexagrams to the reader's particular circumstances. Unless the interpretation of the hexagram addresses our personal and social needs, it loses its significance. Our interpretation is not complete until it meets our needs. How does one make the interpretation meaningful in respect to one's own experience? This question will be covered fully in the next chapter, where the human predicament is interpreted in light of the hexagrams as attained through the manipulation of the stalks. However, using the three hexagrams covered in this chapter, let me attempt to relate them to my experience in writing this book.

Hexagrams 11 and 21 are taken together for this task. If we look at the structure of hexagram 11 in relation to that of hexagram 21, it is easy to notice that the second and third lines of hexagram 11, or *T'ai,* are transformed from yang (undivided line) to yin (divided line) in hexagram 21, or *Shih Ho;* and that the fourth and sixth lines of hexagram 11 are changed from yin to yang lines in hexagram 21.

T'ai   *Shih Ho*

Hexagram 11 is *T'ai* or Peace, which is the symbol of harmony and concord between Heaven and Earth, between positive and negative—or, in general, between all opposites. The writing of this book must be based upon just this type of harmonious relationship between these polarities. As explained earlier, one thing that motivated me to write the book was the chance to explore the harmony and mutuality between the Christian faith and the *I Ching.* My intention, therefore, was not only to explore the commonality between them but also to help each learn about the other, since popular belief has it that the *I Ching* is completely opposite to the Christian faith.

The I Ching *is still understood by many Christians as a heretical and superstitious book whose impact is contrary to the promotion of the Christian faith. I have attempted to show that the* I Ching *is a book of wisdom par excellence, and is complementary rather than contradictory to the Christian faith. Therefore, when I look at hexagram 11, I can relate the ideas of Heaven and Earth to those of Christianity and the* I Ching *respectively. Christianity can represent Heaven, for it stands for the revelation of God, while the* I Ching *can represent the Earth, for it stands for the wisdom of humanity. Just as Heaven and Earth are brought together in hexagram 11, Christianity and the* I Ching *are contrasted and compared in this book for their mutual enrichment.*

The Judgment on hexagram 11 says, "Peace. The small departs and the great approaches. It is good fortune and success." This seems to suggest the process of bringing Christianity and the *I Ching* together. The small could be the negative, or yin, force that holds me back when I start to write the book. This negative force begins to decrease as I pursue my writing. The idea that I hope to pursue becomes more and more positive, and I am convinced that such mutual enrichment as I had hoped for is possible in this endeavor. Thus, the great approaches. The great is the power of the positive energy, or the yang element, that continues to grow as I pursue this task. I relate this Judgment to my work in this way because I can use hexagram 11 to illustrate my own experience.

As I will explain in the next chapter, the moving lines are important. The moving or changing lines in hexagram 11 are, as we have already indicated, the second, third, fourth, and sixth lines. The second line changes from yang to yin. This moving line tells me that I should walk in the middle way in dealing with the subject matter. The purpose of this book is to introduce the *I Ching* to Christians by highlighting their mutual understandings. I have been tempted to weigh things more heavily on the side of the *I Ching*. However, I have consciously tried to provide some Christian counterparts to help balance the subject. This has not been an easy task. Keeping the middle path is difficult.

The third lines moves from yang to yin again. This line indicates the difficulty of maintaining such evenness of treatment in the subject matter. I know that although I have tried to maintain evenness, I have failed to do so.

The fourth line talks about sincerity. Certainly, what I have attempted to say here is sincere. When I come to the top line, however, I begin to see that sincerity alone fails to whet my enthusiasm. It may be that my humiliation will begin when I finish this book. I will no doubt feel the inadequacy of any treatment that I can provide regarding a book that has been honored for centuries by the most brilliant scholars in the East.

Hexagram 21, *Shih Ho* or Chewing, seems to describe the struggle I have had in writing this book. I have had to overcome many obstacles in order to continue this book. My teaching at the university, my service to local congregations, and my family life have continuously obstructed my work on this project. My persistent will to pursue this task, or my strong will to "chew up" the obstacles, has been essential to its completion. I can, therefore, relate this hexagram to my determination to overcome the difficulties I have encountered while writing this book.

Let me now relate hexagram 31, or Influence, to my present experience. The idea that comes to mind is the influence this book could exert upon the world. Is this hexagram telling me the effect of the book? I would, of course, like to believe that the book carries the power of influence that the hexagram describes. The structure of this hexagram shows the mutual attraction between youthful boy and youthful girl. This seems to indicate a universal attraction. The Judgment speaks of "taking a maiden." This also suggests a joyous occasion of celebration. I want to believe that all of these positive forces will influence my work. Of course, this will not remain as a mere wish if the hexagram really represents the germinal situation of my work on this book. I will discuss in detail in the next chapter how we can pinpoint the right hexagram for symbolizing the germinal situation that we are in.

An existential interpretation is also essential to the Christian faith. Unless an interpretation is meaningful, addressing the condition that we find ourselves in, it is ineffectual. Interpretation involves personal participation. For example, Christ-events on the cross are meaningful when they are related to our personal life. We can participate in these events when they are related to the condition we experience. That is why any interpretation is incomplete if we don't relate it to our personal concerns. A proper attitude we should take in the interpretation of a passage of Scripture, for example, is to contemplate and reflect upon the passage with open-mindedness. Let the Word speak to me, to my particular condition of existence! This seems to be the traditional Christian attitude. Let the Word be active and us passive. Yet many of those who follow the traditional approach, in particular those who hold to a propositional view of inspiration, often speak as if the Word is outside of—and separate from—us. They also speak as if the event of Christ is a past, and not a present, reality. However, the I Ching reminds us that it is a part of us and is a present reality. In the dialectical theology of Karl Barth, the word of God is not somewhere outside of us, and the event of the cross is not in the past, but is in us now. We are the bearers of the cross that Jesus bore. The cross represents the germinal situation that is in process of realization now. Our interpretation is, then, the conscious realization of that potential condition that is buried within us. Thus, interpretation is none other than an uncovering of the Christ-event in us. This may be a radically different approach to the interpretation of the Christian faith from that of Luther, Calvin, and Moody. However, this is a challenge that we must take seriously as we study the interpretation of the I Ching.

In summary, there are six steps or guidelines for interpretation of the *I Ching*. This sixfold approach is coincidental with the structure of a hexagram. Just as there is a definite direction of movement within the hexagram, there is also a definite step to be taken as we interpret the hexagram. The first step corresponds to the beginning line of the hexagram. Just as the beginning line deals with the innermost structure of the hexagram, the first step has to do with the most inner symbol—that is, with the lineal symbol, or the hexagram itself. At this stage, a careful observation is made of the structure of the hexagram without any reference to the written words. This, of course, presupposes some basic knowledge of the nature and characteristics of the lines and trigrams that constitute the hexagram. The hexagram is not to be interpreted logically at this stage, but intuitively. The second step is to concentrate upon the written words, especially the Judgment, without reference to the structure of the hexagram. Since the written words bear rich cultural and historical heritages, we receive much wisdom through careful interpretation of the Judgment. The third step is to bring the first and second steps together and integrate them. The correlation of the primary symbols (the hexagrams) and the secondary symbols (the Judgments) is indispensable in the process of interpretation. The fourth step is to relate the judgments on the lines with the Judgment on the hexagram. Since the lines are relative to the hexagram as a whole, they must be interpreted within the delimitation of the Judgment as a whole. The fifth step is to consult the Ten Wings, the standard commentaries on the *I Ching*. These commentaries are supplementary and should illuminate and enrich our interpretation of the hexagram. The sixth step is to make this interpretation meaningful to our existential condition. Unless our interpretation is related to our personal situation, it is incomplete. The hexagram that we interpret is, in a way, our own germinal condition. An interpretation, therefore, is merely the conscious actualization of that germinal situation within us.

5

The Method and Implications
of Divination

The Nature of Divination

The *I Ching* is most of all a book of divination. The word "divination" is best understood as "primordial prognostication." Although originally associated with divinity, prescience or skill at foretelling has almost nothing to do with divine nature. It belongs not to revelation, but to the domain of human wisdom. Since the *I Ching* is a book of wisdom, its method of divination utilizes human wisdom. Divination deals with the unconscious and spiritual dimensions of human existence. Divination in the *I Ching* reveals spiritual and invisible realities through the symbols of the hexagrams. It is a human tool by which we investigate the potential reality that may be effected in the world. In this respect, its method of self-prognosis is merely an effort to find a germinal situation that describes the question we are asking and answers it in light of our own predicament. Divination is not a magical or religious investigation. As we will see, divination is not superstition, but rather a profound level of wisdom aimed at self-realization.

The divination of the *I Ching* is more closely associated with science than with religion. Carl Jung regarded the *I Ching* as a standard Chinese scientific work. When asked by the president of the British Anthropological Society to explain why a people as highly intellectual as the Chinese had produced no science, Jung replied, "This must really be an optical illusion, because the Chinese did have a 'science' whose 'standard work' was the *I Ching,* but the principle of this science, like so much else in China, was altogether different from our scientific principle."[1] The *I Ching* method of divination used by early Chinese science was holistic and intuitive in approach. If, as many scholars hold, science operates in a different domain from that of religion such that they cannot be in conflict, then the *I Ching*'s divination and the Christian faith may well be mutually inclusive and supportive, too. Divination is a search for self-actualization through human wisdom, while the Christian faith seeks self-transcendence through divine grace. They are thus not contradictory, but complementary to one another.

Preparation for Divination

No one should consult the *I Ching* in order to test the validity of its divination. Because prognostication is much more subjective than objective, its authenticity cannot be tested or validated. Divination is effective only when the mental condition of those who consult it is pure and genuine.

This approach to divination is very similar to our concept of the Christian faith. No one can test the Christian faith scientifically to find out what Christianity is. Faith is also much more subjective than objective. It cannot be validated by intellectual methods. Its authenticity is known only to those who trust in God. Likewise in divination, the element of trust seems to play an important part.

In traditional East Asian thought, especially that of Confucianism, sincerity plays an important role in one's attitude toward divination. The *I Ching* is a book of self-prognostication, which means that those who consult it are also the agents; that is, those who want to know what their predicament is are also the controllers of their own destiny. This factor distinguishes the *I Ching* from all other divination books. Since everyone who consults the *I Ching* is himself the diviner, falsely manipulating the process of divination amounts, in fact, to self-deception. The *I Ching* is only a medium through which one discerns his or her own predicament. Insincerity invalidates the divination.

We can liken the divination potential of the *I Ching* to an electric light bulb that has only the potentiality of lighting. It does not give light by itself. It illuminates only when it is properly connected to the electric current. Likewise, the *I Ching* acts only when genuine contact with the subject is established.

Under what conditions is it possible for us to adopt a genuine and sincere attitude toward divination? Those who are enlightened or who have strong faith can maintain such a genuine attitude at will. However, most of us possess such heartfelt sincerity only when confronted by crises that call for important life decisions. When we cannot decide upon a course of action, we seek assistance from something beyond our own wisdom. Let me illustrate what such a critical moment of decision is like.

A young man has to decide whether he should stay with the wife he has recently married or become a monk under a great Zen master. At that moment, he has to select either the route of "love" or that of "success." He must choose between his wife and his enlightenment. In this devastating moment, he writes the following verses:

> Love or success, the two separate ways.
> Shall I take this or that way?
> I have to make a choice, but I cannot.
> If I take the way of love, the success will cry.
> If I take the way of success, the love will cry.

When we face this kind of circumstance, we may not be able to reach a decision by ourselves. We need assistance or guidance. When the choice is evenly divided, some, possibly most, people will take a chance. We may throw a coin in the air and let chance decide for us. This is why, as Wilfred Smith has indicated, "The mental attitude which leads a person to consult an oracle is, after all, not foreign to our own culture either. We, too, are familiar with symbols, prophets, and places from which prophetic sayings emanate."[2] When we are desperate, we seek assistance from something outside ourselves. Christians pray and meditate on a scriptural passage for answers when they need inspiration. Unless their mental attitude is pure and genuine, however, their prayers may not be answered. In the same manner, the *I Ching* is helpful only when we consult it with a genuine and sincere intent. We must not approach it with fear or awe, however, for it is not an idol or a god. It has no power in itself. Our attitude toward the process of divination is the same as our attitude toward our self, for the source of divination is not the *I Ching,* but our own nature. The *I Ching* is simply a medium through which our unconscious is revealed.

Our attitude toward the I Ching *as an instrument of divination is quite different from the Christian attitude toward the Bible as a focus for contemplation and reflection. For Christians, the Bible is more than merely a medium through which one's real self is understood. The Bible is the witness of divine truth as well as a source of knowledge about our true self. In other words, Christians approach the Bible as the authoritative source through which to know the truth. Reflection on the Bible will yield truths that are not to be found within us. On the other hand, the* I Ching *is a means of reflection on our own self. If we compare the* I Ching *with a light bulb, then the Christian Bible can be compared with the electric current, which brings the electric power, the source of light, to the bulb. Through prayers and contemplation, Christians receive the truth about themselves and their predicaments. On the other hand, through divination the* I Ching *becomes a means through which people can realize their own potentialities or understand the resources of their unconscious depths. The divination of the* I Ching *stresses the attitude of sincerity, while Christian contemplation and prayers stress the attitude of trust or faith.*

The Method of Divination

The method of divination is well explained in the Great Commentary. The technique of manipulating the yarrow stalks for divination is based on a profound philosophy. In order to understand the philosophy of divination through the manipulation of stalks, we must return to the diagram known as the Yellow River Map. This was the basis for the formation of the trigrams and hexagrams, as the Great Commentary indicates.

Heaven, therefore, produced spiritual things perceived by the holy sages. They imitated Heaven and Earth and produced symbols to indicate good fortune and misfortune. The Yellow River brought forth the Map, and the Lo River brought forth the Writing. The holy sages modeled [trigrams and hexagrams] after them. (1:11)

Although the writings from the Lo River may bear no relationship to the formation of the trigrams, the Map from the Yellow River is extremely important for understanding the rationale not only for the formation of the trigrams and hexagrams, but also the method of consulting the *I Ching* for divination.

If we observe the Yellow River Map (see chapter 1), the light circles represent the heavenly, or yang, numbers, while the dark circles represent the earthly, or yin, numbers. According to the Great Commentary, "Heaven belongs to one, Earth belongs to two, Heaven belongs to three, Earth to four; Heaven belongs to five, Earth to six; Heaven belongs to seven, Earth to eight; heaven belongs to nine, Earth to ten" (1:9). All of the odd numbers represent the heavenly quality, while the even numbers stand for the earthly quality. There are five odd numbers and five even numbers. They are, therefore, complementary to one another, As we see from the Map, the five odd circles are distributed among five different places. The center represents earth, the south, fire; the east, wood; the north, water; and the west, metal. Both heavenly and earthly numbers are complementary in all these five places. From the map, one can see that the four elements representing the directions of east, south, west, and north are relative to the Earth, the center, because these four elements are the substances of Earth. Earth, then, comes from the five of Heaven, the core of the Map. Thus, divination has a direct connection with this core. Through this core, which is also called the "Great Overflow" *(Ta Yen),* the divination process is related to the cosmic process. The number of this Great Overflow is fifty; that is, ten of the earthly number complemented by five of the heavenly number. Since ten is complemented by five, the product representing all possible combinations is fifty, or five times ten. This number, fifty, is the total number of the Great Overflow. That is why we use fifty yarrow stalks for divination.

In the process of divination, one stalk is removed from the fifty and the remaining forty-nine stalks are used for manipulation. The fiftieth stalk is removed because it represents the Great Ultimate, which symbolizes the ultimate unchanging overall reality. This stalk represents the starting point of all possible numbers, or zero, the sign of nonbeing, which becomes the source of all changes in the universe. It is, therefore, not counted as a number, since the *I Ching* holds that all numbers come from it. A practical reason for its removal is, as common sense tells us, that when fifty is divided into any two parts, it gives either two odd numbers or two even numbers, which would make the process meaningless.

The remaining forty-nine stalks are now divided into two portions, representing the two great powers, Heaven and Earth, the prototypes of yin and yang forces. One stalk is then set apart from one of the two heaps; it represents persons who occupy the center between Heaven and Earth. Here, the trinity of world principles is attained. The person, together with Heaven and Earth, forms the complete and perfect union symbolizing the wholeness of the universe. This trinity is symbolized in the trigrams that represent the basic units of germinal situations. When one stalk is taken out of the heap of heavenly numbers, it becomes the yang force. When it is taken from the heap of earthly numbers, it becomes the yin force.

To summarize thus far, two steps are taken to form the trigrams. Before we began to manipulate the fifty stalks, we eliminated the one that represents the absolute, for it does not represent any changing number. Thus, among the fifty, forty-nine are used for the process of manipulation. The first step with the forty-nine is to divide them into two groups, because everything is ultimately categorized into either heavenly or earthly realms, or yin and yang forces. The second step is to take one stalk from the left-hand heap, which represents the heavenly numbers. This stalk represents persons. Heaven, Earth, and persons then form the principle of a trinity, which is symbolized in the trigram. This process corresponds to the process of cosmic evolution, which is well expressed in the forty-second chapter of the Taoist scripture, *Tao te Ching:* "The Tao begot one, and the one two; then the two begot three and all else." The Tao is represented by the absolute number, the background of all changing numbers. The one is represented by the aggregate of the forty-nine stalks. The one then begets two, represented by division of the forty-nine stalks into two heaps. The two beget three by taking one stalk from one of the two heaps. The three (stalk + heap + heap) represent the trinitarian principle of the world that is symbolized in the trigrams. These trigrams are, in turn, the foundations for the sixty-four hexagrams that represent everything in the world.

The third step aims at reducing the heaps to small numbers (four or less); it consists of counting through by fours—because the number four represents the four seasons of the year—and retaining only the remainder. It is analogous to the process of casting out nines in arithmetic. The trigrams are now arranged according to seasonal changes. The correlation of the trigrams with the four seasons shows the directions of the changes. This correlation is found in the Writings of the Lo River and corresponds to the Sequence of Later Heaven arrangement made by King Wen. The correlation of the trigrams to the seasonal changes makes a change complete.

A complete change then consists of four operations: 1) the random division of forty-nine stalks into two heaps; 2) among stalks of the left-hand heap (heavenly numbers), one is removed to represent persons; 3) the remaining stalks of the left-hand heap are counted through by fours, and the fours are cast out; and 4) the stalks of the right-hand heap (earthly numbers) are likewise counted through by fours and the fours are cast out. In this way, four operations are needed to produce a change. For our convenience, the one stalk from the second operation is inserted between the ring finger and the little finger. The remainder from the third operation is then inserted between the ring finger and the middle finger; and the remainder from the fourth is inserted between the forefinger and the middle finger. Now the sum of stalks held in our hand must be either five or nine, because the only possible variables are 1+4+4, 1+3+1, 1+2+2, or 1+1+3. The number five, therefore, is three times as easy to obtain as the number nine (three chances in four as compared with one chance in four).

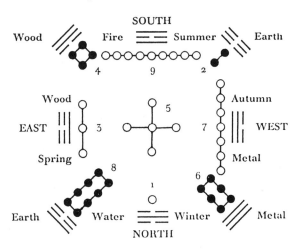

This complete change now must be repeated two more times, according to the Great Commentary, because of the two months intercalated in every five calendar years. It is said, "The remainder is put aside to represent the intercalary month. There are two intercalary months in five years. Therefore, the putting aside is repeated, in order to make the whole possible" (1:9). Let me try to justify what the Great Commentary is saying, According to the traditional Chinese calendar, the days of the year come only to 360, and a month to about 29 days. Since there are 12 months in a year, when 29 days are multiplied by 12 months, the result is 348 days. The Chinese year is, therefore, short by 12 days. Twelve days are then multiplied by 5 to get 60 days, which corresponds approximately to 2 intercalary months in 5 years. Because of these 2 intercalary months, the same process for change is repeated twice more. Altogether, three changes are necessary to derive the value of one line of a hexagram.

I personally disagree with the Great Commentary, which, I believe, is too preoccupied with the number of days and months involved in completing the changing process. Although I have attempted to explain the Great Commentary in this regard, I am not convinced. I believe that the repetition requiring two more changes in order to complete the three changes pertains to a trinitarian principle of cosmic process. Everything in the world consists of three units or evolution: the male, the female, and the offspring. Because three units of change are needed to complete the total divination, the process of change is repeated three times.

Let us now return to the second and third changes. With the stalks that remain in the heaps, we will repeat twice more the same process (the four steps) that complete a change. The possible combinations of remainders from the second and third changes are 1+4+3, 1+3+4, 1+1+2, or 1+2+1. Stalk numbers obtained through these changes are either eight or four, with equal probability of each. The stalk numbers obtained through the first change were, as we recall, nine and five. The nine of the first change and the eights of the second and third changes are now translated into the numerical value two; and the five of the first change and the fours of the second and third changes are translated into the numerical value three.

How did the early sages translate stalk numbers into the value-number? It is difficult to fathom why nine stalks and eight stalks become value-number two, and the five stalks and the four stalks become the value-number three. Although it may be impossible to derive it through a rational process, it might be helpful to think in terms of the trinitarian principle. If we cast out threes from the number nine, its remainder is zero. When we cast out threes from the number eight, its remainder is two. And zero plus two is two. That is, perhaps, why the stalk numbers nine and eight possess the value-number two. Using the same method, when the three is cast out from the stalk number five, the remainder is two. Casting out the three from the number four leaves one. When these two remainders are added together, we obtain the value-number three. That is perhaps why the stalk numbers five and four possess the value-number three. In any case, the stalk numbers are translated into these numerical values.

Consequently, the total numerical value of the three changes can come to either nine or eight or seven or six. There is only one possible chance of obtaining the numerical value nine: the sum of five stalks (numerical value three), four stalks (numerical value three), and four stalks (numerical value three) yields the numerical value nine. The numerical value of six is also obtainable in only one way in three changes: the sum of nine stalks (numerical value two), eights stalks (numerical value two), and eight stalks (numerical value two) is the numerical value six. On the other hand, there are three possible combinations yielding the numerical value seven and the same for eight. The combinations for numerical value seven are: nine stalks (value two) plus eight stalks (value two) plus four stalks (value three); five stalks (value three) plus eight stalks (value two) and eight stalks (value two); or nine stalks (value two) plus four stalks (value three) plus eight stalks (value two). The combinations yielding the numerical value eight are: nine stalks (value two) plus four stalks (value three) plus four stalks (value three) plus eight stalks (value two); or five stalks (value three) plus eight stalks (value two) plus four stalks (value three).

The characteristics of these numerical values are found in the structure of the Map of the Yellow River. In the Map, the dots of the outer circle correspond to those of the inside circle. The six dark dots (●●●●●●) are correlated with the two dark dots (●●); the seven light dots (ooooooo) with the one light dot (o); the eight dark dots (●●●●●●●●) with the four dark dots (●●●●); and the nine light dots (ooooooooo) with the three light dots (ooo). The six dark dots represent the old yin, the changing yin line, because six plus two makes eight dark dots, which represent the young yin, the unchanging yin line. On the other hand, the nine light dots represent the old yang, the changing yang line, because nine minus two makes the seven light dots, which represent the young yang, the unchanging yang line. When the total numerical value of three changes is six, it is the changing yin line; when it is seven, it is the unchanging yang line; when it is eight, it is the unchanging yin line, and when it is nine, it is the changing yang line. As we will see, the changing lines, the old yin and old yang lines, or the numerical values six and nine, become very important in the process of divination.

When the first line of the hexagram has been obtained by means of this process of three changes, all of the forty-nine stalks are again gathered together and the same procedure is repeated to obtain the second line. The rest of the lines of the hexagrams are in turn obtained in the same manner. There are altogether eighteen changes, for each line of the hexagram is derived from three changes. The Great Commentary thus says, "Eighteen mutations give a hexagram" (1:9). As we noted previously, it takes four steps to make a change and three changes to make one line. Since there are six lines in the hexagram, it takes seventy-two steps to form a hexagram. In building the hexagram, one starts from the bottom. That is, the first line is at the bottom and the last line, or the sixth line, is at the top of the hexagram.

It is important to make a clear distinction between the changing lines (the old yin or old yang lines) and the unchanging lines. Changing lines will create a new hexagram. For example, suppose that we have obtained hexagram 1, *Ch'ien* or Heaven, through the process of mutation. Among the six lines of the hexagram, if the beginning line is an old yang or changing line, then a new hexagram, hexagram 44, *Kou* or Encounter, is created.

This hexagram, number 44 or *Kou,* is the by-product of the changing line.

The first line of *Ch'ien* changes from a yang line (unbroken line) to a yin line (broken line). Hexagram *Ch'ien* is the original hexagram *(Yuan kua)* because it signifies the original situation. Hexagram *Kou* here is known as the consequent hexagram *(Chih kua),* because it represents the situation as a consequence of change. As a rule, we consult the judgment on the changing line along with the Judgments on both hexagrams. In interpreting the situations expressed in these hexagrams, it is helpful to follow the practical suggestions for interpretation that are given in the preceding chapter.

It is difficult to relate this divination process to the Christian faith. The only idea that comes to my mind is the use of the rosary for prayers in the Roman Catholic church. The activity of dividing and counting the yarrow stalks during the process of divination takes a great deal of concentration. In the same manner, counting the beads of the rosary is a means of concentrating the mind for prayer. Concentration is easily attained through the method of counting. That is why the counting of breaths is used in the beginning of meditation. Counting the yarrow stalks itself yields a great reward because it transmutes into medita- tion itself. Prayer and meditation must be one. Prayers must be done meditative- ly, just as meditation must be done prayerfully. In the Protestant tradition, more attention should be paid to meditation. The process of counting yarrow stalks is a meditation that connects us to the cosmic principles. Likewise, through Christian prayers and meditation, we are connected to God.

Since the use of yarrow sticks was a time-consuming process, simpler forms of divination processes were devised later. One involved the use of coins. In early China, the coins were made of bronze with a hole in the middle; they were inscribed on one side and blank on the other. Since these coins are not available today, it is practical to use any coins at hand. Three coins are needed for divination. By tossing three coins together, we get a line. The inscribed side counts as yin, having the numerical value two, while the reverse side counts as yang, having a numerical value of three. If we decide to use nickels or dimes, heads should be yin and tails yang. Adding these numerical values, we can obtain a line. If all three coins are yang (tails), the sum of the numerical values is nine, that is, the changing yang line. If all three coins are yin (heads), the sum of the numerical values is six, the changing yin line. However, two yins (heads) and one yang (tails) produces a seven, and two yangs and one yin produce an eight. Both the seven and the eight are unchanging lines. We notice that each coin represents a change. Three coins, therefore, represent the three changes that make a line possible. This means that the eighteen changes are possible through only six tosses of the three coins. This is certainly a simpler method of divination. However, its accuracy is much lower than that of the yarrow stalk method. Great concentration is needed to toss the coins in a way that achieves the accurate results required for divination.

Correlation as a Basis of Divination

As we have already discussed, divination is merely a process by which to relate ourselves to cosmic principles. Certain ways of manipulating the divining stalks or of tossing the coins are employed according to the cosmic principles of change and transformation. The process may be regarded in part as a primitive attempt to do what is done in modern physics today. In both the ancient and modern cases, *a priori* laws of change are employed to develop theory, and theory is then correlated with empirical fact. In the *I Ching,* the numerical considerations reflect laws of cumulative chance, while the appeal to the solar- and lunar-based calendar reflects an effort to correlate theory with fact. Similarly, in his *Fundamental Theory,* Eddington begins by assuming particles in purely random condition and then develops in highly mathematical detail a statistical formulation of the situation—the statistics reflecting, of course, the *a priori* laws of change. He then computes the values of several of the most fundamental constants of nature (fine-structure constant, ratio of electron to proton, cosmological constant, etc.) and finds that they often accord precisely with observed values. The essential principles employed are thus analogous to those of the *I Ching,* but of a radically different order of sophistication. In the *I Ching,* the process of divination is correlated with the process of cosmic change. Thus, correlation with the seasons of the year or spatial directions is a key to understanding the *I Ching*'s implications for divination.

The importance of this correlation can be illustrated in our daily experience of correlating the movement of the sun with our watch. Because our watch is correlated with the sun, we do not have to look at the sun to know where it is; we can simply look at the watch. The *I Ching* is analogous to the watch, and the sun to the cosmic phenomena. Through the sixty-four hexagrams in the *I Ching,* every cosmic phenomenon is understood. The process of divination correlates the *I Ching* and the cosmos. The *I Ching* is the microcosmos, and the world is the macrocosmos. Thus, knowing the hexagram (the germinal or microcosmic situation) is to know the cosmic situation. Even at the moment of this writing, this type of knowledge, under the rubric "joint relativity-quantum theory," is being vigorously pursued by cosmologists, most notably by the Cambridge physicist Stephen Hawking.

If divination is a means of correlating microcosm to macrocosm, it is quite similar to the Christian idea of prayer. In prayers, our thought is related to God's thought. Just as the effectiveness of divination is based on the precise correlation of the divining process with the cosmic process, the effectiveness of prayer is based on the correlation of our thought with divine thought. This correlation is possible only when we are in tune with the divine will. Just as the divination process conforms to the cosmic process, our thought in prayer must conform to

*the divine mind. It is wrong, therefore, for us to change divine will by our will.
Rather, we must conform to the divine. In prayer, we learn to conform to the
divine. When we pray, therefore, we ask "Thy will be done." This is the essential meaning of correlating our thought with divine thought through prayer.*

The divination process is correlated with the cosmic process because it is
initiated by human thought. Any act of divination is commenced by the diviner's
question. Thus, our thought on the question we ask must be correlated with the
divination process which, in turn, correlates with the cosmic process. We, therefore, must correlate three distinct processes: the process of thinking about the
question we ask at divination, the process of divination itself, and the process of
cosmic change and transformation. These three processes must be interrelated so
that divination can win its results in a most meaningful and efficient way. Since
we have already dealt with the relationship between the process of divination and
the expression of cosmic principles, let me examine now the correlation between
the process of the questioning mind and the process of divination itself.

The correlation between our mental activity and divination is complicated.
Most of our objective thinking must be done in terms of space and time, just as
the hexagram or the germinal situation also deals with these two categories.
However, since the hexagram depicts the germinal situation, the situation where
time and space dimensions are not yet differentiated, it presents a featureless
continuum. In order to correlate our questioning minds with the process of divination, we must inject our thought into this undifferentiated space-time continuum. Since we are the diviners who pose the question to ourselves through the
divination process, our thoughts on the question and our act of divination must
be united. The unity of thought and action in the divination process can be
expressed in the form of meditation, which aims at the oneness of all things. In
a moment of deep meditation, we, as the diviners, become one with our thoughts
in the very process of divination. In fact, we become one with the very act of
divination itself. In this total unity, we become a part of the undifferentiated
continuum of space and time. In this continuum, the present, the past, and the
future are also united. The past becomes present, and the present becomes future
in total unity. Moreover, in this kind of continuum or germinal situation, what
is spatially local is also revealed as spatially distant, and what is spatially distant
is also simultaneously revealed locally. In this continuum, our consciousness is
realized in our unconsciousness, for they are undifferentiated. According to the
Great Commentary, reaching this continuum is also known as grasping the seed
of all things (1:10).

*Likewise, the most effective prayer is more than a correlation of our thought
with divine thought. It is, in fact, more than a dialogue between humanity and
divinity. Rather, it is the very unity of our thought with divine thinking. In this
unity, we may also attain the undifferentiated continuum where we can say, as
did Paul, that we have attained the mind of Christ. And we may see, too, that it*

is no longer we who live but Christ who lives in us. The mystical union between God and man enables the most effective prayer. Within this union, everything we do and every thought we possess is prayer. Our very existence is prayer. When our thought is united with God in prayer, God's mind is reflected in our mind. With this reflection we know eternity—where past, present, and future are one. In this eternity, we can know the future, for the future is contained in the present moment. This experience can elicit a Christian understanding of divination.

In the *I Ching,* the undifferentiated continuum brings together the individual and cosmic minds. It is more than the Hegelian notion of the coincidence of the Absolute Mind with the relative mind. In this continuum, the individual mind in fact becomes the cosmic mind. Because the individual mind is a microcosm of the cosmic mind, the correlation between them is complete. Because the continuum, or the germinal situation, transcends time and space, it brings the unity of all things. To obtain the hexagram or the germinal situation is, therefore, to obtain a microcosm of the universe. Thus, the process of divination that obtains the hexagram(s) helps us to understand all things.

Laws of Causality and Chance

Not everything that happens in the world is subject to the laws of causality. Although we use the laws of causality to rationalize everyday life and to relate things to it, chance is at work at the deeper levels of our existence. What divination through the *I Ching* attempts to say is that the laws of chance seem to control the psychic and spiritual world. In other words, divination makes use of chance rather than causality. How do we select one hexagram out of the sixty-four? The mode used in the *I Ching* is that of manipulating the divine stalks or tossing coins. The manipulation of stalks or tossing of coins is an operation of chance. We cannot control the outcome, for the procedures are at random. We cannot utilize logic; instead, we must entrust the result to the law of probability. Therefore, the divination process is not dependent on the principle of cause and effect; it does not belong to the realm of empirical and rational investigation. The divination process employs chance as a means of understanding future predicaments. If all things were governed by the law of cause and effect alone, there would be no room for the *I Ching.* However, the world that we live in does seem to reflect both causality and chance.

The law of chance is important for divination because it is closely related to the world of the spirit and to unconsciousness. Chance is understood by intuition and imaginative insight, while causality is plumbed through logical and rational approaches to reality. Both of them are needed to understand the world as it is. Because of the development of scientific technology in the West, however, we have had a tendency in the past to stress the causality principle as the only viable means of understanding reality. However, as our scientific knowledge evolves further and further, we have come to recognize the limitations of the causality principle. In our time, scientists have begun to admit that both chance and causality must be seen as complementing one another if we are to truly know the reality of natural phenomena. The German theoretical formulation of quantum theory—statistical because it is based on chance—gives us the following account:

> In fact, all primitive polytheistic religions seem to be based on such a conception of nature: things happening in a haphazard way, except where some spirit interferes with a purpose. We reject today this demonological philosophy, but admit chance into the realm of exact science. Our philosophy is dualistic in this respect; nature is ruled by the laws of cause and laws of chance in a certain mixture.[3]

As Born noted, there is room for chance even in the realm of exact science. An interesting example today is the fact that the magnitude of a nuclear explosion can be predicted only within broad limits. The limits are established by the laws of causality, and unpredictability within those limits is a reflection of the fact that the explosion begins on a quantum level with the chance collisions of a very few neutrons. The world we live in, therefore, appears to be governed by a polarity of laws: the laws of causality and those of chance. Just as the world is subject to both necessity and accident, both causality and chance seem to be inevitable for our understanding of reality. If the world were strictly ruled by the law of causality alone, it would be like a great machine in which we are only little cogwheels. This implies a metaphysic of materialistic determinism, which is certainly not the case. If, on the other hand, the world were governed strictly by the law of chance, all would be chaos. Since the world is neither chaotic nor deterministic, both causality and chance must indeed play important roles in the governing of the universe.

What we have attempted to do so far is to legitimize the use of chance as a means of understanding reality. By doing this, we can perhaps restore divination, or something analogous to it, to a place in our lives. If the use of chance is as authentic as that of causality as a means of understanding reality, divination should be as acceptable as science or any other discipline in today's world. If we were to regard the causality principle as the only means of knowing reality, then divination, because it is based on chance, would be regarded as irrelevant and superstitious. By acknowledging the place of chance in the search for reality, however, we can see the relevance of divination. When we learn to appreciate the interdependence and complementarity of causality and chance, our approach to reality will then become holistic.

If the objective of divination is to plumb reality down to the level where chance prevails, then the crucial question is not the legitimacy of hope—its fulfillment is commonplace in physics today. The crucial question is, instead, whether or not the methods of the *I Ching* are adequate to plumb this depth. When regarded only as the blind movement of objects, they are not. The yarrow stalks and the coins are *molar* objects, which means that they are so large as compared with nuclear particles as to transcend, by many orders of magnitude, the realm of chance that science has legitimized. In nature, aside from intricate scientific apparatus and theory, only the human brain—with a nerve network capable of perceiving a chance occurrence by three hundred thousand in one-fiftieth of a second—is sensitive enough to plumb this realm. Thus the *I Ching* can be faulted not so much for its underlying principle as for its failure at the task. But as we shall see in the next section, the *I Ching* in fact did *not* view the stalks and coins as mere blind objects, but as receptive to very subtle influences from the mind of the manipulator. Viewed in this light, the use of yarrow stalks, being a digital procedure, would be strikingly more dependable than the tossing of a coin, with which it is hard to imagine how even the unconscious mind could control the outcome.

The relationship between causality and chance is like that between reason and faith in religion. There is a long history of efforts to resolve the conflict between reason and faith. The soundest approach to reality has always been to grasp the complementarity of the two. It is not possible to understand the Christian faith without reason, for our thinking is subject to the laws of rational categories. Moreover, it is not possible for us to understand the reality of God without faith in God. Faith and reason are inseparable in our search for religious truth. The Reformation tradition in the past few centuries has too much stressed faith over reason. The idea of sola fidei, *or faith alone, dominated the Reformation tradition. Although the synthesis of reason and faith is inevitable in theology, the priority of faith has been emphasized, for grace has been closely related with faith. Just as the priority of chance over causality is emphasized in the process of divination, so also the theological enterprise has emphasized the priority of faith over reason. This seems to imply that spiritual truth transcends reliance on the rational alone. Just as faith alone is not possible in the Christian faith, so also chance alone is insufficient for divination. But, just as faith includes reason, so also chance displays a certain reliability of its own kind, which makes it a meaningful process.*

Synchronicity as a Key to the Reliability of Divination

The *I Ching* divination techniques have been felt to be reliable for many centuries in East Asia. The reason for this reliability ties in with a meaningful correlation found with the law of chance. Divination would be meaningless if it had to do only with sheer chance. If it were based only upon chance, there would be no reason to go through a serious process of manipulating stalks or of tossing coins. There is, on the contrary, some sort of authenticity to be credited to this chance operation. For example, some meaningful correlation between the conscious and unconscious as well as between time and space must be found in the process of divination. In particular, the specific process of divination used by the *I Ching* is a means of tapping the hidden principle of correlation existing in the realm of chance. This kind of meaningful correlation can be considered a real possibility when we think of everything, whether spiritual or material, conscious or unconscious, past or future, far or near, as an interdependent and interrelated aspect of an organism to be taken as a whole. In this regard, Paul Veide is right when he says, "There is no such thing as sheer chance."[4] This hidden principle of correlation, which can be tapped by the divination process, is called by Carl Jung "synchronicity," which means "the coincidence of events in space and time as meaning something more than mere chance."[5] Synchronicity is, then, an acausal connecting principle, i.e., one which is opposed to the principle of physical causality. "The *I Ching* presupposes," said Jung, "that there is a synchronistic correspondence between the psychic state of the questioner and the answering hexagram."[6]

The acausal principle of synchronicity can be applied to the astrological zodiac as well. Its significance is illustrated through a study of the horoscope of married couples. One of Jung's summaries of such studies reads as follows:

> Together with my co-worker, Mrs. Liliane Frey-Rohn, I first proceeded to collect 180 marriages, that is to say, 360 horoscopes, and compared the 50 most important aspects that might possibly be characteristic of marriage, namely the conjunctions and oppositions of ☉ ☽ ♂ (Mars), ♀ (Venus) *Asc* (Ascendent) and *Desc* (Descendent). This resulted in a maximum of 10 percent for ☉ ♂ ☽ As Professor Markus Fierz of Basel, who kindly went to the trouble of computing the probability of my result, informed me, my figure has a probability of $1:10,000$.[7]

A similar evaluation of his second group of 220 marriages yielded a maximum figure of 10.9 percent for ☽ ♂ ☽ . The probability of this figure is about $1:10,000$ again. Some of these experiments suggest that the correlation of the positions of the horoscope in marriage is more than that of mere chance. Jung, therefore, concludes: "Their concurrence . . . is so improbable that one cannot help assuming the existence of an impelling factor that produced this result."[8]

If we were to make a statistical study of the reliability, and thus the credibility, of the *I Ching*'s divination for individual cases, we might find a surprising result—a coincidence of the condition of the questioner with the answering hexagram. In default of studies, however, we can still urge that without this kind of meaningful result, the *I Ching* would not have continued for centuries to be the favored book of divination in East Asia. Its popularity throughout the centuries has sometimes been seen as enhancing the reliability of divination. One of the great commentators on the *I Ching,* Wang Fu-Chih (1619–92), illustrates the synchronicity of two basic strata of existence. He correlates one's immediately experienced reality with the invisible order of existence that is not immediately accessible. His idea of such an invisible order is similar to the Kantian notion of noumena. These two differentiated orders, noumena and phenomena, are brought together in the process of divination. The meaningful correlation of the two strata can be understood as a synchronistic process; and to one who acknowledges the possibility of such a process, the divination of the *I Ching* may seem more reliable than mere chance.

Such a synchronistic correlation between the questioning and the answering hexagram is possible because of the interrelatedness of all things in an organic world. If the world is understood reductively in terms of sheer mechanical structure, there is no possibility of synchronicity. In the mechanical worldview determinism based on the causality principle prevails. In this kind of worldview, everything is a separate entity that is connected to other things only by the causality principle. Because of this agglutinative metaphysic, there is no room for chance or for synchronistic relationship. In an organic view of the world, however, different strata are mutually related and interconnected. Because of this organic connection among things, synchronicity is possible. Tun Chung-shu, a thinker of the early Han period, said:

> In all things there must be correlations. Thus there are such correlations as upper and lower, left and right, external and internal, beauty and ugliness, obedience and disobedience, joy and anger, cold and heat, day and night. These are all correlated. The yin is the correlate of the yang, the wife of the husband, the son of the father, the subject of the ruler. There is nothing that does not have such correlations, and in each such correlation there is yin and yang.[9]

Because of such mutual dependence, things seemingly unrelated to one another occur simultaneously. There are coincident appearances of identical thoughts, symbols, or spiritual experiences. Belief in the organic continuum is, therefore, essential for understanding the synchronistic principle.

Various examples of such organicism are acknowledged. The relationship between the dreaming and waking states seems to be based on synchronistic correlation. From the conventional point of view, human beings and trees, for example, seem to be totally unconnected—a solipsism so distressing that an encounter with this so-called fact can cause *nausea,* as it did in existentialist Jean-Paul Sartre's novel of that title. However, many mystics in East and West alike believe that a personal relationship between men and trees is possible. For example, Martin Buber, an outstanding Jewish existentialist philosopher, indicated that the "I-Thou" relationship—that is, a truly personal relationship— is possible not only between persons but between personal and impersonal objects as well. If we believe that the world consists of the two forces of yin and yang, everything is then interdependent, just as yin and yang are interconnected. Because of this mutual interconnection and interdependence, the idea of synchronicity is possible.

Let me now apply the concept of synchronicity directly to the process of divination. One's mental attitude should be correlated with his physical activity at the moment when he casts the coins or divides the stalk-piles. If one's mental attitude, which is conscious, is affected by the unconscious, one's activity can also be influenced by the unconscious. Physical activity can be affected by spiritual forces, and the movement of the hands in the process of dividing the stalk piles or tossing the coins can be influenced by the unconscious forces.

In Christianity, we read of the event of Pentecost in the Acts of the Apostles. When the Holy Spirit came, the people spoke in tongues. Here, the Holy Spirit in fact controlled the movement of their tongues. The idea of spiritual healing is also related to the concept of synchronicity. For example, Christian Scientists believe that the healing of the physical body can be brought about through spiritual exercises. Thus, the spiritual and psychic powers can restore the body to its healthy state.

There are also shamans who dance by moving their hands, arms, and legs according to the directions of the spirit. There are, in fact, countless examples that the seen is influenced by the unseen, and vice versa. It is, therefore, not totally strange for us to believe that our unconscious minds can influence our conscious minds when we go through the process of divination. If our conscious mind is a part of the cosmic consciousness, the process of divination is precisely the correlation of our conscious activity with the activity of cosmic consciousness. When these two activities coincide, the questioner will receive a reliable answer through the hexagram.

I have said before that prayer is more than a dialogue between God and believers. Such dialogue presupposes that God and human beings are separate. Genuine prayer, as I said, is only possible through personal participation in the divine nature. When divine thought and human thought are united and become one, prayer becomes genuine. Within this unity, a mutual influence occurs. In fact, meaningful correlation between divine will and human thinking occurs. This is a synchronistic correlation, and it represents, then, the reliability of prayer.

Some Practical Suggestions for Divination

To conclude this chapter, I would like to suggest some practical guidelines for divination. I also believe that these guidelines can help Christians develop their own form of prayer. First of all, we must be sure to refrain from repeating the divination again for the same question. Once divination is done for a given question, this should be sufficient; repeating it shows a lack of sincerity and also shows our mistrust in divination itself. Moreover, what is once done cannot be repeated, for everything is changing continuously. Strictly speaking, nothing can revert to a former state and then be repeated. Thus, repetition of a divination for the same question is self-defeating.

In prayer, sincerity is also one of the most important attitudes to be assumed. It is better not to pray at all if we do not pray sincerely. Insincere prayer will harm more than help us, for insincerity is a betrayal of God's concern and love for us. If our prayer is sincere, we do not need to pray again and again for the same thing. If we believe that God is everywhere and is aware of everything, He certainly hears us even if we say it only once. If we pray the same prayer again and again, we are doing it for our own sake, not to persuade God. Of course, the repetition of certain prayer formulas, such as the Lord's Prayer in Christianity or the Nembutsu in Amida Buddhism, helps us to focus and concentrate our minds. Ritualistic repetition of prayer is done for the sake of our own concentration, not to importune the will of God. If we ask a certain thing in prayer, it is best to pray sincerely just once. One sincere prayer is better and more powerful than hundreds of insincere prayers.

Secondly, the question that we ask at divination must be acceptable to the community at large. We should not ask anything that is immoral or unethical. Since purity of heart is a prerequisite to the mental concentration called for in the process of divination, anything unacceptable for the good of the community or the self should not be asked for in the first place. Some of the questions that we may be tempted to ask can be disruptive to our community and ourselves, and we should eschew all such questions. In short, our intentions should be good and pure when we consult the *I Ching*.

The same principle is also applicable to prayers. We should not ask God for anything that is unethical or immoral. Our intention must be pure and good when we pray. We cannot ask God to wreak revenge upon others. We cannot ask Him to destroy others because we detest them. We should not pray, for example, for God to destroy fascist nations, but rather we should pray for the liberty and freedom of the people of such nations. We should not use prayer as a means of justifying or advancing our own interests. God does not answer prayers that arise out of impure or unethical motivations.

Thirdly, we should not ask questions that we can resolve by ourselves.

When our wisdom is exhausted and we cannot find the means to solve the problem, we can then approach the *I Ching* for divination. If the answer can be found by some manner other than divination, then we should not consult the *I Ching*. The *I Ching* must be the final appeal for help. Unless we are desperate for help, it is difficult for us to have a sincere and pure intention. If we know that divination is the only means available for resolution of our question, we will certainly take it seriously and do our very best to make it meaningful for us.

In the same manner, we should not pray for something that we can do by ourselves. We have developed a tendency to pray for everything. Prayers are often used to make our lives easy. We should not make prayer into a sort of magic that solves everything. Moreover, we should not ask God for such things as making money in business, getting a good grade in school, or catching a lot of fish on a fishing trip. When we do, we debase prayer into magic. Why does God give us wisdom and strength? We should use them as effectively as we can. Only when the powers of our minds and strength are exhausted should we pray for help. We should ask God only when things are beyond our control. The prayer for help should be our last appeal. Unless we adopt this kind of attitude in prayer, our prayer cannot be genuine. Most of our prayers, therefore, should be expressions of thanksgiving rather than petitions or appeals for help.

Fourthly, when we formulate the question, we must be careful not to make it absurd, vague, or ambiguous. The question we ask must be specific in nature. We should not ask a question that involves many different answers. For example, we should not ask a question like, "What shall I do in the future?" This kind of question is not specific enough for divination; it is too broad and abstract. Rather, the question should be focussed: "Shall I take a trip to Japan this summer" Unless the question is specific, simple, and as concrete as possible, we cannot expect a reliable answer.

This is also true in our prayers. We have a tendency to pray for abstract and general themes, such as for peace and the welfare of humankind. While there is nothing wrong with praying for such things, this kind of prayer becomes so ritualized that the real meaning of prayer is lost. When we direct our prayers toward more specific and concrete events, we become more closely identified with them and get better results. One of the best prayers I've ever heard was one offered many years ago by a kindergarten student. He asked specific things from God; and he did not make anything abstract or general. If we look at the Lord's Prayer, what strikes us is how simple and concrete it is. We discern very little that is abstract or general in this prayer. A simple, concrete prayer is not only more effective but also more personal than a complex and abstract one. The more specific the prayer is, the more meaningful it becomes for us.

Fifthly, concentration is the key to the divination process. Without concentration, divination is impossible. When we count the stalks or toss the coins, we have to concentrate on the question. When we become one with the question that we ask, our act of divination is also united with our thought. In this movement we become nothing; it is our own thought that motivates and becomes the process of divination itself. This abnegation is similar to the Buddhist idea of no-mind. We do not have any independent mind; we enter the process of divination. This kind of state can be attained through the ritualistic performance of counting stalks or tossing coins. The constant repetition of counting, for example, becomes a means for us to become no-mind, or to become one with the process. Thus, when we perform divination, we should do it ritualistically, avoiding anything that detracts us from undivided concentration.

Likewise, it is my opinion that prayer should be performed ritualistically and holistically. Prayer in the proper sense is a holy conversation with the divine. It must be done, therefore, as in a worship service. A proper physical position should be maintained and anything that detracts from our attention to God should be avoided. We should try to lose ourself by deeply participating in prayer. We should, in fact, become the prayer when we are deeply involved in it. Some of us can use the rosary as a means of concentrating our thought. Whatever means we use, concentration is the key to effective prayer. We should learn how to get into the state of no-mind, so that we become a part of the mind of Christ when we are in prayer.

Sixthly, we must remember that the hexagram we have received through the divination process is only a means for us to understand ourselves. It is a symbol that helps us to project our own unconscious. It does not have any inherent power. We must carry it with us until we understand the answer. The hexagram thus is similar to the Zen Buddhist idea of *koan* or *kung-an,* which is an intellectual puzzle. Just as the monks are asked to concentrate on the koan day and night, so also we should carry the hexagram with us continuously until we solve it. Whatever we do through the day, we should be bound to the hexagram. Whether we eat, sleep, walk, or work, we should at no time be free from it. Through ceaseless meditation and contemplation on this hexagram, we may find the answer and this answer will eventually free us.

I believe that the most effective form of prayer involves the reception of a vision, similar to the generation of a hexagram. The vision that we receive in prayer should remain with us until we find peace in a solution to the problem. Many times God answers us through visions. I do not refer to visions in dreams, but to visions in prayer. When we are deeply involved in prayer, God often gives us a vision. Jeremiah, for example, was given a vision of two baskets of figs (24:1–4). If we contemplate for a long time, God may likewise give us a vision today. We may accept the vision as God's answer to our prayer before grasping its meaning. We must then carry it with us and contemplate and meditate on it until we find the answer from it. This vision may become a powerful symbol that can transform our lives. Prayer is, therefore, more than a communication between God and a person; it is the power that transforms us from what we are to what we shall be.

Finally, we should not feel guilty when we consult the *I Ching*. The divination of the *I Ching* does not depend upon a supernatural power. It has nothing to do with the divine. Belonging to the depth of human wisdom, it provides a means for realization of our own self. We should not fear that we are betraying our loyalty to our own religious beliefs when we consult the *I Ching* for divination. Our reliance on divination is no more a betrayal of our faith in God than is our reliance on scientific knowledge. Further, as I have noted previously, the divination of the *I Ching* is different from most foretelling. It is based on a primitive cosmology and is applied to an understanding of the unconscious. It is, therefore, to be understood as a creation of human ingenuity rather than practice of a religious belief. In this respect, the divination of the *I Ching* may be understood as a gift of God.

It is then my conclusion that the divination of the I Ching *has a place in the Christian faith. I regard it as a wisdom book, one that belongs to human investigation, although some others may think differently than I. What I have attempted is to show that the* I Ching *is a book of profound human wisdom that belongs to all of humanity. The* I Ching *is a means for self-understanding. It has no authority in itself. It cannot, therefore, claim to have the authority to reveal ultimate reality. In fact, it can help us enrich our Christian tradition if we approach it as a book of human wisdom. It is my hope that students of theology will study the* I Ching *just as they apply their minds to any other books of wisdom.*

6

The Significance of the *I Ching* in our Time

What does this archaic book, the *I Ching,* have to do with the twenty-first century civilization nearly upon us? Is it relevant to our postmodern world? Is it compatible with today's scientific technology? Unless it is compatible with the contemporary scientific worldview, it cannot be relevant to us. Since the *I Ching* may be understood to elucidate microcosms of the universe, let us begin by considering the relevance of this book to today's cosmology. However, a comparison of the worldview of the *I Ching* with that of postmodern science is difficult in principle because of their different orientations. The *I Ching* is not written as a textbook for science; as a wisdom book, it is quite different from empirical science. Since, in a strict sense, a comparison of the two worldviews is almost impossible, what I will attempt to do here is to show the compatibility between them.[1] This investigation will attempt to discover some common denominators between the *I Ching* and today's science.

The *I Ching* and the Postmodern Worldview

Wilfred C. Smith, former director of the Center for the Study of World Religions at Harvard University, said, "Some observers hold that twentieth-century science in the West is moving closer to a fundamental yin-yang type of interpretation of the natural universe than traditional Western view."[2] Until recently, the traditional Western view of the world was, in fact, materialistic, mechanistic, and deterministic. This worldview saw things as consisting of impenetrable particles of material moving in time and space in accordance with fixed laws. Space and time were independent, so that the particles could move by themselves within these fixed dimensions. This traditional Western view was framed in terms of the commonsense notion of a three-dimensional Euclidean space. Everything in the world was related mechanically and ruled by inexorable laws, so that the future state of the world could be easily predicted, at least in principle. All existence could conform to the law of nature and the principle of cause and effect. This kind of worldview prevailed until the beginning of the twentieth century. Newtonian physics, for example, did not make any radical break with the Euclidean concept of space and time. For Newton, the categories of space and time were absolute and prior to all other existence in the universe.

A radical break with the traditional Western view of the world came, however, with Albert Einstein, Max Planck, and Niels Bohr, who brought us a new understanding of the universe and ushered us into postmodernity. This new understanding, which is radically different from the traditional Western worldview, is much closer to that of the *I Ching*. In this understanding of the world, the idea that space and time are absolute is gone. Space and time are no longer independent realities and *a priori* categories antecedent to all other existence in the universe. They are no longer used as stationary reference points in relation to which we understand other entities. According to the theory of relativity and the empirical results of the Michelson-Morley experiment, nothing can be stationary. Everything moves and changes according to certain principles of transformation. Einstein's theory of relativity means that—apart from rotation, rest-mass, and charge (and such quantities as the velocity of light and the fine-structure constant)—there are no absolutes in all of existence. Nothing is absolute in itself, for everything changes and transforms itself. Moreover, nothing is independent from all others, for everything is a part of the whole and the whole is also in each part. According to the cosmologist William Bonner, "The theory of relativity acknowledges that frames of reference are relative, and that one is as good as another."[3] Since time and space are not stationary, nothing acts as a steady frame of reference. All things are relative to one another. As James Coleman said:

> There is no heavenly body in our universe that we can use as a stationary reference point. The earth rotates on its axis; it travels in its orbit around the sun; the sun and the solar system are moving about within our galaxy, the Milky Way, which is itself rotating. And our galaxy is also moving relative to the other galaxies. The whole universe is filled with movement. And in all this seemingly haphazard turmoil, no one can say what is moving and what is stationary. We can only say that all the heavenly bodies are moving relative to one another and no one of these is different in this respect.[4]

Stars age and die, often with supernova explosions; and new stars are formed by condensation out of the debris. The new stars take the place of the old in this process of change. Galaxies recede from one another. The whole universe, in fact, is in the process of constant movement and change, with no static point of reference.

Since relativity presupposes the idea of change in all things, we begin to see the relationship between the theory of relativity and the idea of change in the *I Ching*. Thus, the idea of change is basic to that of relativity. The contemporary worldview based on relativity is much closer to the worldview of the *I Ching* than was the traditional view of a static world, since the worldview of the *I Ching* depicts a constantly moving and changing universe.

Moreover, this changing world is more organic than mechanistic. Hellmut Wilhelm makes a distinction between the traditional Western and Eastern views of the world: "According to Western ideas, sequent change would be the realm in which causality operates mechanically, but the *Book of Changes* takes sequent change to be the succession of the generations, that is, still something organic."[5] In view of the twentieth-century development of quantum theory, we can no longer hold to the mechanistic worldview. Thus, Max Born denounces the purely mechanistic view ruled by the strict causality principle:

> An unrestricted belief in causality leads necessarily to the idea that the world is an automaton of which we ourselves are only little cogwheels. This means materialistic determinism. It resembles very much that religious determinism accepted by different creeds, where the actions of men are believed to be determined from the beginning by a ruling of God. I cannot enlarge on the difficulties to which this idea leads if considered from the standpoint of ethical responsibility. The notion of divine predestination clashes with the notion of free will, in the same way as the assumption of an endless chain of natural causes.[6]

If we believe that nature as well as human affairs is subject to both necessity and accident, we cannot regard the world as a machine. The mechanistic worldview based on the law of cause and effect cannot be held in view of the theory of quantum mechanics. This is why the worldview of modern science is closely related to that of the *I Ching*.

The organic view of the world that the *I Ching* presupposes is also closely related to the aspect of Einstein's theory that explains the equivalency of mass and energy. The energy-mass equivalency formula, $E = mc^2$, says that the energy, *E*, and mass, *m*, are not independent; they are one and inseparable. The continuity between energy and mass makes mutual interaction possible, in which one is precisely the manifestation of the other. Einstein also developed the formula $GM = fl\pi C^2 R$ for the whole universe, where *M* and *R* are its mass and radius of curvature and *G* is the gravitational constant.[7] If one ignores the $fl\pi$—which is close to 1—and multiplies both sides by M/R, the formula then becomes $GM^2/R = MC^2$. Since the left-hand member represents the potential energy of the total universe (as represented by the degree of dispersion of its matter) and the right-hand member depicts the energy equivalence of its mass, the formula makes the overall energy of the universe a reflection of how much matter there is in it—such that the total mass-energy is zero. The universe is thus holistic—its parts are a function of the whole.

This kind of worldview is close to the organic view of the world that the *I Ching* presupposes. In other words, the world depicted by today's quantum physics and the theory of relativity is more organic than mechanical. To this may be added what L. C. Birch said, "If physics and biology one day meet, and one of the two is swallowed up, that one will not be biology."[5] The integration of biology and physics would make the world closer yet to an organism. Whitehead remarks, "Biology is the study of the larger organism, whereas physics is the study of smaller organisms."[9] The integration of biology, the study of the macrocosm (the molar level) and physics, the study of the micro-cosm, may produce a worldview similar to the micro- and macrocosmic ideas of the *I Ching*.

The philosophy of change in the *I Ching* presupposes that the world is finite and self-contained. Change operates according to the process of expansion and contraction between growth and decay. This process is possible because the universe is self-contained. The world that the *I Ching* presupposes can be compared with a balloon, which can expand and contract within its limit. Such a self-contained world would be limited in total volume, but infinitely unbounded. The world of the *I Ching,* because of its organic nature, is constantly changing and reproducing according to the process of expansion and contraction. The Great Commentary says, "Contraction and expansion act upon each other to produce that which increases" (2:5). Today it is well known that most of the matter in space is hydrogen, and that wherever it condenses into stars, the hydrogen converts constantly into helium in their fiery cores. This changing of hydrogen into helium goes on throughout the universe wherever there are stars.[10] This ever-changing flow of energy forms the background of today's astrophysical theory.

Within our own Milky Way galaxy, as also in the billions of other galaxies, this flow of energy carries each star through an evolutionary life cycle of growth and decay. Any large region—as, for example, a spiral arm—is dotted with stars that have aged and reached the verge of exploding. In supernova explosions, in particular, a large fraction of the total mass is sprayed out into space to become clouds of dust and gas. These clouds, in turn, condense and form new stars to replace the old. Thus the spiral arm will retain much of its overall shape even as the stars of which it is composed are in gradual flux. In this way, constant change occurs in the universe. Old stars disappear and new ones are formed, just as old yang and old yin are changed into new yang and new yin. The process of change according to growth and decay, formation and destruction, and expansion and contraction is thus operating throughout the universe. In this kind of process of change spatial extension is correlated with time and forms a more fundamental space-time continuum. In such a process of continuous creation of new stars from the old, it might seem that the universe has no beginning and no end, and is subject to just the kind of endless cyclic change that is expressed in the *I Ching*.

Such a beginningless and endless cosmology, however, seems very dubious today. By far the most widely accepted hypothesis in our time is the "big bang" theory of the universe, which was first proposed in 1929 by the Belgian astrophysicist Georges Lemaitre. According to this hypothesis, all of the concentrated mass and energy of the universe exploded at the zero point of time from a primordial state. As a result of this primeval explosion, the bodies condensing from the products of that explosion—the galaxies—are continuously moving outward and away from each other forever, like spots on the surface of an expanding balloon. The fact that all of the distant objects are moving away from us at a rate that is proportional to the distance is an indication that the whole universe is expanding. As George Gamow says, "The present rate of expansion is about 0.000,000,01% per year, so that each second the radius of the universe increases by *ten million* miles."[11] The evidence of this expanding universe lies in the "red shift," the slight increase in the wavelength of light observed from faraway galaxies, with the magnitude of the shift proportional to the distance of the galaxy. This slight increase is observed in the light from faraway galaxies because of the receding motion of that which emits the light, just as the pitch of a train whistle sounds lower when the engine is receding than it would if the engine were approaching.[12]

In light of these observations, the older concept of a static overall universe —which Einstein himself supported at first—was overthrown. The overall universe is now seen to be in constant motion and change. Currently it is in an expansion phase. The question is, will this expansion stop? If the curvature of interstellar space is negative, the expansion could prove to be permanent. The universe will then expand forever without end. This idea of an open universe is, in fact, quite possibly true. However, the most likely geometry of the universe is one in which the curvature of space is positive, which in turn indicates that space is finite in volume. If this is the case, relativity theory then predicts that, for certain values of the cosmological constant, the expansion will eventually come to a halt and the universe then begin to contract again. As Coleman said, "We can conclude that according to the general theory of relativity, the universe is finite and unbounded."[13] In this finite and unbounded universe, the expansion stage stops when it reaches its maximum and the universe then contracts again to its minimum. If this view is accepted, we have in effect a pulsating universe. Inasmuch as the pulsating universe "ends" by passing through a radically constricted "throat" and then opening out into a new universe that expands again as before, the cycles can go on forever even in a big bang type of cosmology. Likewise, in the philosophy of change in the *I Ching,* when everything reaches its maximum it returns to its minimum, and, after that, toward its maximum again. We now see that the universe might constitute no exception to this principle. In sum, the contemporary worldview has, in recent years, moved close to that of the *I Ching*.

What then would be a Christian response to this worldview? The Christian faith, if it is to be relevant to the present day, must accommodate the contemporary worldview. Since this worldview is similar to that of the I Ching, *the Christian faith can be conveyed through the worldview of the* I Ching. *In other words, the organic worldview of the* I Ching *seems to provide a better understanding of our Christian faith than does the mechanical worldview traditional in the West. Because we take the images for our thinking from the world, our worldview affects our way of thinking. Just as the Copernican system did in the sixteenth century, so also the theories of relativity and quantum mechanics provide a new way of thinking. Among those Christians who take the contemporary worldview seriously are the process theologians. They, following the process philosophy of Alfred North Whitehead, have attempted to reconstruct Christian theology from the perspective of "becoming." Following the philosophy of the* I Ching, *we can similarly reconstruct Christian theology from the perspective of change.* [14] *We can take this as a challenge as the West comes closer in its metaphysics to the East.*

The *I Ching* and Quantum Mechanics

Let me further comment on the compatibility of the philosophy of the *I Ching* with that of quantum mechanics. In the organic view of the world, where everything is organically interdependent, chance plays an important role, especially in regard to the subatomic world. The causality principle seems to fail to predict the location and movement of electrons. As Eddington said, "Anything which depends on the relative location of electrons in an atom is unpredictable more than a minute fraction of a second ahead."[15] This seems to echo the famous Principle of Indeterminacy or the Principle of Uncertainty proposed by Werner Heisenberg. Yet not all scholars have welcomed the idea of indeterminism. Einstein himself found it unacceptable. "God does not throw dice" was his well-known challenge, to which Niels Bohr replied, "Nor is it our business to prescribe to God how he should run the world."[16] However, the majority of quantum theorists seem to have accepted the Principle of Indeterminacy. Koestler says, "Heisenberg will probably go down in history as the man who put an end to causal determinism in physics—and thereby in philosophy—with his celebrated Principle of Indeterminacy for which he got the Nobel Prize in 1931."[17] For the subatomic world Heisenberg describes, "we cannot make observations without disturbing the phenomena—the quantum effects we introduce with our observation automatically introduce a degree of uncertainty into the phenomenon to be observed."[18] According to this principle, the more precisely the location of an electron is determined by the observer, for example, the more uncertain its velocity becomes; and vice versa. This paradox seems to be a result of the interdependent relationship between the observer and the observed.

Although the *I Ching* comes from a totally different culture, it seems to share the ethos of Heisenberg's idea of indeterminacy. According to the principle of change in the *I Ching,* yin and yang are primarily relational and operative in a paradoxical manner. Because of its relational nature, yin alone is not known without yang. When yin is objectified, yang becomes absurd. If we focus on one, the other becomes blurred, because they are two but also one simultaneously. If yin decays, yang grows, and vice versa. As in the case of the Indeterminacy Principle, the more precisely we define yin, the more uncertain we become with yang, for they are complementary to one another. Although it is difficult to articulate the idea of indeterminacy through the philosophy of change in the *I Ching,* we can see the compatibility of this philosophy with the basic spirit of the Indeterminacy Principle.

It is interesting that both the *I Ching* and quantum physics share the idea of the complementarity of opposites. According to the *I Ching,* everything consists of yin and yang. When there is yin, there must be yang. One does not exist without the other. Yet they are opposite in character. This idea seems to be expressed in quantum mechanics as well. An important discovery by Paul Adrian Maurice Dirac of Cambridge University deals with anti-electrons. This discovery was made during his study of space as a limitless sea of electrons or negative energy. He found a "hole" or bubble in the sea of negatively charged electrons. This hole is the negation of an electron; therefore, it has a positive charge. Since the discovery of anti-electrons, many anti-particles have been discovered. They seem to possess opposite electric charges, magnetic movements, and spin. Although we do not call yin "anti-yang" or yang "anti-yin," the principle of the coexistence of opposites is implicit in the yin/yang relationship. Yin is the opposite of yang, and vice versa. Yin is negative while yang is positive. Yin is passive but yang is active, and so on. They are exclusive, but complementary to one another.

The Principle of Complementarity was discovered by the Danish physicist Niels Bohr, who recognized that light behaves as both a wave and a corpuscle. Heisenberg, one of his associates, said, "After the discovery of the quantum of action by Planck, the first and most important step was the recognition (achieved by Lenard's investigations and their interpretation by Einstein) that light, in spite of its wave nature as shown by countless experiments of interference, nevertheless does show corpuscular properties in certain experiments."[19] It seems to deny the exclusion of opposites. "The electron," as de Broglie said, "is at once a corpuscle and a wave."[20] It means then that light as a wave is also light as a corpuscle, i.e., we have the simultaneous coexistence of opposite phenomena. This kind of relationship is fundamental to the yin and yang relationship in the *I Ching.* Just as yin and yang are opposite but complementary, the two different modes of light are exclusive but complementary. Bohr's concept of complementarity, according to Heisenberg, is "to describe a situation in which it is possible to grasp one and the same event by two distinct modes of interpretation. These two modes are mutually exclusive, but they also complement each other, and it is only through their juxtaposition that the perceptual content of a phenomenon is fully brought out."[21] We see a similar juxtaposition in the yin and yang relationship. Yin and yang are mutually exclusive but also mutually complementary in the process of change and transformation.

We see some similarities of structure between quantum mechanics and the *I Ching.* Even though it is impossible to make a real comparison between them, we see similar patterns existing in atomic nuclei and the hexagrams. As atomic nuclei are basic building blocks of the universe, hexagrams are symbolic of germinal situations of the universe. They are like seeds which contain the potentialities of everything in the universe. Thus it is said, "The seeds . . . are the slight beginnings of movement and the initial indications of good fortune and misfortune. The superior person sees the seeds [hexagrams] and acts immediately without a delay of a single day."[22] In this respect, hexagrams are similar to atomic nuclei. The constitutive elements of hexagrams are yin and yang lines. A similar phenomenon is also found in atomic nuclei, which are also believed to consist of positive and negative electronic states.[23]

We see a similar phenomenon in the process of transformation. The pattern of the hexagram changes through the transformation of yin to yang or yang to yin. This transformation is due to the separation and union of lines. Yin, or the divided line (— —), changes to yang, or undivided line (———), by union; and the yang line becomes a yin line by separation. This seems to be similar to the addition and emission of an electron to change the structure of an atomic nucleus. It becomes clear when we consider the addition and subtraction of yin and yang numbers in the transformation of lines in hexagrams. As the reader will recall, yin represents the value-number two, and yang represents the value-number three. Yin changes to yang when one value-number is added to it, and yang changes to yin when one value-number is deducted. Here the addition and deduction of the value-number transforms one hexagram to another. Likewise, the addition and emission of quanta seem to cause the alteration of nucleus structures. Thus, we see the compatibility of the *I Ching* with a general philosophy of quantum physics.

Let us now conclude with a discussion of the poetic and symbolic images that both the *I Ching* and quantum physics utilize. Unlike classical physics, quantum physics cannot use a descriptive language. In his conversation with Werner Heisenberg, Niels Bohr said, "We must be clear that, when it comes to atoms, language can be used only in poetry. The poet, too, is not nearly so concerned with describing facts as with creating images and establishing mental connections."[24] The *I Ching* also avoids descriptive language. It is poetic and symbolic in its attempt to convey the inner and spiritual meaning of the universe. Hexagrams themselves are symbols, and the judgments are written in the form of oracles and poetry. Both the *I Ching* and quantum physics in their own ways respond to a world of great mystery and wonder. Koestler describes the beauty and wonder of the quantum world: "It is also a world of great mystery and beauty, reflected in those fantastic photographs of events in the bubble-chamber, which show the trajectories of unimaginable small particles, moving at unimaginable speeds in curves and spirals, colliding, recoiling or exploding and giving birth to other particles or wavicles."[25] We, in fact, become speechless before the mystery of the world that God has created. In reality, neither poems nor symbols are adequate to express that mystery. Perhaps silence is the only language that brings both science and wisdom together in our postmodern world.

The *I Ching* and a New Understanding of Time

Our new understanding of the curvature of space based upon the general theory of relativity brings our contemporary view of time closer to the concept of time in the *I Ching*. Newtonian laws were predicated on the assumption that light travels in straight lines. The general theory of relativity, on the contrary, showed that light rays are deflected by gravitational masses. If we travel along a straight line on a finite but unbounded surface such as that of the earth, we eventually come back to the same point where we started. This would also be the case in a finite, unbounded, curved space—though the limit on one's speed of travel makes the exercise theoretical. Because space itself is curved, all things, including light, move along the curve. Time is no exception to this. Time is a part of the process of change in the universe, a process of change that is based upon movement that is curved. More specifically, as measured by the Mossbauer effect, time slows down in the vicinity of heavily gravitating bodies in proportion to the gravitational force,[26] which means that its vector is viewed askew—that time is curved, just as light is, in such a field. Thus, time also moves, as it were, along the curvature of space.

It is enormously suggestive to hear the statement made by the emergent evolutionist Samuel Alexander, who said that "time is the mind of space."[27] By this he meant that it is a new emergent quality arising from space but still organic. Time is the mind of space, and time moves along space that is curved. Since space and time are one complex continuum that cannot be differentiated, the curvature of space is also the curvature of time. If the curve is positive, time moves cyclically, for the universe is finite and unbounded. The *I Ching* and Eastern philosophy as a whole envision the movement of time as cyclic. In view of the curvature of space, it is certainly difficult to assert the linear concept of time that has been traditionally accepted in the West. The general theory of relativity helps us to see that the view of time in contemporary physics moves closer to the cyclic movement of time that the *I Ching* presupposes.

Some may argue that the cyclical nature of time in cosmology has nothing to do with time in history. However, cosmic time and historical time cannot be separated, just as the universe and human civilization are inseparable. If cosmic time is cyclic, historical time, which is a part of the cosmos, must also be cyclic. The separation between the cosmic process and human activities in the West is partly responsible for our perception of historical linear time.

In view of this analogy between the two time concepts, we may have to rethink the history of salvation in Christianity. Salvation history does not move in a linear way. It moves not only from the promise to the fulfillment, but also from the fulfillment to a new promise. Thus, the last day, or eschaton, *need not be the absolute end. It is the end of the old, but the beginning of the new. The new world and the New Jerusalem pictured as marking the end of the world in the Book of Revelation seem to attest to this cyclic movement of time in Christianity. If our contemporary view of time is to see it as cyclic, following the curvature of space, and if historico-cosmic analogizing is valid, then the history of salvation cannot be independent of ordinary time. On this basis, sacred time and secular time would have to be interdependent.*

Moreover, time is not a principle of abstract progression in the *I Ching.* Time is the locus of that which is immediately experienced and perceived. Time in the *I Ching* is not an *a priori* principle such as Newton prescribes, but an event in relation to what is right or wrong as well as to what is favorable or unfavorable. Within the undifferentiated continuum of space and time, we see that time is not an *a priori* principle, but is a concrete event in relation to the process of change. Time is as concrete as the event itself, and it is known as a hexagram, a germinal situation.

> The situation represented by the hexagram as a whole is called time. . . . In a hexagram in which the situation as a whole has to do with movement, "the time" means the decrease or growth, the emptiness or fullness, brought about by this movement.[28]

Just as time is part of space, it is also part of the event itself. This nondualistic approach to understanding time is closely related with the ethos of postmodernity. Time is not only the mind of space but also the creative and changing dimension of existence.[29]

Change is the process of production and reproduction, or expansion and contraction. Time as a unit of change thus never comes to an ends or repeats itself. Every production and reproduction has an element of the new, because of the constant change arising through the new relationship between yin and yang forces. As long as the universe is in the process of change, time never repeats itself. The cyclic movement of time is not a repetition of the same thing, but movement into a similar cyclic pattern without repetition. The birth of new stars and the decay of old ones recur in the process of change, but they never repeat it in precisely the same way. Just as a son may follow a similar life pattern to that of his father without repeating his father's life, time never repeats itself. What the *I Ching* suggests, then, is a theory of cyclic time without repetition. Time in this way renews itself without repeating the same old time, for time is a dimension of the process of constant change and transformation.

Let's return to the Christian understanding of time. As we noted previously, salvation history is cyclic. But that does not mean that the end of time is identical with the beginning of time. In the Book of Revelation, we see the destruction of humanity coincides with the end of time. The last day is the day of cosmic judgment. However, the destruction of the world is the end of the old and also the beginning of the new world. "Then I saw a new heaven and a new earth; for the first heaven and first earth had passed away, and the sea was no more" (Rev. 21:1). The passing away of the old world is accompanied by the coming of a new world. In Christ, who is the Alpha and Omega, the beginning of the new and the ending of the old are one. However, the unity of beginning and ending does not imply that the beginning is identical with the ending. Although the end is renewed in the new beginning, what is renewed is different from what was in the beginning of the old. Because change itself is creative, the end is not identical with the beginning. That is why the cycle is open-ended, and there are infinite cycles of beginning and end, or promise and fulfillment in Christ, for Christ is infinite. Therefore, we should not conclude that returning to the new from the old or returning to the beginning from the end is a meaningless cycle of time. Rather, an open-ended cyclic time is more meaningful than closed linear time, in which beginning and end are so distinct that they are unrelated. The biblical concept of time appears to be linear, but in reality it is an open-ended cyclic time. Just as the cycle of day and night or the seasons of the year repeat themselves without repetition, so the history of salvation repeats without repetition.[30]

Another important contribution that the *I Ching* can make is to help us to recognize the reality of changes in our world. We have a tendency to deny the fact of change. We think that we can stay the same, although basically we know that we cannot. Anxiety, fear, and despair in our time may have a great deal to do with our inability to accept seriously the reality of change. The *I Ching* tells us that our existence itself is, in fact, change. We cannot stop the fact of change. To do so means to stop living. Yet, paradoxically, we resist change. We want to stay young and youthful, but we know that we cannot be young forever; it is impossible to stop our aging. Change, thus, becomes a source of problems for those who do not want to change. However, those who want to accord with normal processes of change can find peace and tranquility in life. The *I Ching* teaches us that the best way to live in the world is to flow along with changing process. Accepting change as the absolutely given, we become a part of the natural flow. Those who wish to be changeless in the midst of constant change will likely experience an existential threat, but those who are in the stream of change experience changelessness, their own eternal presence in the midst of transitoriness. In other words, to be one with change means to be changeless, for change that changes is also changeless. Avoiding change means, then, to avoid changelessness. From the perspective of time, we can say that we become timeless when we are truly in time. This timelessness or no-time is eternal time, which includes all time. As the center of a wheel does not move because of its hollowness, eternity is not only empty and changeless, but is also the source of all transitory states. Thus, Richard Wilhelm said, "By entering into change, while continuing to maintain the center in change, it is quite possible to raise the transitory state to the state of eternity."[31]

It is also true that the Christian concept of eternity does not negate time but includes it without identifying itself with time. When we are in eternity, we become one with the divine. In this oneness, we become spontaneous and unconscious of our existence in time. I believe that Jesus experienced this in his prayers. When he said that he was in God and God was in him, he was in eternity, where he and God were one. At that moment of oneness, eternity is experienced; and when it is experienced, all times are experienced also. In this respect, the "now" can become eternal; or, as expressed in the Christian experience, the Kingdom of God is within us. This is the experience to which the Apostle Paul was attesting when he said, "It is no longer I who live, but Christ lives in me." When we become one with Christ, we experience changelessness in the midst of change, what Paul Tillich called (in a book of that title) "the eternal now."[32]

The *I Ching* as a Wisdom Book of our Time

The significance that the *I Ching* has for today's scientific thinking is certainly important, but what makes the book truly significant is the profound wisdom that it offers to us in our lives. The *I Ching* can be regarded as an old, wise counselor who attempts to answer the questions that we raise in our lives. What makes wisdom different from divination is precisely that it does not directly answer the question we ask, but rather provides a guideline or way of life that eventually solves the ills of life. The *I Ching* is, therefore, more than a divination book; it is a book of wisdom for our time.

The *I Ching* helps us live in a way that heals the ills of contemporary living. One of the life-styles we have developed through industrialization, modern technology, and capitalistic economy is competition. A competitive way of living divides us between right and left, above and below, rich and poor, and educated and uneducated. Competition is a device that emphasizes differences rather than harmonious cooperation. It creates fear and anxiety in our lives. Competition produces enormous emotional stress and harms the spiritual development of humanity. It not only promotes the strong over the weak, but nurtures a dualistic way of either/or thinking. In response to our competitive life-style, the *I Ching* provides us with a cooperative life-style that promotes the unity of opposites and harmony amidst differences. It is based on the yin/yang idea of mutual dependency and complementarity. Yin and yang are not competitive, but inclusive. Yin needs yang to be yin; and yang needs yin to be yang. Thus, by cooperation with their counterparts or opposites, they can truly be what they are meant to become. In this kind of *Weltanschauung,* no member is excluded from the whole. The organic view of the cosmos provides a cooperative style of life that not only enriches the entire society but also heals the wounds created by today's civilization.

This organic and holistic approach to life is also known in the New Testament idea of the church. In Paul's letter to the Corinthians, he describes the ideal community of believers as the body of Christ:

> *For as the body is one, and has many members, and all the members of that body, being many, are one body; so also is Christ. For by one Spirit are we all baptized into one body, whether we be Jews or Gentiles, whether we be bound or free; and have been all made to drink into one Spirit. . . . And those members of the body, which we think to be less honorable, upon these we bestow more abundant honor; and our uncomely parts have more abundant comeliness. For our comely parts have no need; but God has tempered the body together, giving more abundant honor to that part which lacked; That there should be no schism in the body; but that the members should have the same care for one another. And whether one member suffer, all the members suffer with it; or one member be honored, all the members rejoice with it. Now you are the body of Christ, and members in particular. (I Cor. 12:12–27)*

The idea of cooperation and complementarity is beautifully expressed in this letter. What is most impressive is the idea of honoring the insignificant members of the body in order to bring harmony for the whole. Like the body of

Christ, our society is an organic entity that needs cooperation rather than competition.

The *I Ching* also sheds a new light on our understanding of the relationship between man and woman. According to the *I Ching,* man and woman are not the same, but they are equal. Yin, which represents woman, is equal with yang, which represents man. What makes them different are their characteristic emphases. Like yin, woman tends to be more passive, nurturing, intuitive, and tender than man. For his part, man tends more toward an aggressive, rational, and firm character. In a traditional society, the characteristics of women were clearly differentiated from those of men. Women were believed to possess only feminine characteristics, and men only masculine characteristics. This view was based on the dualistic outlook of the roles of man and woman in early days. The *I Ching* opposes the dualistic roles and stresses the unity of roles with different emphases. Men, for example, possess feminine characteristics, but the primary emphasis of their character is masculine. Likewise, women possess masculine characteristics, but the primary emphasis of their character is feminine. Because of the influence of the Confucian school of thought, many judgments in the *I Ching* appear to elevate the masculine character. This was, no doubt, a result of the cultural and historical condition of that time. Nevertheless, the essence of the *I Ching* does not value masculine character over feminine character. They are equal at the same time they are different.

In our time, women seek to liberate themselves from the past oppression of patriarchal emphases and valuations that deny women their full worth as human beings. According to the *I Ching,* liberation of women is not possible without also liberating men to accept and honor their own feminine characteristics. Liberation must be mutual. Moreover, liberation is a recovery of human authenticity, which means the rediscovery of the inherent potentiality of each person. The liberation of women means to rediscover that authentic womanhood that comes out of a total affirmation of their value as human beings. Women cannot assume the male nature without loss of at least a degree of their female nature, because changing is a mutual process. Women's becoming "masculine" means an equivalent redefinition of what it means for a man to be "feminine." In this respect, we cannot hold a monolithic character of value system. We cannot say, for example, that masculine traits such as strength, assertiveness, and "positiveness" are better than feminine traits of gentleness, responsiveness, and "negativeness." The problem in today's society is that such masculine characteristics have been valued, and feminine characteristics have been devalued. As long as women have to compete under a masculine value system, they can never liberate themselves, because liberation for them means to acquire value by becoming "like men," by acting or thinking like men. This only strengthens the monolithic value system so that both men and women become victims. Women become victims because they lose their intrinsic feminine characteristics, and men become victims because they lose as well their own feminine qualities. Neither gender can be wholly human without a balance of the masculine and feminine qualities.

The wisdom of the *I Ching* seems to suggest that the genuine liberation of both males and females in our time requires a change in the value system of our society. We need to value not only the masculine virtues and traits, but also the feminine virtues and traits. We must value and respect the passive, responsive, and negative characteristics as much as the active, unyielding, and positive.

This principle of liberation is applicable to other areas as well. The liberation of ethnic minorities in America, for example, is possible only when their unique cultural characteristics are recognized and valued by the dominant groups of American society. Moreover, their liberation is incomplete without the liberation of the whole nation. This holistic approach to human liberation brings us to another area of concern: the ecological situation of our time.

The wisdom of the *I Ching* also suggests that we must change our outlook on nature. In the past, we have taken an individualistic and anthropocentric approach to nature. We have stressed our independence from the cosmos. The basic objective of people in the past was the conquest of nature. Thus, William Braden said:

> Western man appears to be engaged in a kind of rape of mother nature. And we all know what that makes Western man, in the common parlance. One price he pays for this is alienation and isolation, the loss of cosmic connection: the feeling that he is not at home in his own universe, like a cat burglar who has crept through a window to steal the silverware. He also pays another price: the loss of wonder.[33]

There is no doubt that the Judeo-Christian interpretation of the creation story in Genesis has had something to do with the mental formation of the idea of dominance over nature. If we take up the passage in Genesis 1:28 and interpret it literally, we get the idea of domination over nature as a God-given right. God said, "Be fruitful and multiply, and fill the earth and subdue it; and have dominion over the fish of the sea and over the birds of the air and over every living thing that moves upon the earth." This passage has often been used to justify our engagement in the destruction of nature and, ultimately, the present ecological crisis. We must supplement this passage with the second story of creation in Genesis (chapter 2), where man not only came after the creation of other species, but was also formed out of dust from the ground (2:7). In a way, human beings are products of the earth. The Psalmist reminds us that we are "made of dust," and to dust we shall return. Thus, earth is the mother of humanity. The human being is more than merely a product of the earth, but when we stress the power of humanity over nature, we justify and perpetuate ecological disaster. This one-sided emphasis should be corrected by stressing the earthly nature of humanity in Scripture.

As Franklin Woo said, the cause of the ecological crisis is not only one of the improper use of technology but of our relationship with nature. "In short," he said, "it is a question of our 'cosmology'."[34] The *I Ching,* as a book of cosmology, teaches us that we are part of the cosmos. Our independence from the cosmos means the end of our lives. As a part of the cosmos, we are organically related to nature. The pollution of water, air, and soil eventually pollutes our body and our mind. According to the *I Ching,* we are microcosms of the universe, and products of Heaven and Earth. The trinitarian view of the world—Heaven, Earth, and human beings—is a helpful paradigm for restoring the ecological balance. We must turn away from our anthropocentric approach and reorient ourselves with a cosmological approach to our lives. We need to replace our anthropocentric approach with a cosmo-anthropological perspective. This new orientation in thinking may provide a new framework for cultivating our spirituality and achieving holistic living.

7

Conclusion

It seems to be appropriate to conclude this book with some issues and challenges arising out of the study of the *I Ching*. Although many of them have been discussed previously, let me try to recapture some of the most salient of them as a way of concluding our study.

One of the most significant issues is that of the authenticity of the origin of the *I Ching*. This question forms the crux of all other issues dealing with the authority of the book. As we discussed in the first chapter, the real authorship of the *I Ching* should be credited to the wisdom accumulated by the early Chinese and East Asian peoples rather than credited to a few prominent leaders. Also, the evolution of this wisdom is attributable to the careful discernment of human experience. Nevertheless, through the long history during which the tradition began to emerge, people developed a tendency to believe that the book had a mystical origin. They traced it back to the mystical chart on a legendary dragon-horse, known as the River Map or *Ho T'u,* which came to be viewed as the basis not only of the eight trigrams, but also for understanding the method of divination. Critical scholarship often considers the map as a reconstruction of the Yin-yang School and Five Movements school during the Han period (206 B.C.–A.D. 220). However, tradition attributes the discovery of the mystical map to the legendary King Fu Hsi. I personally believe that the book's authenticity cannot be proven by the mystical origin theory. Rather, the true authority of the *I Ching* lies in its preservation of the collective wisdom of the extraordinary people of those early days, a wisdom later enshrined in myth and legend. Although the tradition is indeed filled with myths and legends, it is still the most reliable source of our understanding of the *I Ching*. I have thus used existing tradition to support my theses in this book. However, in order to avoid mere blind acceptance of these traditions, I have attempted to interpret them, keeping in mind that the myths and legends attesting to the origin of the *I Ching* were themselves creations of the tradition.

The problems concerning the interpretation of the *I Ching* are even more complex than those of its origin. As discussed in the third chapter, the problem

176

of interpretation arises because of the symbolic nature of this book. Since the *I Ching* is a book of unusual symbols, the problem of interpretation becomes much more difficult than it is for an ordinary book. Unlike other books, it contains two distinctive levels of symbolism: primary symbolism, expressed in the primitive form of lines that make up hexagrams; and secondary symbols, the texts, which express the content of the primary symbols through words. There are also two distinctive forms of word symbolism: the Judgment of the hexagram as a whole, and the judgments on the lines. The latter is subordinate to the former. In a strict sense, then, there are three orders of symbolization in the *I Ching:* the hexagrams, the Judgments of the hexagrams, and the judgments on the lines. Because of the hierarchical symbolization in the *I Ching,* then, the problem of interpretation is extremely complex.

Another problem concerns some inconsistencies in the interpretations of the hexagrams. Sometimes the hexagrams are interpreted according to their structure as a whole, while at other times they are interpreted according to the attributes of the constituting trigrams. Let me illustrates these problems with hexagram 11, *T'ai* or Peace, and hexagram 20, *Kuan* or Contemplation. Hexagram 11 is interpreted according to the constituting trigrams; however, hexagram 20 is interpreted according to its whole structure. Hexagram 11 consists of the trigram Heaven below and the trigram Earth above. The concept of Peace in this hexagram is definitely derived from the attributes of the trigrams, which naturally move toward the center for peaceful harmony. If we look at hexagram 20, however, we see that its interpretation is based on its overall shape, which is that of a tower climbed to win a wider view:

| *T'ai* | *Kuan* | *I* |

Thus, it is *Kuan,* which literally means "view" or "to behold."

Let me take another example of this type of investigation. Hexagram 7, *I* or Jaws, received its name from its appearance. Observing the structure of this hexagram, we see that it resembles a picture of an open mouth. These examples make clear that the interpretation of the hexagrams is based on either the attributes of the constituting trigrams or its overall structural appearance. We can offer no guidelines by which to judge whether one form of interpretation is more appropriate in a certain situation than another. The lack of guidelines makes it difficult to interpret the hexagrams.

Besides these difficulties, we have the task of considering these symbols in relation to their cultural and historical backgrounds. Since the symbols grew out of such backgrounds, we cannot understand them unless we know their cultural and historical roots. According to the Great Commentary, the hexagrams were not only the basis of early Chinese civilization but were also the by-products of it. The intimate relationship between the hexagrams and Chinese civilization is unquestionable. In particular, the secondary symbols, which are the products of the early Chou dynasty, must be studied in relation to the early agrarian civilization of that period. We need also to consider the problems associated with the Chinese language. The lack of grammatical precision and the consequent ample room for ambiguity in Chinese make it far more difficult to comprehend the original meaning of the text than with most languages. Those who do not read classical Chinese must remember that translations are interpretations. Clearly, the problem of interpretation is enormous. (Almost the same kind of issues and problems confront those who would interpret the Bible.) The complex symbols, with their rich cultural and historical backgrounds, cannot be neatly classified in terms of some simple system of thought.

Divination is another issue, and one which seems to create more problems than any other consideration. As indicated in the fifth chapter, the divination method of the *I Ching* is more reliable than that of a mere chance operation. In order to examine the reliability of divination, we need to consider the relationships between freedom and fate, the material and the spiritual, space and time, and the conscious and the unconscious. All of these relationships are vital factors in supporting the reliability of divination. An important aspect in dealing with divination is our freedom to make decisions. As we have already indicated, divination in the *I Ching* presupposes a relative and limited freedom, because the human being is relative to time and space. Absolute freedom is an impossibility. Thus, human freedom is relative to the actualization of the potentialities of a given situation. This kind of limited freedom is not only a realistic aspect of our existence, but is the correlative of the organic world in which we live. Because of the human freedom to actualize the germinal situation in which one finds oneself, the *I Ching* denies any all-powerful fate that would eliminate freedom of choice. The primary purpose of divination through the use of the *I Ching* is not to win a blind acceptance of fate, but to urge the control of one's own destiny before it is too late. That is why divination in the *I Ching* is unique in comparison with other divination methods. The *I Ching* points out the future for us so that we can actualize it by ourselves. We all know that we are not totally free to alter our own destiny. We depend upon many factors that control our destiny. That is why the relative and limited freedom that the *I Ching* presupposes is reasonable. But our freedom cannot transcend the germinal situation in which we are placed. This idea is compatible with the Christian faith as well.

We Christians likewise believe that we are finite. Because we are not absolute, we cannot possess absolute freedom; our freedom is, thus, limited and conditioned. God alone possesses absolute and unconditional freedom. When we try to transcend our limited freedom, we commit sin. That is why the Christian

concept of freedom is compatible with the concept of freedom suggested in the
I Ching.

Another problem regarding divination pertains to the correlation between the spiritual and the material, or between the inner and outer phenomena of the world. The *I Ching* presupposes that spiritual activities are correlated with physical symbols. Without this presupposition, the reliability of divination could not be established. As we have already pointed out, there are many examples that suggest that physical activities are influenced by spiritual powers. Speaking in tongues, spiritual healings, and ecstatic prophecies are good examples of such influence. Also, materials like water and fire have inner meanings. Water, for example, symbolizes washing and purifying. Fire symbolizes clinging and lightness. External objects such as a mountain, a lake, metal, wind, thunder, earth, or heaven also have correspondent inner or symbolic meanings. The meaningful correlation between these external and internal natures is a vital aspect of divination. The validity of these correlations must be experienced by those who divine through the use of the *I Ching*. As previously noted, the psychoanalytic thinker Carl Jung seemed to believe in the reliability of these correlations. If we are interested in the *I Ching,* as Carl Jung was, we should practice it ourselves. Only by taking up the challenge can we really know the effectiveness of divination in the *I Ching*. Divination also deals with the concept of time. If the function of divination is to predict future situations, it must stress the element of time as of decisive importance for its reliability. It can predict the future only if the future is understood as the pointedness of present experience. In the germinal situation, or the hexagram, there is no distinction between past, present, and future. Within this undifferentiated continuum of time, the past and the future are in the present. According to the Western linear concept of time, time moves from one point to another, so that the distinction between past and future is clear. The *I Ching,* however, rejects the linear movement of time that is deeply rooted in the minds of Western peoples. This then challenges the West to reexamine its concept of time. What the *I Ching* suggests in divination is not so much the cyclicity of time, but time as a decisive moment. In a way, this view can be compared with the Christian idea of *kairos,* or opportune time. *Kairos* is an occasion that contains all dimensions of time: the past, the present, and the future.

Divination is also closely related to the psychic condition of humanity. It is reliable because correlation between the conscious and the unconscious is possible. The reliability of this correlation is reflected in the idea of synchronicity, the acausal principle of coincidence. The principle of synchronicity is to be identified neither with the law of causality nor with that of probability. It is less reliable than the causality principle, but more reliable than the probability principle. As we have pointed out, Carl Jung has done an extensive study on it and has given us reliable data to support the possibility of a synchronistic principle in divination. This is an area that merits further study and experiment.

The last issue that challenges us is one concerning our way of thinking. The process of change consists fundamentally of the interplay of yin and yang forces. The characteristic emphasis of this interplay is not the conflict between, but the complementarity of, opposites. Everything in the universe is in the process of change and transformation through the eternal interplay of yin and yang. All things are to be described in terms of this complementary relationship. Our way of thinking is no exception to this. The way of complementary thinking can be described in terms of the category of "both/and" thinking, which is the denial not only of the absolute, but also of one-sidedness. The category of both/and thinking is a counterpart to "either/or" thinking. The former deals with the most inclusive approach to the integral reality of the whole of existence, while the latter embraces an exclusive and analytical approach to the reality of the world. The either/or category of thought made possible the analytical and logical mentality of the West, while the both/and category of thinking provided the East with intuitive and aesthetic insight. There is a growing trend in the West to recognize the validity of both/and thinking. Many observers feel that contemporary science is moving closer to the complementary kind of thinking. For example, they do not accept either the wave theory or the quantum view of light, but accept them both at the same time. *Nels Ferre, a well-known theologian in America, recognizes the necessity of using the category of both/and thinking, which he calls "contrapletal logic." He has said, "There is here no place for paradox, excluded middle,* toum simul *or* Alles auf einmal. *What we need is a contrapletal logic.*"[2] *The prime example of the use of such contrapletal logic, he admitted, is the Chinese use of yin and yang.*[3] *Wilfred Smith also expresses his personal penchant for the both/and category of thinking:*

> *What I myself see in the yang-yin symbol with regards to this matter, if I may be allowed this personal note, is not the first solution only, nor merely an image that would reduce Christian Truth to a part of some larger Truth. Rather I find it a circle embracing Christian Truth itself. . . . In this, the image says to me, as in all ultimate matters, Truth lies not in an either/or, but in a both/and.*[4]

I use the category of both/and thinking to explain the inclusive nature of the Christian faith. The yin-yang way of thinking has become a hermeneutical principle of my theological work.[5]

A growing interest in the both/and category of thinking, or in contrapletal logic, is evident in the West. However, the question is whether it can replace the either/or category of thinking that is so deeply ingrained in the Western mind. Just as the Einsteinian concept of relativity needed time to replace the Newtonian concept of absolute time and space, it will also take time for the category of both/and thinking to come to dominate the mental activity of the West. Whatever our future way of thinking may turn out to be, the *I Ching* has, at least, taught the West that there is a possibility of altering its way of thinking.

Appendix: The Main
Text of the *I Ching*

Key for Identifying the Hexagrams

TRIGRAMS UPPER ➤ LOWER ➤	Ch'ien ☰	Chên ☳	K'an ☵	Kên ☶	K'un ☷	Sun ☴	Li ☲	Tui ☱
Chi'en ☰	1	34	5	26	11	9	14	43
Chên ☳	25	51	3	27	24	42	21	17
K'an ☵	6	40	29	4	7	59	64	47
Kên ☶	33	62	39	52	15	53	56	31
K'un ☷	12	16	8	23	2	20	35	45
Sun ☴	44	32	48	18	46	57	50	28
Li ☲	13	55	63	22	36	37	30	49
Tui ☱	10	54	60	41	19	61	38	58

1. CH'IEN / Heaven

Heaven *(Ch'ien)* above

Heaven *(Ch'ien)* below

The Judgment
Heaven is originating, successful, advantageous, and correct.

The Lines
1. The dragon is hidden. It is no use to act.
2. The dragon is seen in the field. It is advantageous to see the great person.
3. The superior person is creative and creative all day long, but he rests with care in the evening. It is dangerous but no mistake.
4. Leaping over the depths. There is no mistake.
5. Flying dragon in the sky. It is advantageous to see the great person.
6. The arrogant dragon will be remorseful.

All six: There is a herd of dragons without heads. It is good fortune.

2. K'UN / Earth 坤

Earth *(K'un)* above

Earth *(K'un)* below

The Judgment
The earth will bring great success and advantage through the correctness of a mare. When the superior person makes any movement, she will go astray if she leads; but she will gain the way if she follows. It will be advantageous for her to find friends in the west and south, but she will lose her friends in the east and north. Peace in correctness brings good fortune.

The Lines

1. Treading on frost. The firm ice will come.
2. She is straight, square, and great. Everything is advantageous without practice.
3. Concealing her ability she can maintain her correctness. If she happens to serve the king, she should not aim at success, but at the completion of her work.
4. A sack is tied up. There will be neither mistake nor honor.
5. The yellow dress. There will be great fortune.
6. Dragons fight in the field. Their blood is dark and yellow.

All six: It is advantageous to be perpetually correct.

3. CHUN / Difficulty

Water *(K'an)* above

Thunder *(Chên)* below

The Judgment

Difficulty is originating, penetrating, advantageous, and correct. Do not make any movement. It is advantageous to find an assistant.

The Lines

1. When one faces hindrance, it is advantageous for him to remain in correctness. It is advantageous to find an assistant.
2. Difficulty is mounting, and a horse and chariot are separated. He is not a robber, but seeks her to be his wife. She maintains her correctness and does not consent. She consents to marry in ten years.
3. If one follows the deer without the forester, one becomes lost in the forest. The superior person knows it and prefers not to chase. Advancement will bring humiliation.
4. A horse and chariot break apart. He seeks her to be his wife. Advancement brings good fortune. Everything is advantageous.
5. Difficulty in blessings. A little correctness brings good fortune. Extreme correctness brings misfortune.
6. The horse and chariot break apart. Blood and tears flow in streams.

4. MÊNG / Immature Youth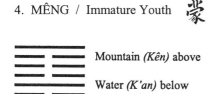

Mountain *(Kên)* above

Water *(K'an)* below

The Judgment

Immature youth will bring success. I do not seek the immature youth, but he seeks me. I speak to him at the first divination. But if he wants me to answer a second and a third time, it is boring. If I am bored, I do not continue to speak to him. It is advantageous to be correct.

The Lines

1. Foolishness develops. It is advantageous to see punishment; even the fetters may be used. Afterward humiliation will come.
2. To bear an immature youth will bring good fortune. To take a woman brings good fortune. The son can take care of the family.
3. Do not take a girl who sees a man of wealth and loses herself. There is nothing advantageous in doing this.
4. Annoying the immature youth will bring humiliation.
5. A childish, immature youth will bring good fortune.
6. Attacking the immature youth is not advantageous, but it is advantageous to treat the injury.

5. HSÜ / Waiting

Water *(K'an)* above

Heaven *(Ch'ien)* below

The Judgment

Waiting. Your sincerity gives you light and success. Correctness brings good fortune. It is advantageous to cross the big river.

The Lines

1. One is waiting in the meadow. It is advantageous to be constant. There will be no mistake.

2. One is waiting on the sand, complaining. There will be good fortune at the end.

3. One is waiting in the mud, thereby inviting enemies.

4. One is waiting in blood. He gets out of his own cave.

5. One is waiting at the meat and drink. Correctness brings good fortune.

6. One gets into the cave. Three guests are coming. To receive them with respect will bring good fortune at the end.

6. SUNG / Conflict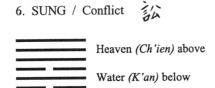

Heaven *(Ch'ien)* above

Water *(K'an)* below

The Judgment
Conflict. Sincerity is obstructed. The middle way brings good fortune. The end brings misfortune. It is advantageous to see the great person, but it is not advantageous to cross the big river.

The Lines
1. Do not perpetuate the affair. Say little. There will be good fortune at the end.

2. One cannot overcome the conflict. He goes to his home town, which has three hundred families. There is no remorse.

3. Ancient virtue is nourished, but correctness is in danger. Nevertheless, the end will bring good fortune. If one is engaged in the business of the king, one cannot accomplish it.

4. One cannot overcome the conflict. One returns and submits to the fate, and it changes to peace. Correctness brings good fortune.

5. Conflict brings the supreme good fortune.

6. If one is awarded the leather belts, they will be taken away three times by the end of the morning.

7. SHIH / The Army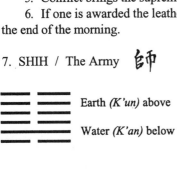

Earth *(K'un)* above

Water *(K'an)* below

The Judgment

The army. The correctness of a strong person brings good fortune. There is no mistake.

The Lines

1. The army must go forth in order, otherwise it will bring misfortune.
2. They are in the army. It is good fortune. There is no mistake. The king gives them awards three times.
3. The army may have to carry corpses in the wagon. It will bring misfortune.
4. The armies in retreat. There is no mistake.
5. Birds are in the field. It is advantageous to take hold of them. There is no mistake. Let the elder lead the army, and the youngest transport corpses. Correctness will bring misfortune.
6. The great ruler is in charge of rescuing the nation and heading families. The small person is useless for this.

8. PI / Uniting Together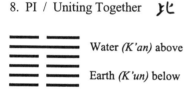

Water *(K'an)* above

Earth *(K'un)* below

The Judgment

Uniting together brings good fortune. Let the primal cast of divination be original, consistent, and correct. There is no mistake. The restless ones are coming. There will be misfortune to latecomers.

The Lines

1. There is sincerity in uniting together. There is no mistake. Let sincerity be like a clay bowl. In the end good fortune will come from without.
2. Uniting together within oneself. Correctness brings good fortune.
3. Uniting together with the bad people.
4. Uniting together with others. Correctness brings good fortune.
5. It expresses the most illustrious instance of uniting together. The king pursues in three directions. The front animal escapes. He fails to warn the villagers. Good fortune.
6. There is no head (leader) in uniting together. It brings misfortune.

9. HSIAO CH'U / The Small Power of Taming

Wind *(Sun)* above

Heaven *(Ch'ien)* below

The Judgment

The small power of taming is successful. There are dense clouds, but no rain from the western sky.

The Lines

1. They return in their own way. What mistakes have they committed? There will be good fortune.
2. They are allowed to return together. It will bring good fortune.
3. The spoke comes out from the wheel, and the husband and wife look on each other with wrangling eyes.
4. If they are sincere, the bloodshed will be over and fear will depart. There is no mistake.
5. If they are sincere and draw others, they will be rich with their neighbors.
6. When rain comes, they rest and accumulate virtue. The correctness of women is dangerous. As the moon approaches its fullness, the superior persons overcome their misfortune.

10. LÜ / Treading

Heaven *(Ch'ien)* above

Lake *(Tui)* below

The Judgment

People tread upon the tail of the tiger, which does not bite them. It is successful.

The Lines

1. By treading simply they go forward. There will be no mistake.
2. People tread step by step. The correctness of solitariness will bring good fortune.

3. The one-eyed person can see, and the lame person can walk. They tread on the tail of the tiger, which bites them. It is misfortune. Thus warriors act as great rulers.

4. People tread on the tail of the tiger. They become cautious and apprehensive. There will be good fortune in the end.

5. People tread decisively. Correctness will be dangerous.

6. People see and tread carefully and thoughtfully. When it is fulfilled, there will be supreme good fortune.

11. T'AI / Peace

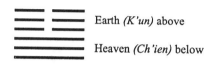

Earth *(K'un)* above

Heaven *(Ch'ien)* below

The Judgment

Peace. The small departs, and the great approaches. It is good fortune and success.

The Lines

1. When ribbon grass is pulled up, it brings the sod with it. Advance will bring good fortune.

2. One who embraces the unsophisticated people can cross the river without a boat. He does not neglect those friends who are far away. Thus he can walk in the middle.

3. There is no evenness that is not liable to be disrupted. There is no going that is not followed by a return. It is difficult to maintain righteousness without mistake. Do not complain about this truth. Enjoy the blessings that you still possess.

4. One flutters down and does not boast of his wealth. He calls his neighbors in sincerity.

5. King I gives his daughter in marriage. By doing this there will be blessing and supreme good fortune.

6. The wall [town] returns into the moat. Do not use the army. Announce your orders to the people of your own city. Correctness will bring humiliation.

12. P'I / Stagnation 否

```
━━━━━━━  Heaven (Ch'ien) above
━━ ━━
━━ ━━   Earth (K'un) below
━━ ━━
```

The Judgment

When the evil one is stagnant, the correctness of superior persons is disadvantageous. The great go and the small come.

The Lines

1. When ribbon grass is pulled up, it brings the sod with it. Correctness brings the supreme good fortune and success.

2. Continuing to endure, the small persons receive good fortune. The great persons also attain success in stagnation.

3. Shame is covered up.

4. There is no mistake in acting according to the fate. Their companions share the blessings.

5. Stagnation ends. The great persons are fortunate. It is finished, it is finished! Things are tied up like a mulberry shoot.

6. Stagnation is removed. The beginning was stagnation, but the end is joy.

13. T'UNG JÊN / Fellowship 同人

```
━━━━━━━  Heaven (Ch'ien) above
━━━━━━━
━━ ━━━━  Fire (Li) below
━━━━━━━
```

The Judgment

Fellowship is possible in the open. Success. It is advantageous to cross the big river. The correctness of superior persons brings advantage.

The Lines

1. Fellowship at the gate. There will be no mistake.

2. Fellowship with kinsmen will bring humiliation.

3. People hide their arms in the bushes and climb up the high hill. For three years they cannot be restored.

4. They climb the wall, but do not attack. It is good fortune.

5. People in fellowship wail and lament at first, but they laugh later. The great armies are engaged together.

6. Fellowship in the meadow brings no remorse.

14. TA YU / Great Possessions 大有

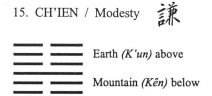

Fire *(Li)* above

Heaven *(Ch'ien)* below

The Judgment

Great possessions have supreme success.

The Lines

1. Keep away from what is harmful. There will be no mistake. Difficulty is to be faced up to, but there is no mistake.

2. A big wagon is fully loaded. It may go in any direction. There will be no mistake.

3. The rulers offer sacrifice to the Son of Heaven. The small persons cannot do this.

4. They do not expand their power. There is no mistake.

5. Their sincerity is well received and dignified. It is good fortune.

6. They will receive heavenly blessings. It is good fortune. Everything is advantageous.

15. CH'IEN / Modesty 謙

Earth *(K'un)* above

Mountain *(Kên)* below

The Judgment

Modesty is successful. The superior persons work out things for completion.

The Lines

1. The superior persons are truly modest, modest enough to cross the big river. There will be good fortune.

2. Their modesty becomes evident. Correctness brings good fortune.

3. With modesty and diligence the superior persons carry out their work to the end. It brings good fortune.

4. Everything is advantageous, for they freely act in modesty.

5. They are not rich but they have their neighbors. It is advantageous for them to use force. Everything is advantageous.

6. Their modesty becomes evident. It is advantageous to mobilize the army to conquer the city and nation.

16. YÜ / Eagerness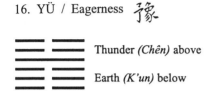

Thunder *(Chên)* above

Earth *(K'un)* below

The Judgment

Eagerness. It is advantageous to install rulers and to mobilize the army.

The Lines

1. Proclaiming eagerness. It brings misfortune.

2. It is firm as a rock, but it does not last all day. Correctness brings good fortune.

3. Eagerness looks upward. If it is delayed, it brings remorse.

4. Eagerness is motivated. It achieves great things. Be not suspicious of friends who are around you.

5. Correctness brings illness, but no death.

6. Eagerness is misled into darkness. Things change after their completion. There is no mistake.

17. SUI / Following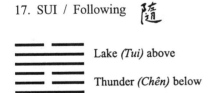

Lake *(Tui)* above

Thunder *(Chên)* below

The Judgment

Following brings great success. It is advantageous to be correct. There is no mistake.

The Lines

1. The official position is changing. Correctness will bring good fortune. Going outside the gate to join the company will produce merit.

2. If you cling to the small boy, you will lose the grown person.

3. If you cling to the grown person, you will lose the small boy. By following you get what you seek. It is advantageous to maintain correctness.

4. Following gains. Correctness brings misfortune. If you are sincere in your way, you will find brilliance. How could this be a mistake?

5. Sincerity excels. There will be good fortune.

6. Cling tightly. Your followers are still further tied to you. The king presents offerings on the western mountain.

18. KU / Decaying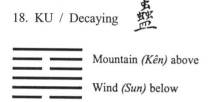

Mountain *(Kên)* above

Wind *(Sun)* below

The Judgment

Decaying is supremely successful. It is advantageous to cross the big river. Prepare it three days before; prepare it three days after the beginning.

The Lines

1. Setting straight father's decaying. If you are a filial son, it is no mistake. There is danger but good fortune in the end.

2. Setting straight mother's decaying. Don't be too correct.

3. Setting straight father's decaying. There will be small remorse, but no great mistake.

4. Allow father's decaying indulgently. If you go forward, you will be humiliated.

5. Setting straight father's decaying. Be glorified.

6. Do not serve kings and lords, but prefer higher goals for yourself.

19. LIN / Approach 臨

Earth *(K'un)* above

Lake *(Tui)* below

The Judgment

The approach will bring great success. It is advantageous to be firm. There will be misfortune in the eighth month.

The Lines

1. Approach together. Correctness brings good fortune.
2. Approaching together will bring good fortune. Everything is advantageous.
3. Sweet approach brings no advantage in any way. If you are anxious about it, there will be no mistake.
4. Approaching completely will bring no mistake.
5. To know the approach is the duty of a great leader. It brings good fortune.
6. Generous approach brings good fortune. There is no mistake.

20. KUAN / Contemplation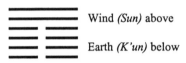

Wind *(Sun)* above

Earth *(K'un)* below

The Judgment

Contemplation cleansed but not yet consecrated. Be sincere and dignified in your appearance.

The Lines

1. Childlike contemplation. It is no mistake for small persons but humiliation for superior persons.
2. Deep contemplation. The correctness of women is advantageous.
3. Contemplation of my own life. I must either advance or retreat.
4. Contemplating the glory of the nation. It is advantageous to become a guest of the king.
5. Contemplation is my own life. The superior persons do not make a mistake.
6. Contemplation of their lives. The superior persons do not make mistakes.

21. SHIH HO / Chewing

Fire *(Li)* above

Thunder *(Chên)* below

The Judgment

Chewing brings success. It is advantageous to use the punishment.

The Lines

1. His feet are in the stocks, and his toes are cut off. It is no mistake.
2. He chews on the skin and bites off the nose. It is no mistake.
3. He chews on dried salted meat and meets with poisons. It will be a small humiliation, but no mistake.
4. He chews on dried gristly meat and gets metal arrows. It is advantageous to be firm at the time of difficulties. It is good fortune.
5. He chews on dried meat and gets yellow gold. Correctness brings danger, but there is no mistake.
6. He wears the cangue, and his ears are cut off. There will be misfortune.

22. PI / Adornment 賁

Mountain *(Kên)* above

Fire *(Li)* below

The Judgment

Adornment is successful. There will be a small advantage in undertaking something.

The Lines

1. Adorn one's toes. Abandon the vehicle and walk.
2. Adorn one's beard.
3. Be adorned and moistened! Perpetual correctness brings good fortune.

4. Be adorned simply. One comes on a white horse as if on wings. He does not come to steal, but to marry her.

5. Adornment in hills and gardens. The roll of silk is very small. It brings humiliation, but good fortune in the end.

6. Adorned in white. There is no mistake.

23. PO / Breaking Apart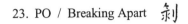

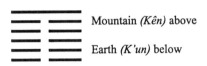 Mountain *(Kên)* above

Earth *(K'un)* below

The Judgment

Breaking apart. It is disadvantageous to move in any direction.

The Lines

1. The leg of the couch is breaking apart. The destruction of correctness brings misfortune.

2. The edge of the couch is breaking apart. The destruction of correctness brings misfortune.

3. Things break apart. There is no mistake.

4. The cover of the couch is breaking apart. It is misfortune.

5. The string of fish. Affection comes from the court ladies. Everything is advantageous.

6. The great fruits are not eaten. The superior persons gain vehicles, while the small persons break their own house apart.

24. FU / Returning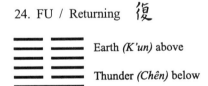

Earth *(K'un)* above

Thunder *(Chên)* below

The Judgment

Returning is successful. Going and coming with no disease. Friends come without mistake. Back and forth on the way, one returns on the seventh day. It will be advantageous in all directions.

The Lines

1. Return from not far away. Remorse is unnecessary. There will be great good fortune.

2. Restful return. It will be good fortune.

3. Endless return. It is dangerous, but there is no mistake.

4. Walking in the center, one returns alone.

5. Noble return. There is no remorse.

6. Confused return. It is misfortune. There will be calamity and trouble. If one mobilizes his army, the end will be a great defeat. It will bring misfortune to the ruler of the nation. For ten years he cannot overcome the disaster.

25. WU WANG / The Unexpected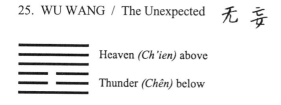

Heaven *(Ch'ien)* above

Thunder *(Chên)* below

The Judgment

The unexpected brings great success. It is advantageous to be correct. If you are not righteous, you are in trouble. It is not advantageous to undertake anything.

The Lines

1. The unexpected advance brings good fortune.

2. One expects harvest without plowing, and the product of the third year's field without cultivating the first year's field. It is advantageous to go in any direction.

3. Calamity happens unexpectedly. The cow that was tied becomes the possession of a passerby, while citizens are in calamity.

4. It is possible to be correct. There is no mistake.

5. An unexpected disaster. Use no medicine. There will be joy of recovery.

6. Walk unexpectedly in the midst of calamity. It will be disadvantageous to undertake anything.

26. TA CH'U / The Great Power of Taming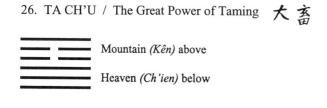

Mountain *(Kên)* above

Heaven *(Ch'ien)* below

The Judgment

The great power of taming. It is advantageous to be correct. Not eating at home brings good fortune. It is advantageous to cross the big river.

The Lines

1. Danger is near. It is advantageous to stop it.
2. The axle of the vehicle is removed.
3. Chase a good horse. It is advantageous to face up to the difficulty and to be correct. Daily practice in riding and defense brings advantage in any direction one moves.
4. Taming the young bull brings great good fortune.
5. The tusk of the gelded boar. It is good fortune.
6. Commanding the way of Heaven. There will be success.

27. I / Jaws

Mountain *(Kên)* above

Thunder *(Chên)* below

The Judgment

Jaws. Correctness will bring good fortune. Observe the jaws and find out what one fills his own mouth with.

The Lines

1. Leave the magic tortoise, and look at me with your lower jaw dropping. It is misfortune.
2. Jaws are turned over. It is abnormal to move the lower jaw upward to the hill. It will bring misfortune.
3. Jaws are abandoned. Correctness brings misfortune. Do nothing for ten years, for there is nothing that would be advantageous.
4. Jaws are turned over. It is good fortune. The tiger glares unwaveringly with desire to pursue you. It is not your mistake.
5. Abandon what is expected to be done. Remaining in correctness brings good fortune. It is not possible to cross the big river.
6. Because of jaws it is dangerous, but good fortune. It is advantageous to cross the big river.

28. TA KUO / The Great Excess 大過

Lake *(Tui)* above

Wind *(Sun)* below

The Judgment

The great excess. The beam is bending. It is advantageous to move in any direction. There will be success.

The Lines

1. Place the white rushes underneath. There is no mistake.
2. If a withered willow produces shoots, an older man takes a young wife. There is nothing that would not be advantageous.
3. The beam is bending. It is misfortune.
4. The beam is rising. It is good fortune. Looking to others for help brings humiliation.
5. If a withered willow produces flowers, an old woman takes a young husband. There will be neither humiliation nor honor.
6. You must pass through the water, which comes over the head. It is misfortune, but not your mistake.

29. K'AN / Abysmal 坎

Water *(K'an)* above

Water *(K'an)* below

The Judgment

The abysmal practiced. Have sincerity and a penetrating mind. Any action will be appropriate.

The Lines

1. The abysmal practiced. Getting into the pit of the abysmal. It is misfortune.
2. The abysmal is dangerous. Seek a small gain.
3. Come and return to the depth of the abyss. Pause and contemplate, for it is dangerous. Getting into the pit of the abysmal. Do not act.

4. A bottle of wine and two bowls of rice made of clay. Enter simply through the window. In the end there is no mistake.

5. The abysmal does not overflow. It is filled to the brim. There is no mistake.

6. Bound with black ropes, and placed in the thorn-hedged prison. For three years you do not attain liberty. It is misfortune.

30. LI / Flaming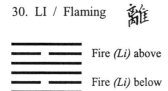

Fire *(Li)* above

Fire *(Li)* below

The Judgment

The flaming. It is advantageous to be correct. There will be success. Raise the cow. There will be good fortune.

The Lines

1. Walk with confused steps. If you tread reverently, there will be no mistake.

2. The gold flaming. It is great good fortune.

3. In the flame of the setting sun, one does not beat the drum or sing a song. Rather, he utters the groan of old age. There will be misfortune.

4. Its coming is sudden, as the flaming fire is extinguished and as the dead is thrown away.

5. Tears flowing in torrents and lamenting in sorrow. It will bring good fortune.

6. The king uses you to march forth. You earn merit, kill the enemy leaders, and take captive their followers. There is no mistake.

31. HSIEN / Influence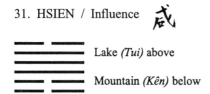

Lake *(Tui)* above

Mountain *(Kên)* below

The Judgment

Influence brings success. It is advantageous to be correct. To take a maiden will bring good fortune.

The Lines

1. The influence affects the big toe.

2. The influence affects the calves of your legs. There will be misfortune. It will be good fortune to remain in your place.

3. The influence affects the thighs. Hold on to followers. However, going forward in their way will bring humiliation.

4. Correctness brings good fortune. Remorse disappears. If your thoughts are not settled, they go in any direction. Remember that your friends will follow your thoughts.

5. The influence affects the nipples. There will be no remorse.

6. The influence affects the jaws, cheeks, and tongue.

32. HÊNG / Endurance 恒

Thunder *(Chên)* above

Wind *(Sun)* below

The Judgment

Endurance has success. There is no mistake. It is advantageous to be correct and move in any direction.

The Lines

1. Desiring endurance too hastily. Correctness brings misfortune. There will be no advantage.

2. Regret disappears.

3. The virtue that does not last may bring shame. Correctness brings humiliation.

4. No game in the field.

5. Endurance maintains right virtues. It is good fortune for a wife, but misfortune for a husband.

6. Endurance is disrupted. It brings misfortune.

33. TUN / Withdrawal 遯

Heaven *(Ch'ien)* above

Mountain *(Kên)* below

The Judgment

Withdrawal has success. It is a small advantage to be correct.

The Lines

1. Withdrawal to the tail is dangerous. Do not move in any direction.
2. Hold fast with the hide of a yellow ox. No one can break it loose.
3. A halted withdrawal is harmful and dangerous. To take care of courtiers and courtesans brings good fortune.
4. Wish to withdraw. It brings good fortune to the superior person. But the inferior person cannot withdraw.
5. Joyful withdrawal. Correctness brings good fortune.
6. Creative withdrawal. Everything is advantageous.

34. TA CHUANG / The Great Power 大 壯

```
══ ══
══ ══   Thunder (Chên) above
═══════
═══════  Heaven (Ch'ien) below
═══════
```

The Judgment

The great power. It is advantageous to be correct.

The Lines

1. The power manifests itself in the toes. Advance brings misfortune.
2. Correctness brings good fortune.
3. The small persons use power, but the superior persons do not. Correctness is dangerous. A ram butts against the hedge so that its horns are entangled.
4. Correctness brings good fortune. Remorse disappears. The hedge is removed without entangling the horns. The power is like the axle of a great vehicle.
5. The ram is easily lost. There is no remorse.
6. The ram butts against the hedge. It is not possible to retreat or advance. Nothing is advantageous. It is difficult, but good fortune.

35. CHIN / Progress

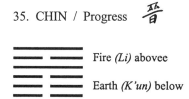

Fire *(Li)* abovee

Earth *(K'un)* below

The Judgment

Progress. The strong noble person has many great horses. He gets three receptions in a day.

The Lines

1. Progress and retrogress simultaneously. Correctness brings good fortune. If you are not sincere, you should be calm. Then there is no mistake.
2. Progress in sorrow. Correctness brings good fortune. Receive great blessings from the grandmother.
3. A confident group. Remorse disappears.
4. Progress like a marmot. Correctness is dangerous.
5. Remorse disappears. Do not concern yourself with gain or loss. Advance will bring good fortune. Everything is advantageous.
6. Progress with the horns punishes its own city. It is dangerous, but good fortune. There is no mistake. Correctness will bring humiliation.

36. MING I / The Twilight 明 夷

Earth *(K'un)* above

Fire *(Li)* below

The Judgment

The twilight. It is advantageous to be correct in time of difficulties.

The Lines

1. The twilight flies with drooping wings. When the superior persons go away, they do not eat for three days. Whenever they go, the hosts gossip about them.

2. The twilight is wounded in the left thigh. Help is needed with the power of horses. It is good fortune.

3. The twilight on a southern hunt. The great general is captured. Do not expect to be correct too soon.

4. Enter into the left side of the belly and attain the core of the twilight. Then, leave the courtyard through the gate.

5. The twilight with Prince Chi. It is advantageous to be correct.

6. There is no light, but obscurity. Ascend first to Heaven, and then descend into the Earth.

37. CHIA JÊN / The Family 家 人

Wind *(Sun)* above

Fire *(Li)* below

The Judgment

The family. The correctness of women is advantageous.

The Lines

1. Seclusion within the home. Remorse disappears.

2. She should not go on her own way. Her central place is to prepare food. Correctness brings good fortune.

3. When the family is excited, there will be remorse and danger, but there will be good fortune. When women and children titillatingly laugh, it will eventually lead to humiliation.

4. The rich family. There will be great good fortune.

5. The king expands his family. Do not frighten the family. There will be good fortune.

6. You possess majesty and sincerity. There will be good fortune in the end.

38. K'UEI / Estrangement 睽

Fire *(Li)* above

Lake *(Tui)* below

The Judgment

Estrangement. There will be good fortune in small affairs.

The Lines

1. Remorse disappears. A horse is lost. Do not chase it. It will return by itself. Seeing the evil person is not your mistake.

2. Unexpectedly confront the master in a narrow path. It is not a mistake.

3. One observes the vehicle dragged forward. The ox is pulled back. Someone's hair and nose are cut off. There is no beginning, but there is an end.

4. The estranged person in loneliness meets an authentic person. They sincerely like to get together. There is danger, but no mistake.

5. Remorse disappears. The elder bit through the piece of skin. When he advances, how can he make a mistake?

6. Estrangement in isolation. One sees a pig covered with mud, and the vehicle loaded with ghosts. First he draws a bow and then releases it. He is not a robber, but wants to get married. When they go away, rain suddenly falls. Then, there is good fortune.

39. CHIEN / Hindrance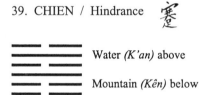

Water *(K'an)* above

Mountain *(Kên)* below

The Judgment

Hindrance. There is advantage in the west and south, and disadvantage in the east and north. It is advantageous to see a great person. Correctness will bring good fortune.

The Lines

1. Going in hindrance, but coming with praise.

2. The servants of the king struggle with hindrance upon hindrance. But they are not blamed for it.

3. Going in hindrance, but coming in revolt.

4. Going in hindrance, but coming in unity.

5. A great hindrance, but friends come.

6. Going in hindrance, but coming with merit. It is good fortune. It is advantageous to see a great person.

40. HSIEH / Liberation 解

Thunder *(Chên)* above

Water *(K'an)* below

The Judgment

Liberation has advantage in the west and south. If there is no place to go, it is good fortune. If there is some place to go, hastening brings good fortune.

The Lines

1. There is no mistake.
2. Three foxes are hunted in the field, and a yellow arrow is found. Correctness brings good fortune.
3. One rides a vehicle with his baggage on his back; thereby he attracts robbers. Correctness will bring humiliation.
4. Liberate yourself from your big toe. Then the friends whom you trust come to you.
5. The superior person alone is capable of liberation. It is good fortune. He proves his sincerity to the inferior person.
6. The prince shoots at the hawk on the top of the high wall and kills it. Everything is advantageous.

41. SUN / Loss 損

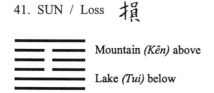

Mountain *(Kên)* above

Lake *(Tui)* below

The Judgment

Loss. Sincerity will bring supreme good fortune without mistake. Correctness is appropriate. It is advantageous to go forward. How can this be done? Two baskets of grain are appropriate for the sacrifice.

The Lines

1. Go away when your work is finished. There is no mistake, but consider the loss of others.

2. It is advantageous to be correct. Marching forth brings misfortune. Increase is possible without loss.

3. If three people go together, one of them will be lost. If one goes alone, he will find a friend.

4. If you give up your ill desire, other people will come and make you glad. There will be no mistake.

5. If you gain ten pairs of tortoise shells, no one can oppose you. It will bring supreme good fortune.

6. Increase without a loss. There will be no mistake. Correctness brings good fortune. It is advantageous to move in any direction. Obtain servants, but not family.

42. I / Gain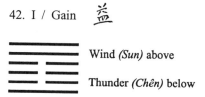

Wind *(Sun)* above

Thunder *(Chên)* below

The Judgment

Gain. Movement in any direction is advantageous. It is advantageous to cross the big river.

The Lines

1. It is advantageous to perform a great contrivance. It will bring supreme good fortune. There is no mistake.

2. If you gain ten pairs of tortoise shells, no one can oppose you. Perpetual correctness will bring good fortune. A king's sacrifice to God brings good fortune.

3. Gain is brought about by the use of evil things. It is not your mistake. Pursue the middle way in sincerity, and report it to the prince with a seal.

4. Pursue the middle way and then report it to the prince. It is an advantage to rely on the removal of the capital.

5. Have sincerity and a benevolent heart. Do not ask the question as to the supreme good fortune. Sincerity and benevolence will be known as your virtues.

6. Nothing is gained. If you are attacked, your mind acts inconsistently. This will bring misfortune.

43. KUAI / Resolution 夬

Lake *(Tui)* above

Heaven *(Ch'ien)* below

The Judgment

A resolute decision is proclaimed at the king's courtyard. It must be a sincere appeal. There is a danger. Inform your own town that it is not advantageous to engage in a war. There will be an advantage to move in any direction.

The Lines

1. One's strength advances with his toes. Going forward does not bring him the victory. It is a mistaken act.

2. He appeals for help, for he sees the danger at evening and at night. Let him fear nothing.

3. The strong face brings misfortune. The superior person makes a firm resolution. He walks alone and suddenly encounters the rain. If he is soaked through, he becomes patient with people's complaints. There will be no mistake.

4. The skin of his ass is stripped. Thus he walks with difficulty. If he is led like a sheep, his remorse will disappear. He hears the word, but does not believe it.

5. Firm resolve is needed to deal with the bed of purslane in the ground. If you pursue the middle way, there is no mistake.

6. No need to scream. In the end there will be misfortune.

44. KOU / Encounter (Intercourse) 姤

Heaven *(Ch'ien)* abovee

Wind *(Sun)* below

The Judgment

Encounter with a strong woman. Do not marry such a woman.

The Lines

1. It must be kept by a metal brake. Correctness brings good fortune. Its movement in any direction will bring misfortune. Even a weak pig will rage about it.

2. A fish is in the bag. It is no mistake. There is no advantage for the guest.

3. The skin of one's ass is stripped. Thus he walks with difficulty. It is dangerous, but there is no great mistake.

4. A fish is not in the bag. This will cause misfortune.

5. A willow tree overshadows the gourd. If the gourd hides its brilliance, goodness comes down from heaven.

6. Encounter with horns. It is humiliation, but no mistake.

45. TS'UI / Gathering Together 萃

Lake *(Tui)* above

Earth *(K'un)* below

The Judgment

Gathering together has success. The king takes care of the ancestral temple. It is advantageous to see a great person. There is success. It is advantageous to be correct. The use of great offerings will bring good fortune. It is advantageous to move in any direction.

The Lines

1. You are sincere, but unable to complete things. Thus, confusion is created in gathering together. If you scream, at once it becomes the occasion for laughter. Do not be afraid. There is no mistake in going.

2. You are led into good fortune. There is no mistake. If you are sincere, it is to your advantage to offer a small sacrifice.

3. Gathering together is similar to sighing together. Nothing is advantageous. If you advance, you make no mistake. There will be a small humiliation.

4. There will be a supreme good fortune. There is no mistake.

5. Gathering together in the position of dignity. There is no mistake. If you are not sincere, you need supreme and perpetual correctness to be free from remorse.

6. Sighing and weeping with floods of tears. There will be no mistake.

46. SHÊNG / Moving Upward 升

Earth *(K'un)* above

Wind *(Sun)* below

The Judgment

Moving upward has supreme success. It is necessary to see the great person. Fear nothing. Going toward the south will bring good fortune.

The Lines

1. Moving upward is welcome. It will bring great good fortune.
2. If you are sincere, it is advantageous to bring a small offering. There is no mistake.
3. Moving upward in an empty city.
4. The king must offer sacrifice to Mount Ch'i.
5. Correctness will bring good fortune. Moving upward in steps.
6. Moving upward blindly. It is advantageous to be correct ceaselessly.

47. K'UN / Annoyance 困

Lake *(Tui)* above

Water *(K'an)* below

The Judgment

Annoyance has success. The correctness of a great person brings good fortune. There will be no mistake. When the word is spoken, it is not believed.

The Lines

1. The bare ass gives annoyance on the stump of a tree. A person enters into a dark valley and is not seen for three years.
2. He is annoyed with wine and meat. The officer with the knee-covered uniform is coming to him. It is advantageous to offer a sacrifice. Any aggressive project leads to misfortune, but it is not his mistake.

3. He is annoyed with a stone. He leans on thorns and thistles. He enters his palace and does not see his wife. It is misfortune.

4. He comes slowly, being annoyed by the golden vehicle. He is humiliated, but carries things through to completion.

5. His nose and feet are cut off. He is annoyed by the official with a red uniform. Slowly, the official explains to him. It is advantageous to offer a sacrifice.

6. He is annoyed by creeping vines. He is in a dangerous position. He says to himself: "If I move, I will be remorseful." If he is remorseful, he should go forward. This will bring good fortune.

48. CHING / The Well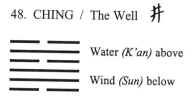

Water *(K'an)* above

Wind *(Sun)* below

The Judgment

The well changes the town, but the well cannot be changed. It neither decays nor grows. People come and go and draw the water from the well. When the drawing is almost accomplished and the rope does not go all the way, the bucket is broken. Thus it brings misfortune.

The Lines

1. The well is polluted and people do not drink of it. It is an old well which even birds avoid.

2. The well has a hole and fishes spurt out. The water jug is broken and leaks.

3. The well is cleaned, but people do not drink of it. They are sorry, for it could be used for drinking. If the king were intelligent, they could receive the blessings.

4. The well is repaired with bricks. There is no mistake.

5. Clean and cold water for drinking springs from the well.

6. The water is drawn from the well without hindrance. Sincerity brings supreme good fortune.

49. KO / Revolution 革

Lake *(Tui)* above

Fire *(Li)* below

The Judgment

Revolution comes from sincerity in its own day. There will be supreme success. It is advantageous to be correct. Remorse will disappear.

The Lines

1. Tied up with the leather of a yellow ox.
2. Revolution takes place in its own day. Going forward brings good fortune. There will be no mistake.
3. Going forward brings misfortune, and correctness is dangerous. When "revolution" is said three times, it is taken seriously.
4. Remorse disappears, and things are reliable. Reforming the governing body brings good fortune.
5. The great person transforms like a tiger. Even before divination his sincerity is known.
6. The superior person transforms like a leopard, but the inferior person revolutionizes his own face. Going forward brings misfortune, but it is good fortune to remain in correctness.

50. TING / The Cauldron 鼎

Fire *(Li)* above

Wind *(Sun)* below

The Judgment

The cauldron will bring supreme good fortune and success.

The Lines

1. The cauldron with its feet is turned over. It is advantageous to get rid of what is stagnating. One takes a concubine to have a son. There is no mistake.

2. The cauldron is full of food. My enemy envies it, but he cannot approach me. It is good fortune.

3. The ears of the cauldron have been changed. It hinders the movement of the cauldron. The fat flesh of the pheasant in the cauldron should not be eaten. But the rain will come and remorse will be removed. There will be good fortune in the end.

4. The feet of the cauldron are broken, and the prince's food is spilled over him. The prince looks ugly and is misfortune.

5. The cauldron has yellow ears and golden rings. It is advantageous to be correct.

6. The cauldron has jade rings. It is supreme good fortune. Everything is advantageous.

51. CHÊN / Thunder

Thunder *(Chên)* above

Thunder *(Chên)* below

The Judgment

Thunder is successful. Thunder comes, "Ho, ho!" and laughs, "Ha, ha!" Thunder terrifies for a hundred *li,* but the sacrificial spoon and wine cup are not disturbed.

The Lines

1. Thunder comes, "Ho, ho!" and then laughs, "Ha, ha!" It is good fortune.

2. Thunder comes and brings a danger. Finding treasures that would be lost a hundred thousand times, the nine hills must be ascended. Do not go after them. They will come to you in seven days.

3. Thunder revives again. If thunder is active, there is no mistake.

4. Thunder pursues you to the mud.

5. Thunder comes and goes. It is dangerous. Nothing is lost. There are things to accomplish.

6. Thunder has ruined everything. One looks around with trembling. Going forward brings misfortune. Thunder has not directly reached to his body, but has reached to his neighbors. There is no mistake. People talk about his marriage.

52. KÊN / Stillness (Meditation) 艮

━━ ━━ Mountain *(Kên)* above

━━ ━━ Mountain *(Kên)* below

The Judgment

When a person keeps his back still, he no longer senses the existence of his own body. When he goes to his courtyard, he does not see anyone. There is no mistake.

The Lines

1. Stillness in the toes. There is no mistake. It is advantageous to be perpetually correct.
2. Stillness in the calf of the legs. One cannot help his followers, and his heart is not glad.
3. Stillness in the hips. It makes the sacrum pinch. It is dangerous, for there is a glowing heat in the heart.
4. Stillness in the body. There is no mistake.
5. Stillness in the jaws. Consistent speech removes remorse.
6. Stillness in the sincere heart. There will be good fortune.

53. CHIEN / Advance 漸

━━━ Wind *(Sun)* above

━━ ━━ Mountain *(Kên)* below

The Judgment

Advance. A marriage of a young girl brings good fortune. It is advantageous to be correct.

The Lines

1. The wild goose gradually advances to the shore. A young son is in danger. There are rumors, but no mistake.

2. The wild goose gradually advances to the cliff. They (husband and wife) eat and drink in peace and harmony. There will be good fortune.

3. The wild goose gradually advances to the plateau. The husband goes forward, but does not return. The wife conceives, but does not nourish her child. There will be misfortune. It is advantageous to protect oneself against attack.

4. The wild goose gradually advances to the tree. If she lands on a flat branch, it is not her mistake.

5. The wild goose gradually advances to the summit. The wife does not conceive for three years, but in the end nothing can stop her conception. There will be good fortune.

6. The wild goose gradually advances to the dry land. Her feather can be used for rituals. There will be good fortune.

54. KUEI MEI / The Marrying Maiden 歸 妹

Thunder *(Chên)* above

Lake *(Tui)* below

The Judgment

The marrying maiden. Going forward brings misfortune. It is advantageous.

The Lines

1. The maiden marries as a concubine. The lame person can still walk. Going forward brings good fortune.

2. The person with one eye can still see. The correctness of the solitary person is advantageous.

3. The maiden marries as a servant. She then returns and marries as a concubine.

4. The maiden's marriage is delayed. There will be time for a late marriage.

5. King I marries his maiden. The garments of the princess were not as good as those of the concubines. When the moon is almost full, there will be good fortune.

6. The young lady takes a basket, but there is no fruit in it. The gentleman kills the sheep, but no blood flows. Nothing is advantageous.

55. FÊNG / Abundance 豐

```
▬▬  ▬ ▬   Thunder (Chên) above
▬▬▬▬▬
▬ ▬  ▬   Fire (Li) below
▬▬▬▬▬
```

The Judgment

Abundance has success. The king will grant it. Do not be anxious. Do it while the sun shines at midday.

The Lines

1. A person meets his destined master. Although they are together for ten days, they do not make a mistake. Going forward meets with appreciation.

2. The folding screen is so overshadowing that the Little Dipper is seen at midday. Going forward brings suspicion and hostility. If you are sincere and arouse the hearts of others, there will be good fortune.

3. The banners are so overshadowing that the small stars are seen in the midday. He breaks his right arm, but it is not his mistake.

4. The folding screen is so overshadowing that the Little Dipper is seen at midday. He meets his friendly master. It brings good fortune.

5. There comes a brilliant person. He receives praise and congratulations. It is good fortune.

6. His household is shaded away as by a folding screen eclipsing the room. When he peeps through the door, he does not see anyone. For three years no one will be seen there. It is misfortune.

56. LÜ / The Traveler 旅

```
▬▬  ▬ ▬   Fire (Li) above
▬▬▬▬▬
▬▬▬▬▬   Mountain (Kên) below
▬▬  ▬ ▬
```

The Judgment

The traveler has a bit of success. The correctness of the traveler brings good fortune.

The Lines

1. When the traveler is preoccupied with tiny details, he invites disaster.

2. The traveler occupies an inn. He has with him money and a faithful servant.

3. The traveler's inn burns down, and he loses his faithful servant. Correctness is dangerous.

4. The traveler is in a resting place, having money and an ax. But he says, "My heart is not glad."

5. He shoots a pheasant. He loses the first arrow, but in the end he will obtain praise and high reputation.

6. The bird's nest burns up. The traveler first laughs and then cries out in tears. It is very easy to lose the ox. There will be misfortune.

57. SUN / Gentleness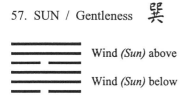

Wind *(Sun)* above

Wind *(Sun)* below

The Judgment

Gentleness has a bit of success. It is advantageous to move in any direction. It is also advantageous to see a great person.

The Lines

1. In advancing and retreating, the correctness of brave soldiers is advantageous.

2. The gentle person crawls under the couch. He uses a diviner and exorcists to deal with confusion. There will be good fortune and no mistake.

3. Constrained gentleness brings humiliation.

4. Remorse disappears. One hunts in the field and gets three kinds of game.

5. Correctness brings good fortune. Remorse disappears. Everything is advantageous. There is no good beginning, but a good end. It takes three days before the correction and three days after the correction. There will be good fortune.

6. The gentle person crawls under the couch. He loses his money and his ax. Correctness brings misfortune.

58. TUI / Joy 兌

Lake *(Tui)* above

Lake *(Tui)* below

The Judgment

Joy is successful. It is advantageous to be correct.

The Lines

1. The joy of inner harmony brings good fortune.
2. The joy of inner sincerity brings good fortune. Remorse disappears.
3. The joy of coming brings misfortune.
4. The joy of commerce is relentless. Get rid of that insidious joy. Then, there will be real happiness.
5. Sincerity that encourages disintegration is dangerous.
6. Leading others to joy.

59. HUAN / Disintegration 渙

Wind *(Sun)* above

Water *(K'an)* below

The Judgment

Disintegration is successful. The king goes to the temple. It is advantageous to cross the big river. Correctness brings advantage.

The Lines

1. Helping others with the power of a horse. It brings good fortune.
2. At the disintegration one hurries to his desk for security. Remorse disappears.
3. The disintegration of one's own body. There will be no remorse.
4. The disintegration of his group. There is great good fortune. Disintegration in turn leads to integration. This is something that ordinary people cannot understand.
5. His great cries are as disintegrating as the sweat. The royal residence is disintegrated. It is not his mistake.

6. The disintegration of his blood. He stays away from it. It is not his mistake.

60. CHIEH / Regulation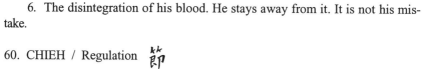

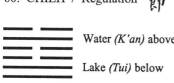

Water *(K'an)* above

Lake *(Tui)* below

The Judgment

Regulation is successful. Bitter regulation cannot be maintained correctly.

The Lines

1. One does not go out of the door and the courtyard. This is not his mistake.
2. He does not go out of the gate and the courtyard. This is misfortune.
3. If he does not regulate, he will be lamented. There is no mistake.
4. Peaceful regulation has success.
5. Sweet regulation has success. Going forward brings admiration.
6. Bitter regulation. Correctness brings misfortune. Remorse disappears.

61. CHUNG FU / Inward Trust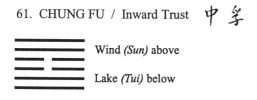

Wind *(Sun)* above

Lake *(Tui)* below

The Judgment

Inward trust. Pigs and fish have good fortune. It is advantageous to cross the big river. Correctness brings advantage.

The Lines

1. Preparation brings good fortune. If you seek something outside of your self, you will find no rest.
2. The crane calls from her hiding place, and her young one answers. "I have a good goblet," the crane seems to say. "I will share it with you," the young one seems to respond.

3. One finds his mate. Now he beats the drum, and now stops. Now he weeps, and now he sings.

4. When the moon is nearly full, the team horse disappears. There will be no mistake.

5. It is the trust that links together. There is no mistake.

6. The sound of the cock crow penetrates to Heaven. Correctness will bring misfortune.

62. HSIAO KUO / The Small Excess ·小 過

```
═══ ═══
═══ ═══   Thunder (Chên) above
═══════
═══════
═══ ═══   Mountain (Kên) below
═══ ═══
```

The Judgment

A small excess has success. It is advantageous to be correct. It is possible to carry out small affairs, but not great affairs. A flying bird leaves the sound behind. It is not good to go upward, but it is good to come down. There will be great good fortune.

The Lines

1. The flying bird meets with misfortune.

2. One passes by his grandfather, but meets his grandmother. He does not reach his prince, but meets the minister. There will be no mistake.

3. Unless he takes extraordinary precautions, somebody may come up from behind and strike him to death. There will be misfortune.

4. It is not his mistake to meet someone without passing by. Going forward is dangerous. He must be cautious. Do not try to be correct all the time.

5. Dense clouds but no rain from our western border. When the prince shoots the arrow, it hits the bird in a cave.

6. Do not meet him and go too far. The bird flies far away. It is misfortune. This is known as calamity and self-injury.

63. CHI CHI / After Harmony 既 濟

```
═══════
═══ ═══
═══════   Water (K'an) above
═══ ═══
═══════
═══ ═══   Fire (Li) below
```

The Judgment

After harmony. It has success in small affairs. Correctness brings advantage. It is good fortune in the beginning, but disorder in the end.

The Lines

1. One drags the wheels and gets his tail wet. There is no mistake.
2. The wife loses her carriage-screen cover. Do not go after it. She will find it in seven days.
3. It took three years for Kao Tsung to take over the demonic regions. Do not use inferior persons.
4. The fine clothes turn to rags. Be on your guard all day long.
5. The neighbors in the east slaughter an ox. They are not like the neighbors in the west, who make the spring sacrifice in order to obtain happiness.
6. The head is immersed. It is dangerous.

64. WEI CHI / Before Harmony 未 濟

Fire *(Li)* above

Water *(K'an)* below

The Judgment

Before harmony. It is successful. After nearly completing the crossing of the river, the little fox gets his tail wet in the water. There is nothing that would be advantageous.

The Lines

1. One gets his tail wet in the water. It is humiliating.
2. He drags the wheel. Correctness brings good fortune.
3. Attacking before harmony brings misfortune. It is advantageous to cross the big river.
4. Correctness brings good fortune. Remorse disappears. He needs to arouse people to conquer the demonic regions. It will take three years to get the reward for the great nation.
5. Correctness brings good fortune. There is no remorse. The light of the superior person is reliable. It is good fortune.
6. Drink the wine in sincerity. There is no mistake. But if one gets his head wet, his sincerity is lost.

Notes

Chapter 1. About the *I Ching*

1. See my "Can God Be Change Itself?" *Journal of Ecumenical Studies*, Fall 1973. See also my book *The Theology of Change* (Maryknoll, N.Y.: Orbis Books, 1979), pp. 29–48.

2. Irving M. Copi, *Introduction to Logic,* 7th ed. (New York: Macmillan, 1986), pp. 295, 296.

3. In his address "In Memory of Richard Wilhelm," delivered in Munich on 10 May 1930. Reprinted in the appendix of *The Secret of the Golden Flower: A Chinese Book of Life,* trans. Richard Wilhelm (New York: Harcourt, Brace and World, 1962).

4. Those interested in the gradual textual origin and development of the *I Ching or Book of Changes* should consult *Researches in the I Ching* by Iulian Konstantinovich Shchutskii, especially pages 13ff.

5. D. Howard Smith, *Chinese Religions* (New York: Holt, Rinehart and Winston, 1968), p. 26.

6. Fung Yu-lan, *A History of Chinese Philosophy,* vol. 1 (Princeton: Princeton University Press, 1952), p. 380.

7. F. R. Tennant, *Philosophical Theology,* vol. 2: *The World, the Soul and God* (Cambridge: At the University Press, 1935).

8. Chu Chun-sheng, *Liu-shih-ssu Kua Ching Chieh* (Peking, 1958), p. 2.

Chapter 2. The Philosophy of Change

1. Hellmut Wilhelm, "The Concept of Time in the Book of Changes," in *Man and Time: Papers from the Eranos Yearbooks,* ed. Joseph Campbell (New York: Pantheon, 1957), p. 212 n. 2.

2. John Cage, *Silence: Lectures and Writings* (Cambridge: MIT Press, 1962), p. 44.

3. Robert Kanigel, "The Coming of Chaos," *Johns Hopkins Magazine,* June 1987.

4. William Ernest Hocking, *The Meaning of God in Human Experience* (New Haven: Yale University Press, 1912), p. 188.

5. Jung Young Lee, *The Theology of Change: A Concept of God in an Eastern*

Perspective (Maryknoll, N.Y.: Orbis Books, 1979), pp. 29ff.

6. J. Kitagawa, "Religions of Japan," in *Great Asian Religions* (New York: Macmillan, 1969), p. 296.

7. Chikao Fujisawa, *Zen and Shinto: The Story of Japanese Philosophy* (New York: Philosophical Library, 1959), pp. 5–6.

8. Ch'u Chai and Winberg Chai, eds., *I Ching: Book of Changes,* trans. James Legge (Secaucus, N.J.: University Books, 1964), pp. xl–xli.

9. Ludwig Wittgenstein, *Tractatus Logico-Philosophicus,* ed. C. K. Ogden (London: Routledge & Kegan Paul, 1922), p. 189.

10. Carsun Chang, *The Development of Neo-Confucian Thought* (New York: Goodman Associates, 1962), p. 172.

11. Chu Hsi, *Chu Wen-kung Wen-chi* (Collected writings of Chu Hsi), 58:5.

12. Chu Hsi, *Chu Zau Ch'uan-shu* (Complete works of Chu Hsi), 49:1b.

13. Karl Barth, *Church Dogmatics,* vol. 3 (Edinburgh: T. & T. Clark, 1958), pp. 42ff., 94ff., 228ff.

14. Wang Pi, *Chou I* (Book of Changes), 3:4.

15. Betty Heimann, *Facets of Indian Thought* (London: George Allen and Unwin, 1964), p. 99.

16. G. J. Whitrow, *The Structure and Evolution of the Universe: An Introduction to Cosmology* (New York: Harper & Brothers, 1959), p. 141.

17. B. Kent Harrison et al., *Gravitation Theory and Gravitational Collapse* (Chicago: University of Chicago Press, 1965).

18. Paul Davies, *God and the New Physics* (New York: Simon and Schuster, 1983), p. 122.

Chapter 3. The Symbolic Meaning of Change

1. Adolph von Harnack, *What is Christianity?* trans. Thomas B. Saunders (New York: Harper & Brothers, 1957).

2. Hellmut Wilhelm, *Change: Eight Lectures on the I Ching* (New York: Pantheon, 1960), p. 32.

3. It must be remembered that the characterizations of firmness/strength and softness/tenderness are not meant to be value-laden. They simply reflect contrasting characteristics or natures. Thus, the imputation of either characteristic to gender is not meant as a value judgment nor as in any way definitive, but rather as an observation of commonly observed tendencies of men and women. Like yin and yang, which interact and transform one to the other, these characteristics in human beings are not found exclusively in either gender, but rather are observable in both according to circumstances and individual tendency. Likewise, other characteristics which are in the West commonly ascribable to gender are not meant to be understood as value judgments in the *I Ching* and in the Chinese philosophy of yin and yang.

4. Edmond Jacob, *Theology of the Old Testament* (New York: Harper & Brothers, 1958), p. 142.

5. Alfred Forke, *World Conception of the Chinese* (London: Arthur Probsthain, 1925), p. 68.

6. Louis T. Culling, *The Incredible I Ching* (Toddington, Cheltenham: Hellois Books, 1965), p. 14.

7. Betty Heimann, *Facets of Indian Thought* (London: George Allen & Unwin, 1964), p. 96.

8. Richard Wilhelm, trans., *The Secret of the Golden Flower: A Chinese Book of Life* (New York: Harcourt, Brace and World, 1962), p. 271.

9. See my "Origin and Significance of the *Chongyok* or the Book of Correct Change," *Journal of Chinese Philosophy* 9 (1982): 211–41.

10. Hellmut Wilhelm, *Change,* p. 82.

11. Richard Wilhelm, *Secret of the Golden Flower,* p. 48.

12. Milton Spenser Terry, *Biblical Hermeneutics: A Treatise on the Interpretation of the Old and New Testaments* (Grand Rapids, Mich.: Zondervan, 1974).

Chapter 5. The Method and Implications of Divination

1. Max Born, *Natural Philosophy of Cause and Change* (New York: Dover, 1964), p. 3.

2. Paul Veide, "Poor Man's Computer," *Commonwealth,* 8 March 1968, 693.

3. Ibid.

4. Ibid.

5. Carl Jung, foreword to *The I Ching or Book of Changes,* 3d ed., trans. Richard Wilhelm, rendered into English by Cary F. Baynes (Princeton: Princeton University Press, 1967), p. xxiv.

6. Carl Jung, "On Synchronicity," in *Man and Time: Papers from the Eranos Yearbooks,* ed. Joseph Campbell (New York: Pantheon, 1957), p. 207.

7. Ibid., p. 208.

8. Ibid., p. 209.

9. Tung Chung-shu. *Ch'un-ch'ui Fan'lu* 12:8; also found in Fung Yu-lan, *A History of Chinese Philosophy,* vol. 2 (Princeton: Princeton University Press, 1952), p. 42.

Chapter 6. The Significance of the *I Ching* in our Time

1. Those who are interested in the relationship between the *I Ching* and modern science may wish to see my article "Korea's Taequk Thought: A Paradigm for New Science," in *Papers of the 5th International Conference on Korean Studies: Korean Studies, Its Tasks and Perspectives,* vol. 2 (Seoul: The Academy of Korean Studies, 1988), pp. 296–309.

2. Wilfred Cantwell Smith, *The Faith of Other Men* (New York: New American Library, 1963), p. 67.

3. William Bonner, *The Mystery of the Expanding Universe* (New York: Macmillan, 1964), p. 90.

4. James A. Coleman, *Relativity for the Layman* (New York: William-Frederick Press, 1958), p. 41.

5. Richard Wilhelm, trans., *The Secret of the Golden Flower: A Chinese Book of Life*

(New York: Harcourt, Brace and World, 1962), p. 285.

6. Max Born, *Natural Philosophy,* p. 3.

7. G. J. Whitrow, *The Structure and Evolution of the Universe: An Introduction to Cosmology* (New York: Harper and Brothers, 1959), p. 102.

8. L. C. Birch, *Nature and God* (London: SCM, 1965), p. 69.

9. A. N. Whitehead, *Science and the Modern World* (New York: Macmillan, 1925), p. 105.

10. Bonner, *Mystery,* p. 13.

11. G. Gamow, *Mr. Tompkins in Paperback* (Cambridge: At the University Press, 1967), p. 52.

12. David Dye, *Faith and the Physical World: A Comprehensive View* (Grand Rapids, Mich.: William B. Eerdmans, 1966), pp. 129–30.

13. Coleman, *Relativity,* p. 118.

14. See my *Theology of Change* (Maryknoll, N.Y.: Orbis Books, 1979).

15. Arthur S. Eddington, "The Decline of Determinism," in *Great Essays in Science,* ed. Martin Gardner (New York: Washington Square Press, 1961), p. 253.

16. Werner Heisenberg, *Physics and Beyond: Encounters and Conversations* (New York: Harper and Row, 1971), p. 81.

17. Arthur Koestler, *The Roots of Coincidence* (New York: Random House, 1972), p. 51.

18. Heisenberg, *Physics and Beyond,* p. 78.

19. Werner Heisenberg, *Philosophic Problems of Nuclear Science* (New York: Pantheon, 1951), p. 15.

20. Quoted by Koestler, *Roots,* p. 54.

21. Heisenberg, *Physics and Beyond,* p. 79.

22. *Ta Chuan,* sec. 2, chap. 5.

23. Atomic nucleii are generally believed to be made up of both protons and neutrons. "Protons and neutrons are now considered simply as two different electronic states of the same elementary heavy particle known as the nucleon." See G. Gamow, *Mr. Tompkins,* p. 136. Furthermore, the proton is nothing but a charged neutron, and the neutron is nothing but an uncharged proton. See Kenneth Ford, *The Worlds of Elementary Particles* (London: Blaisdell, 1963), p. 168.

24. Heisenberg, *Physics and Beyond,* p. 41.

25. Koestler, *Roots,* p. 61.

26. R. V. Paund and G. A. Rebka, "Apparent Weight of Photons," *Physical Review Letters* 4 (1 April 1960): 337–41.

27. Samuel Alexander, *Space, Time and Deity* (New York: Macmillan, 1920), p. 44.

28. Richard Wilhelm, trans., *The I Ching or Book of Changes,* rendered into English by Cary F. Baynes (Princeton: Princeton University Press, 1977), p. 359.

29. In the *I Ching,* space as a static position expresses the principle of yin, while time as a dynamic movement represents the principle of yang. Just as yin and yang form a continuum, space and time are inseparable. Since yin includes yang, and yang includes yin, there is no clear distinction between time and space. Space contains time and time contains space.

30. For an extensive account of open-ended cyclic time, see my article "The Open-Ended Circle: An Asian Corrective to the Christian Concept of Time," in *China Notes*

(New York: National Council of Churches, 1990), pp. 595–600.

31. Richard Wilhelm, *Lectures on the I Ching: Constancy and Change* (Princeton: Princeton University Press, 1979), pp. 22–23.

32. Paul Tillich. "The Eternal Now," in *The Eternal Now* (New York: Charles Scribner's Sons, 1956), pp. 122–32.

33. William Braden, *The Age of Aquarius* (Chicago: Quadrangle Books, 1970), p. 233.

34. See (Franklin J.) Jung Young Woo, "'Integrity of Creation': Human-Centered, Creation-Centered, or Both?" in *China Notes* (New York: National Council of Churches, 1990), p. 603.

Chapter 7. Conclusion

1. See *Ta Chuan,* sec. 2, chap 11.

2. Nels F. S. Ferre, *The Universal World: A Theology for a Universal Faith* (Philadelphia: Westminster Press, 1969), p. 80.

3. Ibid., p. 100.

4. Wilfred C. Smith, *Faith of Other Men,* p. 74.

5. See my article "The Yin-Yang Way of Thinking: A Possible Method of Ecumenical Theology," *International Review of Mission* 60, no. 239 (July 1971): 363–70; reprinted in *Mission Trends No. 3: Third World Theologies,* edited by Gerald H. Anderson and Thomas Stransky (Paulist Press and William E. Eerdmans, 1976); reprinted in *What Asian Christians are Thinking: A Theological Source Book,* edited by Douglas Elwood (Manila: New Day Publishers of Christian Literature Society of the Philippines, 1976). See also my *Theology of Change* (Maryknoll, N.Y.: Orbis Books, 1979).

Bibliography

Albertson, Edward. *I Ching for the Millions*. Los Angeles: Sherbourne Press, 1969.

Alexander, Samuel. *Space, Time and Deity*. New York: Macmillan, 1920.

Anthony, Carol K. *A Guide to the I Ching*. Stow, Mass.: Anthony Publishing Company, 1982.

Barth, Karl. *Church Dogmatics*. Vol. 3. Edinburgh: T. & T. Clark, 1958.

Baynes, Cary F., trans. *The I Ching, or Book of Changes. The Richard Wilhelm Translation from Chinese into German*. 3d ed. Princeton: Princeton University Press, 1967.

Bernstein, Jeremy. "A Question of Parity." *New Yorker,* 12 May 1962, 49–96.

Birch, L. C. *Nature and God*. London: SCM, 1965.

Blofeld, John, trans. *I Ching: The Book of Change*. New York: E. P. Dutton, 1968.

Bonner, William. *The Mystery of the Expanding Universe*. New York: Macmillan, 1964.

Born, Max. *Natural Philosophy of Cause and Change*. New York: Dover Publications, 1964.

Braden, William. *The Age of Aquarius*. Chicago: Quadrangle Books, 1970.

Burke, Kenneth. *Permanence and Change*. Los Altos, Calif.: Hermes, 1954.

Cage, John. *Silence: Lectures and Writings*. Cambridge: MIT Press, 1962.

Capra, Fritjof. *The Tao of Physics*. Berkeley, Calif.: Shambhala, 1975.

Chai, Ch'u, and Winberg Chai, eds. *I Ching: Book of Changes*. Translated by James Legge. Secaucus, N.J.: University Books, 1964.

Chang, Carsun. *The Development of Neo-Confucian Thought*. New York: Goodman Associates, 1962.

Chang Chi-yin. "The Book of Changes (*I Ching*): A philosophical masterpiece mirroring the Zeitgeist of the Western Chou Dynasty." *Chinese Culture* 6, no. 4 (October 1965): 1–41.

Chang Chung-yuan. *Creativity and Taoism: A Study of Chinese Philosophy, Art, and Poetry*. New York: Harper, 1970.

Chu Chun-sheng. *Liu-shih-szu kua ching-chieh* (Explanation of the sixty-four hexagrams). Peking: Ku-chi ch'u-pan-she, 1958.

Chu Hsi. *Chu Wen-kung Wen-chi* (Collected writings of Chu Hsi), 58:5.

———. *Chu Zau Ch'uan-shu* (Complete works of Chu Hsi), 49:1b.

Cleary, Thomas, trans. *The Taoist I Ching*. Boston: Shambhala, 1986.

Coleman, James A. *Relativity for the Layman*. New York: William-Frederick Press, 1958.

Copi, Irving M. *Introduction to Logic*. 7th ed. New York: Macmillan, 1986.

Crary, E. M. *The Superior Man in Politics: Selections from the I Ching or Book of Changes*. New York: Vintage, 1972.

Culling, Louis T. *The Incredible I Ching*. New York: Samuel Weiser, 1969.

Davies, Paul. *God and the New Physics*. New York: Simon and Schuster, 1983.

Dhiegh, Khigh Alex. *The Eleventh Wing: An Exposition of the Dynamics of I Ching for Now*. New York: Depp, 1973.

Douglas, Alfred. *The Oracle of Change: How to Consult the I Ching*. London: Victor Gollanz, 1971.

Dubs, Homer. "Did Confucius Study the Book of Changes?" *T'oung Pao* 24 (1927): 82–90.

Dye, David. *Faith and the Physical World: A Comprehensive View*. Grand Rapids, Mich.: William B. Eerdmans, 1966.

Eddington, Arthur S. "The Decline of Determinism," in *Great Essays in Science*, ed. Martin Gardner. New York: Washington Square Press, 1961.

Endo Ryukichi. *Eki no shosei tetsugaku* (Philosophy of behavior in the Book of Change). 2d ed. Tokyo: Waseda Daigaku, 1925.

Feng Gia-fu and Jerome Kirk. *Tai Chi, a Way of Centering, and I Ching*. London: Collier. New York: Macmillan, 1970.

Ferre, Nels F. S. *The Universal World: A Theology for a Universal Faith*. Philadelphia: Westminster Press, 1969.

Ford, Kenneth. *The Worlds of Elementary Particles*. London: Blaisdell, 1963.

Forke, Alfred. *Geschichte der mittelalterlichen chinesischen Philosophie*. Hamburg, 1934.

———. *Geschichte der alten chinesischen Philosophie*. Hamburg, 1927.

———. *World Conception of the Chinese*. London: Arthur Probsthain, 1925.

Fujisawa, Chikao. *Zen and Shinto: The Story of Japanese Philosophy*. New York: Philosophical Library, 1959.

Fung Yu-lan. "I chuan ti che-hsueh ssu-hsiang" (The philosophical ideas of the commentaries in the Book of Change). *Che-hsueh yen-chiu* (Philosophical Research) 7/8 (1960).

———. "I ching ti che-hsueh ssu-hsiang" (The philosophical ideas of the texts of the Book of Change). *Wen-hui-pao* (Journal of Literary Convergence) 6/7 (1961).

———. "Ts 'ung Chou-i yen-chiu t 'an-tao i-hsieh che-hsueh shih fang-fa-lun ti wen-t'i wen-t'i" (Some problems of methodology in studying the history of philosophical discussion from the study of the Book of Changes). *Che-hsueh yen-chiu* (Philosophical Research) 3 (1963).

———. *A History of Chinese Philosophy*. Vol. 2. Translated by Derk Bodde. Princeton: Princeton University Press, 1952, 1953.

Gamow, G. *Mr. Tompkins in Paperback*. Cambridge: At the University Press, 1967.

Gardner, Martin. "Mathematical Games: The Combinatorial Basis of the *I Ching*, the Chinese Book of Divination and Wisdom." *Scientific American*, January 1974, 108–13.

Govinda, Lama Anagarika. *The Inner Structure of the I Ching.* San Francisco: Wheelwright Press, 1981.

Han dong-suk. *U-ju byun-haw ie won-ri* (The principles of cosmic change). Seoul: Kyang-rim Press, 1981.

Harrison, B. Kent, et al. *Gravitation Theory and Gravitational Collapse.* Chicago: University of Chicago Press, 1965.

Hawking, Stephen W. *A Brief History of Time.* New York: Bantam Books, 1988.

Heimann, Betty. *Facets of Indian Thought.* London: George Allen and Unwin, 1964.

Heisenberg, Werner. *Physics and Beyond: Encounter and Conversations.* New York: Harper & Row, 1971.

———. *Philosophic Problems of Nuclear Science.* New York: Pantheon, 1951.

Hocking William Ernest. *The Meaning of God in Human Experience.* New Haven: Yale University Press, 1912.

Hook, Diana Farington. *The I Ching and Mankind.* London and Boston: Routledge and Kegan Paul, 1975.

———. *The I Ching and You.* New York: E. P. Dutton, 1973.

Huang, Kerson, and Rosemary Huang, trans. *I Ching.* New York: Workman, 1985.

Jacob, Edmond. *Theology of the Old Testament.* New York: Harper and Brothers, 1958.

Johnson, Willard. *I Ching: An Introduction to the Book of Changes.* Berkeley, Calif.: Shambhala, 1969.

Jung, Carl. Foreword to *The I Ching or Book of Changes.* 3d ed. Translated by Richard Wilhelm, rendered into English by Cary F. Baynes. Princeton: Princeton University Press, 1967.

———. "On Synchronicity." In *Man and Time: Papers from the Eranos Yearbooks,* edited by Joseph Campbell. New York: Pantheon, 1957.

Kanigel, Robert. "The Coming of Chaos." *Johns Hopkins Magazine,* June 1987.

Kao Heng. *Chou I ku-ching t'ung-shuo* (Explanation of the ancient classic the Chou I). Peking: Chung-hua Shu-chu, 1958.

Kim, Kan-jae, and Chim Chae-yul. *Chum-ja chung-jong chung-hae* (Correct and clear interpretation of divination). Seoul: Sam-shin Su-juk, 1968.

Kim, Kyung-dan, trans. *I Ching.* Seoul: Mun-hwa Dang, 1971.

Kitagawa, J. "Religions of Japan," in *Great Asian Religions.* New York: Macmillan, 1969.

Koestler, Arthur. *The Roots of Coincidence.* New York: Random House, 1972.

Kuo Mo-jo. *Chou I te kou-ch'eng shih-tai* (The Chou I 's time of formation). Shanghai: Shang-wu Yin-shu-kuan, 1940.

Lach, Donald. "Leibniz and China." *Journal of the History of Ideas* 14 (1945): 437–55.

———. *The Preface to Leibniz's Novissima Sinica.* Honolulu: University of Hawaii Press, 1957.

Lee Chung-ho. *Chu-yok cha-gu sa-in* (Concordance of the Book of Change). 2d ed. Seoul: Guk-chae University, 1963.

———. *Chu-yok chung-i* (Correct meaning of the Book of Change). Seoul: Ah-se-ah Mun-hwa Sa, 1980.

————. *Chong-yok yong-ku* (Study of correct change). Seoul: Kuk-chae University, 1976.

Lee, Jung Young. *The Principle of Changes: Understanding the I Ching.* New Hyde Park, N.Y.: University Books, 1971.

————. *The I Ching and Modern Man: Metaphysical Implications of Change.* New Hyde Park, N.Y.: University Books, 1974.

————. *The Theology of Change: A Christian Concept of God in an Eastern Persepctive.* Maryknoll, N.Y.: Orbis Books, 1979.

————. *Patterns of Inner Process.* Secaucus, N.J.: Citadel Press, 1976.

————. "Some Reflections on the Authorship of the *I Ching.*" *Numen* 17, no. 13 (December 1970): 100–210.

————. "Death is Birth and Birth is Death: The Parascientific Understanding of Death and Birth." *Systematics* 9, no. 4 (1972): 188–200.

————. "Can God Be Change Itself?" *Journal of Ecumenical Studies* 10, no. 4 (1973): 752–70.

————. *Death and Beyond in the Eastern Perspective: A Study Based on the Bardo Thodol and the I Ching.* New York, London, Paris: Gordon and Breach Science Publications, 1974.

————. *Cosmic Religion.* New York: Philosophical Library, 1973. New York: Harper and Row, 1978.

————. "The Yin-Yang Way of Thinking: A Possible Method for Ecumenical Theology." *International Review of Mission* 51, no. 239 (July 1971): 363–70.

————. "The Origin and Significance of the Chongyok or Book of Correct Change." *Journal of Chinese Philosophy* 9 (1982): 211–41.

————. "The Book of Change and Korean Thought," in *Religions in Korea: Beliefs and Cultural Values,* ed. Earl Phillips and Eui-young Yu. Los Angeles: California State University, 1982.

————. "The *I Ching* and Its Basic Philosophy of Inner Process." *Chinese Culture* 16, no. 2 (June 1975): 63–70.

————. "Search for a Theological Paradigm: An Asian-American Journey. *Quarterly Review* 9, no. 1 (Spring 1989): 36–47.

Lee, Yong-ku. *Yok-kyong shin-i* (New meaning of the Book of Change). Daejun: Hae-sang Sa, 1976.

Legge, James, trans. *I Book: Book of Changes.* Edited with an introduction and study guide by Ch'u Chai with Winberg Chai. New Hyde Park, N.Y.: University Books, 1964.

Li Ching-ch'ih. "Kuan-yu Chou-i ti chi-t 'ao yao-tz'u ti tsai chieh-shih" (Further explanations of the lines of several trigrams in the Book of Changes). *Hsin Hua yueh-pao* (New China Monthly), 1963, 1.

Li Ching-ch'un. "Kuan-yu yen-chiu Chou-i fang-fa-lun ti t 'ao-lun" (On the discussion of methodology in the study of the Book of Changes). *Che-hsueh yen-chiu* (Philosophical Research), 1963, 2.

Liang Tao-wei. "A Comparative Study of the *I Ching* and Buddhism." *Transactions of the International Conference of Orientalists in Japan* 15 (1970): 111–14.

Lik Kuen Tong. "The Concept of Time in Whitehead and the *I Ching.*" *Journal of Chinese Philosophy* 1, nos. 3/4 (June-September 1974): 373–93.

Liu Da. *I Ching Coin Prediction.* New York: Harper and Row, 1975.

———. *T'ai Chi Ch'uan and I Ching: A Choreography of Body and Mind.* New York: Harper and Row, 1972.

Liu Pai-min. "The Epistemology of the Great Appendix of the Yi-ching." *Journal of Oriental Studies* (Hong Kong), no. 2 (1955).

MacHovec, Frank J., trans. *I Ching, the Book of Changes.* New York: Peter Pauper Press, 1971.

McCaffree, Joe E. *Divination and the Historical and Allegorical Sources of the I Ching, the Chinese Classic or Book of Changes.* Los Angeles: Miniverse Services, 1967.

McClatchie, Canon, trans. *A Translation of the I Ching or the Confucian "Classic of Change" with Notes and Appendix.* Shanghai: American Presbyterian Mission Press, 1876.

McClathie, T. "The Symbols of the Yih-King." *China Review* 1, n.d.

Mears, Isabella, and Louisa E. Mears. *Creative Energy: Being an Introduction to the Study of the Yih King, or Book of Changes, with Translations from the Original Text.* London: Murray, 1931.

Miller, Terry. *Images of Change: Paintings on the I Ching.* Edited with commentaries by Hale Thatcher. New York: E. P. Dutton, 1976.

Morris, Eleanor. *Functions and Models of Modern Biochemistry in the I Ching.* Taipei: Cheng Chung Books, 1978.

Murphy, Joseph. *Secrets of the I Ching.* West Nyack, N.Y.: Parker, 1970.

Nagai Kimpu. *Shueki jigi* (Contemporary meaning of the Book of Change). Tokyo, 1924.

Naito Torajiro. "Ikigi" (Questions about the change). *Shinagaku* (Chinese Study) 3, no. 7 (1923): 1–16.

Nam Man-sung, trans. *The I Ching.* Seoul: Hyun-am Sa, 1967.

Park Sang-sha. *Chong-yok kwa Han-quk* (Correct Book of Change and Korea). Seoul: Kong-hwa Publishing House, 1978.

Paund, R. V., and Rebka, G. A. "Apparent Weight of Photons." *Physical Review Letters* 4 (April 1960): 337–41.

Ponce, Charles. *The Nature of the I Ching, its Usage and Interpretation.* New York: Award Books, 1970.

Progoff, Ira. *Jung, Synchronicity and Human Destiny.* New York: Dell, 1973.

Ritsema, Rudolf. "Notes for Differentiating Some Terms in the *I Ching*." *Spring,* 1970, 111–15; *Spring,* 1971, 141–52.

———. "The Pit and the Brilliance: A Study of the 29th and 30th Hexagrams in the *I Ching*." *Spring,* 1971, 141–52.

Roe Tae-sun, trans. *The I Ching.* Seoul: Hong-sin Mun-hwa Sa, 1977.

Shchutskii, Iulian Konstantinovich. *Researches on the I Ching.* Translated by William L. MacDonald and Tsuyoshi Hasegawa with Hellmut Wilhelm. Princeton: Princeton University Press, 1979.

Shen Tieh-min. "Chou-i kuan-chien" (My limited view on the Book of Change). *Kuang-ming jih-pao* (Kuang-ming Daily), 15 August 1961.

Siu, R. G. H. *The Man of Many Qualities: A Legacy of the I Ching.* Cambridge: MIT Press, 1965.

————. *Ch'i: A Neo-Taoist Approach to Life.* Cambridge: MIT Press, 1976.

————. *The Tao of Science.* Cambridge: MIT Press, 1957.

Smith, D. Howard. *Chinese Religions.* New York: Holt, Rinehart, and Winston, 1968.

Smith, Wilfred Cantwell. *The Faith of Other Men.* New York: New American Library, 1963.

Sung, Z. D. *The Symbols of the Yi King or the Symbols of the Chinese Logic of Changes.* New York: Paragon, 1969.

————, compiler. *The Text of Yi King.* New York: Paragon, 1969.

Tao Meng-chi. *Tu-I-fa I-cho* (Method of reading the Book of Change). Ch'i-yang: Shun-chi-lou, 1843.

Tennant, F. R. *Philosophical Theology.* Vol. 2: *The World, the Soul, and God.* Cambridge: At the University Press, 1935.

Terry, Milton Spencer. *Biblical Hermeneutics: A Treatise on the Interpretation of the Old and New Testaments.* Grand Rapids, Mich.: Zondervan, 1974.

Tto Togai. *Shuekikyo yoku tsukai* (Commentary on the Ten Wings). Tokyo: Goshi kaisha, 1916.

Tung Chung-shu. *Ch'un-ch'ui Fan'lu* 12:8.

Veide, Paul. "Poor Man 's Computer." *Commonwealth,* 8 March 1968.

von Harnack, Adolph. *What is Christianity?* Translated by Thomas B. Saunders. New York: Harper and Brothers, 1957.

Waley, Arthur. "The Book of Changes." *Bulletin of the Museum of Far East Asia* 5 (1933): 121–42.

Wang Ming. "I ching ho i chuan tissu-hsiang t'i-hsi wen-t'i" (The question of the system of thought in the Book of Changes and its commentaries). *Kuang-ming jih-pao* (Kuang-ming Daily), 23 June 1961.

Wang Pi. *Chi I* (Book of Changes). Shanghai: SPTK (Sss-pu Ts'ung K 'an), 1928.

Wei Tat. *An Exposition of the I-ching or Book of Changes.* Taipei: Institute of Cultural Studies, 1970.

Whitehead, Alfred North. *Process and Reality.* New York: Macmillan, 1957.

————. *Science and the Modern World.* New York: Macmillan, 1925.

Whitrow, G. J. *The Structure and Evolution of the Universe: An Introduction to Cosmology.* New York: Harper Torchbooks, 1959.

Wilhelm, Hellmut. *Change: Eight Lectures on the I Ching.* Princeton: Princeton University Press, 1960.

————. *Heaven, Earth and Man in the Book of Changes.* Seattle: University of Washington Press, 1977.

————. "Leibniz and the *I Ching.*" *Collectanea Commissionis Synodalis* (Peking) 16, nos. 3/4 (1943): 205–19.

————."I-ching Oracles in the Tso-chuan and Kuo-yu." *Journal of the American Oriental Society* 79 (1959): 275–80.

————. "Wanderungen des Geistes." *Eranos Jahrbuch* 33 (1964): 178–200.

————. "The Concept of Time in the Book of Changes," in *Man and Time: Papers from the Eranos Yearbooks,* edited by Joseph Campbell. New York: Pantheon, 1957.

Wilhelm, Richard. *Lectures on the I Ching: Constancy and Change.* Translated from the German by Irene Eber. Princeton: Princeton University Press, 1979.

Wittgenstein, Ludwig. *Tractatus Logico-Philosophicus.* Edited by C. K. Ogden. London: Routledge and Kegan Paul, 1922.

Wong, S. Y. "The Book of Change: A New Interpretation." *Eastern Horizon* 2 (1962): 11–18.

Woo, Catherine Yi-yu Cho. *Characters of the Hexagrams of the I Ching.* San Diego: University Press, California State University, 1972.

Woo Jung Young (Franklin J.). "'Integrity of Creation ': Human-Centered, Creation-Centered, or Both?" In *China Notes.* New York: National Council of Churches in U.S.A., Autumn 1990.

Wu Jing-Nuan, trans. *Yi Jing.* Washington, D.C.: Taoist Center, 1991.

Index

Capital letters are used for the Chinese
names of the Hexagrams.